Dog's Best Friend

DOGS IN OUR WORLD

*Man Writes Dog: Canine Themes in Literature,
Law and Folklore* (William Farina, 2014)

*Saluki: The Desert Hound and the English Travelers
Who Brought It to the West* (Brian Patrick Duggan, 2009)

Dog's Best Friend

Will Judy, Founder of
National Dog Week and
Dog World *Publisher*

LISA BEGIN-KRUYSMAN

Foreword by JANE MILLER

DOGS IN OUR WORLD
Series Editor: Brian Patrick Duggan

McFarland & Company, Inc., Publishers
Jefferson, North Carolina

LIBRARY OF CONGRESS CATALOGUING-IN-PUBLICATION DATA

Begin-Kruysman, Lisa, 1959–
    Dog's best friend : Will Judy, founder of National dog week
and Dog world publisher / Lisa Begin-Kruysman ; foreword
by Jane Miller.
      p.   cm.
    Includes bibliographical references and index.

    ISBN 978-0-7864-7120-1 (softcover)
    ISBN 978-1-4766-1626-1 (ebook)

    1. Judy, Will, 1891–1973.   2. Dogs—United States—
Authorship.   3. Authors and publishers—United States—
Biography.   I. Title.
SF422.73.J83B44 2014
636.70092—dc23
[B]   2014029573

BRITISH LIBRARY CATALOGUING DATA ARE AVAILABLE

On the cover: National Dog Week poster (1950) by Albert Staehle
(from the collection of Sharon Damkaer)

McFarland & Company, Inc., Publishers
  Box 611, Jefferson, North Carolina 28640
  www.mcfarlandpub.com

For my beloved brother, Matthew Peter,
and our special dog, Hooper.
Both gone too soon from this earth,
but who live on in our memories
in love and laughter, and watch over and
wait for us from underneath the Rainbow Bridge.

Table of Contents

Acknowledgments

During the writing of this book, I have come to know so many dedicated and talented humans, and some great dogs, too. From the start, my literary agent for this project, Donna Eastman, of the Park East Literary Agency, saw the value in this book and also had the privilege of working with Captain Haggerty in the pet-publishing industry at one time.

Although there are too many to acknowledge personally, many individuals and groups have been very important in my quest to enlighten the world about the role of our companion animals and some of the relevant canine history. These include the group Project Pets—Spay, Neuter, Love; Thomas Cole and his work on behalf of Shelter Revolution; Janice Fisher and her fellow advocates who have successfully banned new retail outlets for the sale of puppies in my New Jersey community; author and advocate Nikki Moustaki and her successful Pet Postcard Project; and Rose Russo, who sustained life-changing injuries on September 1, 2001, and found healing through the caring of many homeless dogs.

Oregon-based artist Donald Brown so generously used his amazing talents to create a stunning National Dog Week poster for its 2011 observance, and pet photographer Joseph Frazz contributed his talents for the Paws to Pose Project for National Dog Week 2012–13. Los Angeles-based veterinarian Dr. Patrick Mahaney has been a champion of the National Dog Week mission from the beginning, and Jane Miller, in her writing of this book's poignant foreword, so passionately celebrates the healing power of canines. Marie Selto and her fabulous dog, Bocker the Labradoodle, and Sean Martin of Kids Adopt-a-Shelter, have also played an important role in educating many about the special bond between dogs and children.

This book would not have been possible without help from Pat Mussleman and the Alumni Office of Juniata College, Will Judy's beloved alma mater, and the Meyersdale Public Library in Pennsylvania. I also extend thanks to the editorial staff at *Dog World*/I-5 Publishing, the Chicago Historical Society, and author Sharon Griese Damkaer for their help with my research.

Behind any creative endeavor there must be support on the home front, and I have been blessed in that regard, also. On my tenth birthday, my parents, Jack and Cindy, yielded to my pleas for a dog and presented me with a tiny chocolate brown toy poodle named Cocoa, instilling in me a lifelong love of dogs. In my salad days as a blogger, my sister, Manette, helped me to muddle through the early stages of blogging, and her husband, novelist David Lender, offered helpful writing and promotional advice. I also thank my brother, John, and his family for their love, fostering and adoption of many companion animals.

Last, but certainly not least, during the course of this labor of love many challenges occurred. My husband, Rich, experienced a health crisis; our beloved Portuguese water dog, Hooper, passed suddenly; and a storm known as Sandy visited our community. But through it all, I kept writing, largely due to the support and encouragement of my husband, close friends, and family members.

I recall speaking with those who knew and admired Captain Haggerty and my disappointment upon realizing he had passed just a few years before I came to learn of National Dog Week. I remember writing to his daughter, Babette Haggerty, in New York, and telling her about my desire to write a book that captured the energy and passion of her father and his fellow dog enthusiasts. A renowned dog obedience trainer in her own right, Babette gave me her blessing and with her encouragement, the venture was launched.

Will Judy once wrote, "There are too many dog books. There never are enuf good dog books." I can only hope that if alive today, he would find this book to be at the very least good "enuf," and I am honored to be the first to record his life's work and his influence on America's dogs and their humans, too.

Foreword

JANE MILLER

In the early 1920s, Will Judy had a radically different perspective on how to treat dogs. At that time, it was not uncommon to find dogs chained outside at all times and generally treated inhumanely. His philosophy, values and ethics recognized the spiritual connection between dogs and humans. He was a leader and in the forefront of advocating for the humane treatment of dogs. To this day, pets are legally considered property, and there is very little in our legal system to protect them. Will Judy recognized long before it was popular that dogs need to be protected against abuse, inhumane conditions, and adverse treatment.

I have always lived with dogs. Like many dog-lovers, I have enjoyed their company and unconditional love. However, it is my experience in working with dogs that has helped me recognize their healing powers. As a psychotherapist, psychiatric service dog (PSD) trainer, author, healer, and animal lover, I adhere to Judy's values and ethical standards when working with dogs. As such, the dogs' well-being is of primary concern. Over and over again, in my psychotherapy practice, I have a chance to observe how the bond between dogs and people struggling with mental illness can strengthen the human will to overcome challenges and recover. These animals are not just simply companions, they are capable of providing support in ways that we do not fully acknowledge. My own dogs, Simcha and Ahava, accompany me to my office where I see psychotherapy clients. I consider them my co-therapists. Their presence has transformed the way in which my clients share their experiences with me, their histories and their traumas. My dogs help them feel safe in expressing painful memories, often providing moments

1

of distraction when the pain becomes too intense, and helping them open up when they are more inclined to shut down. I also see the dogs mirror the emotions of my clients and help me identify the subtleties of my client's feelings. It is through these experiences that I connect with Will Judy's commitment that dogs are integral to our well-being and deserve respectful treatment.

In my book, *Healing Companions: Ordinary Dogs and Their Extraordinary Power to Transform Lives*, I stressed the need for compassion, love and respect for the dog in the chapter "Dogs Have Issues Too: Helping Your Dog Cope with Stress." All of the PSDs that I assess for my clients are rescue or shelter dogs with the potential to be trained to be service dogs. These are not rehab projects, but dogs that save the lives of their companions while the human saves the dog's life—truly a magical win-win situation and a tribute to honoring Will Judy's journey and philosophy toward dogs.

Judy's wisdom, courage, and deep commitment to animal welfare was remarkable, especially for the 1920s. He was preaching for those without a voice way before it was fashionable or imaginable. He was a man setting the stage for the ethical treatment of dogs that were not being treated with the respect, dignity and love that they deserved. Even those among us who have heard of him know very little about his legacy, his mission and his vision that we are still working towards now almost 100 years later.

Will Judy was a forgotten historical figure who paved the way for improved legislation to protect dogs and was the founder of National Dog Week, a celebration of all that they provide us. He created a number of educational formats through publishing *Dog World* magazine and establishing the Dog Writers Association of America, as well as writing a number of his own books. Will Judy was a lawyer, preacher, nonfiction writer, publisher, diarist and poet. He interwove his talents, genius and heart when expressing the human-animal bond. He implemented his skills and knowledge of legal complexities while interspersing his ethics and values as a minister for the treatment of dogs. He stood up for their rights to adequate care, treatment, and even back in the 1920s was advocating against breed-specific legislation while honoring the dogs of war. He was a social reformer by speaking out for the rights of dogs.

Today we still have so much to learn from Will Judy's wisdom, his depth of appreciation of the human-animal bond and the unconditional love that dogs provide and the ways in which they enhance our lives.

My hope is that Will Judy's life, as shared in this historical portrait, will inspire others to join the ranks and stand up for the dogs we love. He started living out his conviction in the 1920s and died 53 years later; many of the changes for which he advocated had not been embraced by the world. Like Gandhi and Martin Luther King, he started the movement, but we still have a long way to go. Changing legislation is a step in the right direction, but changing people's beliefs about how dogs should be treated, as well as fellow humans, is a long stretch from reaching the goals that Will Judy stood for, way before his time.

Join me in learning more about this remarkable historical figure as you read this poignant book. My hope is that his spirit lives on within each of us as we follow this warm, courageous, loving, caring man in achieving the highest gift of all—respect and unconditional love towards the dogs that share our lives. So take time to reach out to a dog you love and make sure you cherish every moment while fighting for the respect, love and adequate care of all the dogs in the world. We have so much to learn from Will Judy. It is our turn to speak for dogs as Will Judy spoke out for them. Take the challenge of opening your hearts and minds in following Judy's footsteps to save the lives of those four-legged paws that we so deeply cherish. To Will Judy and all the dogs that benefitted from his wisdom!

Jane Miller, LISW, CDBC, is a clinical psychotherapist and licensed independent social worker specializing in holistic healing.

Preface

The Legacy of Captain William Lewis Judy, the Man Who Went to the Dogs and Took a Nation with Him

In January 2010 I joined the world of online bloggers. With a Wordpress account I began writing about my growing fascination with Captain William Lewis Judy, one of the most influential dog enthusiasts in American canine history, albeit perhaps one of the least known.

For those not familiar with the term, a blog is an online biographical log kept by a writer; it is filled with personal observations and commentary about life as it is affected by history and current events. It is estimated that there are currently more than 152 million blogs in existence and a multitude of them are dedicated to man's best friend alone. But up until my entry, no one had ever established one that explored the life and work of William Lewis Judy, more commonly known as Will Judy.

Each week I continued to post about how the work of a man born more than a hundred years ago remained relevant to American dog owners and the American dog population, currently estimated to be 83.3 million.[1]

Some blog posts were dark, examining topics like puppy mills and dog fighting, while others were inspiring, like those that centered on the important role of therapy and service dogs for those facing special challenges. Other posts, such as ones that featured events like canine fashion shows, seemed light and frivolous until you learned that these events also raised funds to help homeless and needy companion animals. Four years later I am still at it and have learned that many of the issues facing dogs of the nation are not so different from those covered in the writings of Will Judy.

In his youth, Will Judy was groomed for the ministry, but this multitalented lover of man's best friend went on instead to become a lawyer, soldier and a prolific writer, publisher and mentor; he was called an "American original" by those in the industry.[2]

Dedicated to good books about dogs and good deeds toward them, Judy served as the publisher of *Dog World* magazine for five decades. Admired for his humor and quirky writing habits, Judy enjoyed taking license with his spelling. Words like "ruff," "alfabet," and "filosophy," were generously scattered among his books,[3] columns and articles, imparting a charm to serious subject matter that endeared him equally to the professional and layman. In today's electronic universe, Judy's writing habits would probably exhaust spell check functions.

But what really made Judy a true original in his field was how he embraced the idea of dogs as sentient beings with souls, destined to join their masters in heaven when they departed this earth. At a time in the nation's history when canines were valued primarily for practical functions, such as hunting and guarding, Judy was among the first of his generation to explore the spiritual side of the dog-human connection.

For this revered professional among the dog elite of his time, the divinity of dogs was just as important as their physical well-being, and there would be consequences for the humans who did not grasp this concept. In 1949, Judy wrote, "You strike your dog, you whip, you even lower yourself and debase your soul to kick at him and you really kick your own dignity into the ditch."[4]

In September 1928, Judy and a committee of dog-loving Chicagoans established the National Dog Week movement[5]; seven special days were set aside to officially acknowledge all the ways dogs helped humans. By Chinese astrology, dogs get their years, and as the Greek idiom states, "every dog has its day," but for Will Judy, seven days seemed more fitting.

However, despite Judy's honorable intentions, his mission was slow to catch on, in part due to the onset of the Great Depression. How could a dog have its week when most humans couldn't even have a day? By post–World War II America, though, when spirits were lifted, weary citizens filled with the promise of better times were now ready to embrace National Dog Week with joy and abandon. In New York City, on the Lower Plaza of Rockefeller Center, purebreds pranced and mutts marched as crowds of appreciative onlookers cheered under the watchful eye of sculptor Paul Manship's famous statue, Prometheus.[6] For many city dwellers, it was their first glimpse of working dogs in action, as a multitude of breeds performed the special tasks for which they were bred.

Coverage of National Dog Week events appeared in newspapers around the nation, sharing the stories of similar celebrations in small towns and other cities. National Dog Week even had its own seals and stamps, designed by nationally renowned artists and imprinted with slogans like "Every Dog Needs a Good Home," and "Man's Best Friend in War ... in Peace." Famous dignitaries, sports figures and film and screen personalities were honored to be among those chosen as the event's honorary chairperson or host.

With subsequent observances of National Dog Week over the years, other notable supporters of the event used it as an occasion to educate the American public about issues affecting modern dog owners. Persons such as Blanche Saunders, known as the "First Lady of Poodle Training,"[7] and later Arthur "Captain" Haggerty, a dynamic and pioneering figure who has been referred to as "the most influential [dog] trainer of all time,"[8] helped to present the observance to a new generations of celebrants.

In 2005, Captain Haggerty devoted a tremendous expenditure of time and energy in urging the dog-loving public not to forget about Will Judy's week that went to the dogs. Setting up an elaborate Web site dedicated to National Dog Week,[9] Haggerty became the ultimate cheerleader for Judy's work, presenting a literal blueprint for those wishing to celebrate National Dog Week in a meaningful way. Haggerty's enthusiasm reached out from computer screens across the nation to help keep Judy's dream alive. One year later, the dogs of the nation, their humans and National Dog Week itself lost a great friend and supporter with the passing of Arthur Haggerty. But Haggerty's words had inspired some, including me, to relay the message of Captain Judy, a man he had held in such high regard.

Will Judy's beliefs and views stemmed from his experience as a responsible dog breeder and dog show judge concerned with canine health and temperament and from his years spent at the helm of *Dog World,* one of the most successful magazines of all times published just for dog enthusiasts.

However, Judy held beliefs that might be viewed as controversial by some today. A purist in the old-world sense, Judy believed that there were several advantages of owning a purebred dog and even attributed many of the problems plaguing the dog world in the late 1940s as stemming from mixed-breed dogs, or strays as he called them, and the humans who irresponsibly bred them.[10] Judy also had no patience for humans who let their dogs run wild, spreading destruction in city alleys and country fields and reproducing at will. He further posited that female dogs made better companion animals than males, and gave specific reasons for his belief.

But today, when many dog lovers champion the cause for canines of all mixes and breeds, it is important to remember that Judy clearly stated that in establishing the National Dog Week movement, his main objective was not to bring more dogs into the world but to make humans more responsible dog owners for the ones that were already here.[11]

Judy understood that breed knowledge strengthened the relationship between dog and human, and with this understanding more realistic expectations of a dog's behavior and natural capabilities resulted. Ultimately the beings at both ends of the leash would benefit.

Judy would have a lot to say about the current proliferation of puppy mills that have been established across the nation. Some puppy millers, such as those among the Amish population, believe that a dog does not possess a soul. Because of this conviction, they have no remorse for their mass production of dogs that are housed and bred in subpar conditions. Like livestock, they are bred strictly as a source of income. Will Judy saw things very differently; he most certainly would have condemned this practice, since he believed all dogs had souls.[12]

Even in 1958 the perceptive Judy recognized the growing problem of dogs born and raised in large puppy mills. On this issue he wrote, "One puppy factory can spoil the good work of a dozen serious breeders." He spoke for those dog owners who deserved dogs that were of sound physical and emotional health. He also asked that dog owners be treated fairly by professional breeders, who were to be held personally accountable for the health of the dogs they bred and sold during and after the "acquisition" process.[13]

And what would he think about the overproduction of designer mixed breeds, or dogs bred to be so tiny they can bathe in a tea cup, which are often sold through retail outlets and purchased for large sums of money on impulse? In the late 1940s, Judy had already expressed concern for the Chihuahua breed that had become increasingly smaller in stature through modern breeding. Judy noted that the Chihuahua still carried "in miniature the basic design of nature's breed of dog," and expressed his hope that "breeders will not twist this dog's type too far from the primal type."[14]

He would most certainly have had a few things to say about those who vilify specific breeds and breed-specific legislation that aims to place limits on the kinds of breeds individuals may own. In responding to a *Dog World* editorial that defended the "man-eating image" of German shepherd dogs, Judy wrote, "The dog fancy must fight the propaganda against dogs. The opposition to dogs is increasing and gives indication of becoming a dangerous thing."[15]

In writing this book, I felt compelled to tell the story of a man who possessed a highly technical, often scientific expertise about all things canine, from the building of their kennels to detailed knowledge of their anatomy, but one who also regarded dogs as almost human. To Judy's way of thinking, the only thing that separated dog from man was the former's lack of an "alfabet" and thumbs.[16]

My blog posts continue to present a variety of dog-related issues, but while my knowledge grows, and my perspective widens, important questions cause me growing concern. While Americans have a resounding adoration of dogs, why is it that so many of our companion animals are abused and discarded each year? Why are so many bills to establish laws to protect them not passed, and if they are, why aren't these laws enforced? Why do we continue to shelter dogs the same way year after year when it appears the system is broken? Why don't more people choose to spay and neuter their pets without caring that they may be contributing to our homeless pet population? Why do dog trainers and rescuers spend so much time arguing about the "right" way to carry out their work? And finally, how could it be that in this dog-obsessed nation, an observance like National Dog Week, with so much potential for good, could be destined to become just a footnote in our history books?

Today, while the majority of American dogs do enjoy a comfortable life, there still remains much work to be done on behalf of those dogs that do not. With millions of dogs currently residing in shelters throughout America, many will not find their forever homes, and it is a sad statistic that approximately 2.7 million cats and dogs are euthanized each year (one every 11 seconds).[17]

When I blog about a young autistic girl's challenging journey to acquire a service dog, a woman's effort to organize peaceful protests outside the retail shops that sell puppies, or the dog fashion designer who produces doggy fashion shows in New York City to raise funds for less fortunate animals, I see the work and feel the passion of Will Judy's legacy in all of their actions.

As much as he admitted to having "gone to the dogs,"[18] Judy understood that if we were going to ever truly improve the lot of the dog in our society, those who chose to protect and honor them needed to get along. He wrote that thoughts and actions surrounding these efforts "should be retained within the circle of normal logical human beings."[19]

Judy's writing was not limited to the topic of dogs, and at times the eclectic author focused on more philosophical projects about the human condition, offering books such as *Men and Things: Fifty Essays About Human Nature,* and *The Ways of Men, and Their Private and Public Conduct.* Under the pen name Weimer (Wymar) Port, Judy displayed an affinity for exploring curious topics that appealed to him personally, such as *Chicago the Pagan* and the exotic *Sayings of Rammikar.*

In his understanding of human nature and the value of dogs, Judy declared, "The battle for the kind heart is never won; it must be fought steadily with every child, with every person, with every new generation."[20]

By examining Judy's numerous volumes on dogs and back issues of *Dog World* over the course of five decades, we can gather insightful, real-time snapshots of how our understanding and perception of man's best friend has evolved over time in America.

As a minister, lawyer, educator, author, and publisher, William Lewis Judy set the course for the betterment of the dogs of the nation and enlightened the humans who continue to care about their welfare. Hopefully some perspective can be gained in the preserving and sharing of one man's lifetime dedication to a species that so uniquely serves mankind.

1

The Man Who
Went to the Dogs

Between the attitude toward the dog of those far past
centuries and the attitude of today is a vast journey in the
direction of kindness and a heart of sympathy.
—William Lewis Judy[1]

In his own idiosyncratic style of putting thoughts into the printed word, Captain William Lewis Judy would most likely have concurred that the American canine traveled a "ruff" road to achieve its exalted status of man's best friend.

Cave canem! "Beware of the dog," warns a Latin Proverb. Those words of caution etched upon the structures of Pompeii and other ancient Roman cities portrayed the dog as a vicious entity, omnipresent, on guard.[2]

In centuries past, dogs have made themselves useful to man as guardians and warriors, ready to battle the appointed enemy, much as they do today. While most of us in the modern world have little cause to beware of them, we as a nation are definitely *aware* of them.

In his writings on canines Judy celebrated the "ancient pledge between man and dog"[3] and offered what he termed his "course of thot," that although the dog had served as man's best friend since the beginning of creation, "it had been a very slow process in the opening of a two way street that allowed humans to call themselves the dog's best friend."[4]

Judy proposed that an unwritten contract existed between a man and his dog; one that was forged in the time of Adam and Eve. In minister-like fashion he shared the story of how one day Adam had gathered all the beasts of the field and forest, to assign each a purpose. At the time of this gathering a large gap opened in the earth and the biblical pair drifted apart from the animal kingdom, causing them great emotional anguish. Judy relayed that of all the animals, only the loyal dog risked its life to leap across the vast opening. Upon its safe passage, the dog went to Adam to "live by the side of man forever."[5]

Judy additionally informed readers that the original watch dog guarded the entrance of Hades, ever alert to the first lost soul hailed to the "infernal fires." And when "those cavemen of the hairy chest and swift-swinging club" came out of the hills to seek food, dogs evolved as man's invaluable helpmate.[6]

The man-canine bond began with these four-legged opportunists looking for a share of the remains of the day. But over time dogs learned that a partnership could be forged, as they protected those who helped them hunt for their own food.[7] Judy presented a scenario where dogs followed human hunters at a distance and broadcasted their intent to cooperate by "stopping, looking intently, and moving along when the hunters moved forward."[8]

When the battle between human and prey became intense, the wise dog seized the opportunity to help in the successful acquisition of the prey while protecting the hunter. Eventually the dog developed its reputation as a dependable and loyal servant of man.

Judy noted that even in the earliest chapters of recorded history, the dog was ever present. In ancient Babylon, Persia, and medieval France, the images of dogs remain chiseled on the foots of graves, sarcophagi and tombs, standing guard for eternity. The ancient Egyptians revered dogs and named the brightest of stars in the sky after them: Sirius, the dog star.[9]

Canis familiaris is the Latin name of the domesticated dog. Like their classification implies, the canine remains a familiar fixture in all corners of the world even now. They prance across big screen televisions during commercials and prime-time television shows, share the spotlight in Hollywood movies, pose adorably on the cover of glossy magazines and are featured almost daily in heart-wrenching news items where they are either being rescued, or are rescuing a human from physical hardship or emotional pain.

In America dogs are definitely at the heart of a great animal obsession; they are still omnipresent, sometimes on guard, but more often serving as loving docile companions and helpmates to countless appreciative humans.

There are legions of cat fanciers and horse lovers, too. But no other domesticated animal has ever coexisted in human households quite like the dog, or claimed outright the title of man's best friend. Of cats Judy wrote, "She is a daughter of many moods, royal in her fits of temper."[10] He went on to describe felines as secretive loners, lovers of darkness and basically unconcerned with the moods or needs of their owners. But the major difference between a cat and a dog, according to Judy, was that while a cat might make a good pet, a dog served more as a companion.[11]

Judy also liked and admired horses but observed that equines lacked the protective instincts of the canine. He made the observation that while under enemy attack, a horse, even one raised and cared for by a human over the course of its lifetime, was not capable of offering any concern or aide in times of danger.

Despite America's reverence for the dog and its special abilities, canines have not always been the recipient of our affection and admiration. Well before William Lewis Judy dedicated his life to their welfare, there was a strong and growing movement for animal advocacy in the nation.

In 1866, Henry Bergh became a champion for those unfortunate animals housed at the "pound," the common term for animal shelters at that time. In his founding of the American Society for the Prevention of Cruelty to Animals (ASPCA) in New York City, Bergh initially focused on the abuse of horses used in the transport of people and freight. Within a short period of time, the cities of Boston, Philadelphia and San Francisco embraced his mission.[12]

In 1877 the American Humane Association was established with the purpose of uniting 27 humane organizations culled from ten states. Its mission was to serve as an advocacy group for the welfare of children and neglected and abused livestock.[13]

Will Judy recognized and understood a woman's ability to bring about positive change despite those who underestimated their ability to do so. In 1927 he wrote, "The chief sufferer from custom and the darkness of the past has been woman." He further noted that the world was full of cowards who "hid piously behind the shield of God Almighty." To those who declared that women were inferior to men he posited that he believed God to be "mostly female," likening this higher power to a universal mother.[14]

This was exemplified by the fact that women figured prominently in the evolution of animal advocacy in America. In 1869 Caroline Earle White helped to establish the Women's Branch of the Pennsylvania SPCA. In 1874 this group established and dedicated the City Refuge for Lost and Suffering Animals. This pioneering facility became the first to provide medical treatments, arranging for adoptions for homeless pets and providing a humane method of death when necessary.[15]

Another woman also helped in the welfare of homeless animals. While Judy spoke out against irresponsible dog owners who allowed their stray dogs to roam free and the dog catchers who claimed the strays, another citizen of Chicago named Irene Castle created a refuge for them.

Castle was the female half of the internationally-renowned dancing team of Vernon and Castle, popular entertainers in the period leading up to and during World War I.[16] A lifelong animal lover, she became a tireless defender of the underdog. In 1928, the birth year of National Dog Week, Castle, now Mrs. Frederick McLaughlin, established an animal shelter called the Orphans of the Storm. Located in the city where Will Judy's *Dog World* headquarters stood, Castle founded Orphans of the Storm fueled by her belief that the unwanted dogs and cats of northeastern Illinois deserved loving homes and responsible owners.[17]

Castle's activity on behalf of her causes met with their share of unfortunate consequences and opposition. Just two years after establishing Orphans of the Storm, Castle endured a personal tragedy when 90 of her dogs perished in a fire that destroyed the kennels of her facility. The fire, deemed "incendiary" by officials, was started in three locations. Prior to this tragedy, the caretaker of the kennels had received threats claiming the resident dogs were a nuisance.[18]

Two decades later the headquarters of *Dog World* would meet a similar fate.

Castle was also active in the Illinois Anti-Vivisection Association and worked to educate the public to assuage the public's fear of rabies in the Chicago vicinity.[19]

When writing about the evolution of kindness in the human species, Judy posited that man's greatest achievements did not center on the number of steel mills, inventions or even the spread of "book knowledge." Man's ability to offer help to those humans in need and "the dumb creation who can not speak for themselves" was what propelled the human race to evolve.[20]

Throughout his literary career the eloquent and thoughtful Judy remained ever hopeful that humans would continue to progress in a civilized manner and reminded his followers that kindness was not hereditary but needed to be taught from one generation to the next. He wrote, "Between the attitude toward the dog of those far past centuries and the attitude of today is a vast journey in the direction of kindness and a heart of sympathy." But those who needed to receive this message were not always open to the lesson. "Every child is born tending toward savagery rather than civilization," he wrote.[21] For Judy the teaching of the care of companion animals was a way to develop strong character in the young. In his lifetime, Judy would accomplish this through his prolific literary achievements.

It may be difficult for a generation so accustomed to instantaneous access to facts and figures via electronics to imagine how the arrival of a monthly magazine in the mailbox or newsstand could be so greatly anticipated and appreciated for its cache of information.

But for many canine enthusiasts and those in dog-related professions, Will Judy's *Dog World* magazine, with its myriad of advertisements, quips, cartoons, and photographs of purebred dogs accompanied by a staggering array of statistics on breed standards and dog show results provided a window into national "dogdom" at a time when the internet, with its plethora of blogs, social media and e-mails, was not imaginable.

Judy was many things to many people in his lifetime, but his role as a reformer, who used the power of the pen to make the world a better place for dogs and their guardians, may be his greatest legacy.

William Lewis Judy was born September 20, 1891,[22] the son of Jerome Judy and Barbara Burkholder, a farmer and the village shopkeeper. The founders of the Judy family arrived from Switzerland, where the family name was spelled Tachudy.[23]

His quest for knowledge, sense of patriotism and love of the written word would take him far from his birthplace on the western slopes of the Allegheny Mountains in Garrett, Pennsylvania. Even with a motto like "the town that goes on and on,"[24] Garrett was not big enough to contain the wanderlust and ambitions of a young man like Will Judy.

By the late 1940s, Captain William Lewis Judy had establish himself as a highly successful pioneer in the dog industry and had also benefitted financially. A self-professed millionaire, which in his day was quite exceptional, Judy extolled, "The dog is the only true love money can buy."[25]

But for Judy the business of dogs wasn't only about money; it was also about using his position to impart the message to his followers that dogs were sensitive creatures that desired love and respect as much, if not more, than their human companions. To understand how he came to see things the way he did, it helps to understand the influences that shaped his early life.

Positions of responsibility came early to Judy. In his youth, he was trained for the clergy in the Church of the Brethren faith, also known as the Dunkards for their practice of "dunking" initiates in water. At the age of 13 he was charged with educating 45 mountaineer youth from kindergarten to grade six. At the time this was the highest level of education achieved by most. For his efforts, he was compensated 40 dollars a week and had to provide for his own room and board.[26]

Will Judy graduated from Juniata College in 1911, an institution established by members of the Church of the Brethren in 1867 and created to prepare individuals "for the useful occupations of life."[27] His affiliation with, and fondness for, Juniata College and its teachings influenced the remainder of his life.

The Church of the Brethren sect was founded by a fellowship of

School children outside the school house in Garrett, Pennsylvania, around the turn of the century. Will Judy is in the second row, second from right (head showing only) (courtesy of the Meyerdale Public Library, Pennsylvania).

Christians. Today, the college continues to emphasize the value of simple living combined with a commitment to peace and reconciliation and service to neighbors. These were the enduring qualities that Will Judy exemplified through his writings and actions.

Juniata College was an institute ahead of its time. In its first year of existence Juniata offered a coeducational experience, atypical for most colleges of its day. It is said that Judy walked barefoot to the classes that were housed in a cramped room above a print shop.[28]

Judy went on to earn an LLD from the Hamilton College of Law in Clinton, New York, where he graduated the class as valedictorian. In 1915, he found employment as a lawyer in Chicago, Illinois.[29]

In 1938, Judy was invited to speak to the graduating class of his alma mater in Garrett, Pennsylvania, and shared his personal tale as a man who made plans for himself that were not in keeping of the expectations of others.[30]

As a student at Juniata Academy, Judy recalled that he had enjoyed a strong academic record that included public speaking. However, Judy informed the audience that during his time there, and while at Juniata College, he had won almost every varsity letter possible, with the exception of tennis, and won every public speaking event held during his senior year of college.[31]

Judy informed the graduates that at the age of 15 he had been elected to the local ministry of the Church of the Brethren, but had declined the position, much to the dismay of the Brothers Valley Congregation. Upon his graduation from Juniata College, Judy relayed that he ventured far from home to spend time in British Columbia and Alaska.[32]

Judy shared that he spent time working in an office at the Packard Motor Company in Detroit, and labored as a "shovel stiff" along the Pacific Coast, an owner of a bowling alley, print shop employee, and candidate for Congress.[33] He also served as the Post Commander of the American Legion in Chicago[34] before finding his true life's calling.

In 1917, Judy interrupted his legal career to serve in the United States Army, where he served in the American Expeditionary Force in Europe. Judy rose to the rank of Captain within two years and for his exemplary service was awarded a Silver Star "for gallantry in action against an opposing armed force."[35]

Judy would later capture his wartime experience in a book titled *A Soldier's Diary*, which chronicled his life from August 1917 to June of 1919. The book was eventually published in 1930; in it the unapologetic young author confided that by maintaining a diary during wartime, he had violated Army regulation.[36]

Judy reported that he had kept a diary since the age of 12 and admitted he felt compelled to relay and share an accurate and "naked"[37] account of his Army experience. "All authors are vain," Judy wrote in the book's introduction, concluding that "diarists are most vain of all."[38]

He explained that he had delayed the book's publication for 11 years so as not to offend certain parties, although he did admit to omitting some names, stating, "The law of libel is the friend of truth but not always of the truth teller."[39]

Judy warned his audience that the book contained vivid and realistic scenes and was not intended to be just another heart-warming, glamorized collection of patriotic war stories. He bluntly declared, "A diary must not smell of the doctor else it lose its first virtue of truth-telling."[40]

In 1923 Judy took advantage of an auspicious business opportunity when he purchased *Dog World* magazine, a publication teetering on the brink of failure.[41] At the time, the magazine had been in circulation for eight years, owned by a man by the name of Fred Formaneck. Judy purchased the magazine that he said was "going down for the third time" for the pittance of $1,200.[42]

As the magazine's publisher, Judy now had an expansive and lucrative venue through which to reach the rapidly growing number of dog-loving Americans. Under his direction, *Dog World* went on to be one of the largest and most successful trade publications in pet-publishing history.

"Our resolution for the coming year is to give to the Fancy the best that is possible in news and service.... As your dog is our dog, no one can kick him without kicking us. With you we pledge ourselves to see that he gets a square deal."[43]

With this declaration that appeared on the cover of Judy's first issue of *Dog World*, it was clear he planned to parlay his wisdom, clever way with words and down-home wit to influence a new generation of dog owners and fanciers. But most importantly he hoped to ensure that humans would always be a dog's best friend.

The skills he acquired in his training for the ministry allowed him to speak with equal ease to those who inhabited the elite circle of the show dog world and those who made their living as dog professionals, as well as average dog owners who simply sought sound advice on how to be more responsible guardians to their dogs, all for a mere 20¢ per issue.[44]

This dynamic yet understated young entrepreneur was hard to ignore. As described in a corporate press release, Judy was a debonair figure, with his "handsome moustache flecked with gray," and his "deep set eyes framed by heavy dramatic eyebrows."[45] The refined publisher might have been cast as a sophisticated supporting actor alongside Clark Gable or Errol Flynn in a popular Hollywood production of his time.

Judy wasted no time proclaiming his desire to enhance the quality of life for the nation's dogs. He used his position at *Dog World* to improve conditions for all dogs by advocating the benefits of enlightened dog breeding and ownership.

In the early part of the 1920s there were no national standards in the field of breeding. Judy sought to change this and would not allow "lowball prices on stud fees and puppy sales in the magazine's classified advertising section," and established "a minimum amount of $20 for a stud fee, and $25 for the advertised sale of a puppy."[46]

Throughout his reign as *Dog World*'s publisher, Judy never lacked for writers who wished for their columns to appear in the magazine. Maxwell Riddle, a prolific writer on dogs and a protégé of Judy's, recalled how Judy found "great economy by asking people to guest write columns."[47]

As this was a fortuitous situation for any writer in the dog industry, the opportunity for a byline was always graciously accepted, and the flattered writer would contribute on a monthly basis with no monetary compensation. When the novelty eventually wore off and the writer moved on, a new one gladly replaced them.[48] In many instances Judy was content to conduct his own research and wrote his own columns on a variety of topical issues relating to dogs.

By 1945 *Dog World* was selling for 35¢ a copy, received by mail at a rate of $2 for a year, $3 for two years or the money-saving plan of $5 for five years. In addition to *Dog World*, a pocket-size magazine called *Judy's* was also available. According to a promotional blurb for this publication, "*Judy's* represents a new and different type of American journalism—honest thinking, straight talk, and an absence of pretense and hokum." This publication offered news, articles, literary excerpts and illustrations that focused on "American Viewpoints, and American ways of thot [thought] and life."[49]

"The Story Behind *Dog World* Magazine" was presented in a press release under the title of *The Boxer Review* and distributed in October of 1956; the seasoned editor reflected on three decades of his publishing experience. "Readers criticize its [the magazine's] layout ... advertisers cheer its results ... competitors envy its circulation ... and *Dog World* rolls on each month to an impressive 50,000 circulation," boasted the proud publisher.[50]

Judy took his publishing responsibilities seriously, but always maintained a sense of humor and patience while enduring his critics. Under a bold face heading that declared, "Why editors and circulation managers of day papers die at an early age!" a bemused Judy shared what he referred to as his "boots and bravos," under a sub-heading he called "Brikbats and Bokays."[51]

"*Dog World* is like the Sears Roebuck catalog ... the layouts are lousy—ads, articles, editorials, cartoons, letters all jammed together!" complained one reader.[52] Another carped, "The type's so small, and you can't read it without a magnifying glass."[53] Providing a backhanded compliment, an overly dedicated woman reader penned, "My husband 'hates' me when *Dog World* arrives, for I hibernate for a full day, reading every word."[54]

But readers couldn't get enough of Judy's colorful reporting style. At a time when world travel was not available for many, adoring fans could not get enough of his personal accounts of his traveling adventures as he circled the globe judging dog shows in exotic faraway lands.

Licensed as a dog judge in 26 countries, Judy enjoyed sharing his escapades with his readers during his 28,000-mile dog show circuit from South Africa, Australia, New Zealand, and Cuba.[55] In his "notes to home" style of writing, subscribers learned of his tipping habits and his cocktail of choice, "bourbon straight, a three ounce portion—no ice."[56]

By 1958 Judy had relinquished the publishing helm of the magazine to his business partner, George Berner.[57] In that same year, *Dog World* lost another great asset; its four story home at 3323 Michigan Boulevard was destroyed by a fire. The disaster claimed most of the Judy Publishing Company's records and contents. But an undaunted Judy carried on as the company's president and director in the magazine's new location, not too far away from its previous location.[58]

In the years following his official retirement Judy continued to educate the American dog owner about the importance of proper training through a correspondence course. For $18, dog enthusiasts could purchase a Will Judy "College Course in Canines." For their investment, customers received five autographed copies (at no extra charge) of books written by him.[59]

The Big 6, as he called this course of study, was designed for both professionals and the "just plain dog owner."[60] Book topics ranged from training, kennel building, general care, breeding, and a dog scrapbook filled with stories and anecdotes that paid tribute to man's best friend. The sixth item, touted as a bonus, offered a dozen 16-page pamphlets on a variety of dog-related topics.[61]

Will Judy's *Dog World* magazine, his books on dogs and his mail order courses on their training found their way to millions of American homes via the U.S. Postal Services. However, Judy also took advantage of America's obsession with post card correspondence in fostering the love of dogs.

At a time in American history when most people had no telephones, picture postcards allowed them to send friends and family a brief message in a relatively short period of time, in many cases as frequently as three times a day.

Almost any image could be found on a picture postcard; flowers, birds, babies, romantic couples, bathing beauties, holidays, and views of cities and towns. Whatever image or topic sold well could be produced on a postcard almost on demand. During this golden age of correspondence when Will Judy was in his early teens, images of all kinds of canines were carried in mail pouches from coast to coast.

Postcards bearing images of dogs were popular items, and present day postcard collectors are still discovering cards that were never documented by their publishers.

Post card artists like Vincent Colby specialized in the portrayal of wistful dogs and cats, often pictured side by side. Colby is most famous for a series of black and white images of cats and dogs and often used these images as a platform to call attention to the plights of abused and abandoned pets.

In the 1930s through the 1950s, while Judy produced his volumes of writing on dogs, picture postcards printed on linen paper became readily available. Like the golden age, this so-called linen era of postcards made communications easier during the Depression and throughout World War II. In mail pouches throughout the nation beautiful portrait-like images of pure bred dogs mingled silly and sweet images of all types of dogs.

Copyright, 1906, by V. Colby

ALL I DID WAS GROWL A LITTLE

Above and opposite: Vince Colby black and white postcards c. 1906 and 1909. Postal images with drawings by artists like V. Colby were popular from the early 1900s on, and often conveyed America's attitude and perception of companion animals.

Never one to miss a trend, Judy published his own line of postcards during this time that he advertised as the "Dog Sentiments" series.

By the time he officially retired as the publisher of *Dog World,* Judy had produced 426 issues of his beloved magazine, with his last issue rolling off the press in October 1958.[62] At age 67, dog's best friend, who "went to the dogs and made a million," looked forward to spending more time with his titian-haired wife, Ruth, a prominent dog show professional in her own right.[63]

But as good as he was to the canines, Judy never lost sight of the fact that it took a thoughtful, enlightened human at the other end of the leash to raise a good dog. In 1958, he endowed his alma mater, Juniata College, with a generous donation to its lectureship program.

The Will Judy Lectureship still provides the college with annual visits from leaders in government, education, the arts, natural sciences,

CITY POUND

I don't want to be an Angel!
COPYRIGHT 1909 BY V.COLBY.

and business. In setting up the lectureship, Judy specified that "the detection of fallacies in reasoning" be a feature of at least one lecture, and required that lecturers remain on campus "long enough to enter into the discussion generated by his or her remarks."[64]

In 1959, Henry Margenau, a physicist-philosopher, became the program's first speaker. Since that time, other notables making appearances have included African-American comedian and civil rights activist Dick

A Dog's Prayer

O LORD OF HUMANS, make my master faithful to his fellowmen as I am to him. Grant that he may be devoted to his friends and family as I am to him.

MAY HE BE openfaced and undeceptive as I am; may he be true to trust reposed in him as I am to his.

GIVE HIM a face cheerful like unto my wagging tail. Give him a spirit of gratitude like unto my licking tongue.

FILL HIM WITH patience like unto mine that awaits his footsteps uncomplainingly for hours. Fill him with my watchfulness, my courage, and my readiness to sacrifice comfort or life itself.

KEEP HIM always young in heart and crowded with the spirit of play, even as I. *MAKE HIM as good a man as I am a dog. Make him worthy of me, his dog.*

● By Will Judy

● This is #3

Postcard published by the Judy Publishing Company. Judy used his dog sentiment postcard series to promote responsible pet ownership.

Gregory (1969–70), biochemist and writer Isaac Asimov (1971–72), political activist and presidential candidate Ralph Nader (2002–03), and creativity expert Sir Ken Robinson (2008–09).[65]

Accountability and customer service remained Judy's mission throughout his career. In the early part of the 1960s he championed pioneering concepts such as the importance of obedience training in the first three months of a puppy's life and stated, "The old era of the breeder-seller 'washing his hands' of a sale as soon as the puppy left his place has passed."[66] He also reminded those in the industry that the objective of dog breeding must be based on ethical business practices, because that business depended on their ability to provide healthy dogs to a growing population of American dog owners.

In his lifetime Judy officiated at dog trials in 28 countries, received the Ellie Sheets Memorial Trophy for Outstanding Personage of Fancy in 1936, and went on to be named "Gaines Dogdom's Man of the Year" in 1949, and again in 1958, making him a two-time recipient of their prestigious Fido Award. The Will Judy award is still given to those dogs that earn at least 195 out of 200 points at three high-end obedience competitions during a single season.[67]

He also wrote a syndicated newspaper column, *Dog Talks*; founded the Oldtimers of the Kennel World (a club for seasoned dog professionals); and presided over the Dog Writers Association of America, as well as the Dog Defenders League of America.[68]

Despite his outstanding professional accomplishments in the dog industry and the publishing world, perhaps William Judy's most lasting legacy would come about when he set aside an official week of honor for all the ways dogs had served man throughout time.

For many, the saying "every dog has its day" has come to imply that even the lowliest will achieve revenge on the most powerful oppressor. But to Judy's interpretation, this adage "was based on smug reasoning that it was all right to kick him [the dog] about, to let him fend for himself, except that on one day in his life, you had to be kind to him."[69] With the establishment of these seven days dedicated to kindness toward them, Judy had set out to give dogs their due.

Almost 30 years later, the founder of National Dog Week still held hope for the dogs of the nation. He penned the words, "Between the attitude toward the dog of those far past centuries and the attitude of today is a vast journey in the direction of kindness and a heart of sympathy, toward real civilization."[70]

In 1972 Will Judy wrote his final book, *Dog Shows and Rules*.[71] On December 27 of the following year this icon of the dog world passed away at the age of 82 and was laid to rest in his beloved Chicago. Upon this news, Juniata College proclaimed they had "lost a most faithful and generous friend."[72]

And so had the dogs of America.

2

From Scientific to Soulful: Will Judy's Ultimate Work on the Physical and Emotional Lives of Dogs

Don't Call a Man a Dog, subtitled *Will Judy's Scrap Book on Dogs*, was written and published by Judy in 1949. No other work of Judy's so seamlessly combined the author's scientific knowledge of the canine and his unique spiritual perspective on their place in the universe.

Chapters filled with Judy's personal views on the breeding, training and judging of dogs showcased the author's unorthodox views on their inner workings. But what set this book apart from all others in its category was the influence of Judy's early training in the ministry, present on practically every page.

Don't Call a Man a Dog was the written version of a lecture Judy had delivered to dog enthusiasts across the nation beginning in the mid–1930s. In the book's introduction, the author wrote, "There are too many dog books. There are never enuf good dog books."[1]

He unabashedly acknowledged that dog books and those who authored them comprised a very large portion of the literary world. "We cry out against the flock of volumes on the canine,"[2] he observed, but even this prolific author and publisher of the genre admitted that his complaint was futile, since each book's author fancied their book as "the masterpiece of the pack, the lead dog in the library."[3]

Judy graciously welcomed readers to be the final judge on this matter.

A tough literary critic, Judy condemned many of the offerings of his fellow colleagues. He declared that many writers did not adhere to the "laws of good literature,"[4] and made the wry observation that in no other area of writing had "sentiment, personal viewpoints and the tears of emotion so taken over with disregard to science and intellectual pride."[5]

Judy had earned his right to critique. By the time *Don't Call a Man a Dog* was published, the seasoned publisher's finger was placed adroitly on the pulse of American popular culture, and he understood the enduring appeal of dog books for a multitude of American readers.

In November 2006, an article titled "These Books Have Gone to the Dogs," written by Nancy Pearl, appeared on the National Public Radio website.[6] Pearl stated, "A book about a dog has been at or near the top of nonfiction best-seller lists for about a year now."[7]

But America's fascination with books that celebrated the animal-human bond began well before Will Judy even spoke his first sentence or learned his "alfabet," as he would spell it in his quirky style. The book *Beautiful Joe* was written in 1892, a year after Judy's birth, and is often credited for being the first international bestseller in the rich history of classic dog stories.

The dog on which the story of Beautiful Joe was based was a medium-sized brown colored terrier mix described as a mongrel, to use the then-popular term for a mixed-breed dog. The unfortunate dog was originally owned by an abusive man who severely mistreated the dog, going so far as to cut off the tail and ears of the dog.[8]

In 1890 the dog was rescued from this brutal environment by a woman named Margaret Saunders, who wrote a fictional work based on his harsh life and the family that rescued him. Three years later Saunders submitted the story to a writing contest sponsored by the Humane Society. Her entry won and the following year it was published as a novel and became a huge success.

A woman writing about dogs during this period of time was not the norm. Because she did not think readers would take a woman writer seriously, she wrote under the assumed name of Marshall Saunders. She also chose the novel way of telling the story from a dog's viewpoint.

Saunders' unique storytelling style allowed the reader into Beautiful Joe's mind and evoked more sympathy for this dog than if the author had relied on more traditional narrative forms.

Beautiful Joe made history as being the first book by a Canadian author to sell over a million copies. By 1900, over 800,000 copies had been sold in the United States, 40,000 in Canada and 100,000 in the United Kingdom.[9]

By the late 1930s, the book was still selling over seven million copies, with a sequel published in 1934 titled *Beautiful Joe in Paradise*. Saunders received the Commander of the British Empire in 1934, Canada's highest civilian award.[10]

Many fictional versions of true events joined the ranks of books like *Beautiful Joe*. Over the course of decades, these books dramatized and celebrated the special bond between humans and their dogs. *Lad: A Dog* by Albert Payson Terhune followed in 1919, as well as other classics such as *Old Yeller*, written by Fred Gipson in 1956, and *Where the Wild Fern Grows*, penned by Wilson Rawls five years later.

Don't Call a Man a Dog exemplified Judy's personal view of dogs offered through an assortment of essays, poems and the imaginative and thoughtful works of other dog-centric authors. His regard of dogs as soul mates and valued family members filled every page and he steadfastly defended dogs against those who did not value them or did not live up to the privilege of owning one. The author's sentimental and soft side ruled his words in minister-like fashion.

As he had done in all his previous works, Judy took the time to inform those reading *Don't Call a Man a Dog* that the book's content as well as its physical properties were both of the highest caliber offered in the dog-publishing world.

The proud publisher stated that the volume was "of the Blue Ribbon Series," set on the linotype in 12-point Benedictine type. Detail oriented to the core, Judy went on to inform how this process made for "an excellent book face for readability and design … set in 10-point face on 11-point slug … 25 picas wide."[11]

Judy further offered information on the book's "hardbindings" and pointed out that the "title and backbone on the cloth are stamped in ink with brass dies." He discussed how the book's edges as well as its end sheets were stained in a hue to match its binding, and he praised the quality of paper stock used for its pages and the book's trademark "flyleaf" page that offered a special stamp unique to a "Judy" book, a designated place where the name of the book's owner could be found.[12]

The content of the dust jacket of *Don't Call a Man a Dog* heralded the book as a standard volume of reference that presented the author's heartfelt views on the physical, mental and emotional components of the canine.

Don't Call a Man a Dog offered literate items on all things dog that included prose and poetry and 127 illustrations in the form of drawings, photographs and cartoons that captured the emotional bond between dog and human in a way that engaged and charmed readers.[13]

The book was movingly dedicated to all of Judy's dogs, "past, present and future, and to the occasion when we all shall meet again."[14] Under this inscription, Judy printed a poem he had personally composed years earlier, titled "Purgatory of Dogs," that captured the spirit of this dedication.

In the passage, Judy waxed poetic on his belief that dogs would be waiting for us in the afterlife. Judy's words enabled the reader to experience the loyalty of a dog that preferred to wait in purgatory instead of accepting an invitation to enter into a better place. The last lines of the poem presents a scene where the devoted dog's patience is rewarded as it recognizes his beloved master among the crowd and greets him with yelps of joy.[15]

In the introduction of *Don't Call a Man a Dog,* Judy acknowledged that the sport of dog breeding and the showing of purebred dogs had grown tremendously popular over the years. A perceptive observer of his colleagues, Judy wrote that "with the possible exception of theatrical and stage folks, no other group of humans are as temperamental and emotionally on a spree, as dog fanciers."[16]

By the late 1940s, this legion of professional dog enthusiasts had combined with the multitude of average dog-owning Americans to form a diverse force to be reckoned with. Of this vast army Judy wryly noted, "each one has the best dog in the world," and that the other guy would always have to settle for second best.[17] No one was more capable of understanding these quirky and passionate dog owners than Judy, who was now regarded as the leader of their pack.

Through his years at the helm of *Dog World* Judy had come to understand that there was much more going on in the dog community outside the elite dog show circle to which he was privy. He now endeavored to focus on the more divine side of the dog-human relationship and share his view that a unique spiritual partnership existed between the living entities at both ends of the leash.

Judy understood that people welcomed dogs into their lives for a variety of reasons. Of this he wrote, "The reason is of small consequence, the important item is that owners be worthy of their dogs."[18]

Judy recognized that certain individuals owned dogs for reasons of vanity. For them, the dog was an "expression of self exhibitionism."[19] But even in those cases Judy saw how this vanity might benefit dogs, because at least these dogs would be fussed over by their owners and would never suffer from neglect. Of this group, Judy observed that the dog "feeds the ego, builds confidence and makes life more pleasant."[20]

But he also believed that for another group of people the dog made up for personal feelings of inferiority. These dog owners gained self-worth by possessing award-winning dogs that had received all the accolades and all the right ribbons to prove it.[21]

For the timid souls among the dog-owning populace, Judy noted that a dog provided a sense of self-assurance and comfort.

Long before it was widely accepted, Judy concluded that dogs were natural physicians for the treatment of physical and mental or emotional ailments. He observed that war veterans who suffered from post-war trauma received therapeutic benefits from companion dogs and observed that the lively antics of the canine helped these men to find their way back to functioning in the world.[22]

Judy believed that dogs, with their lack of affectation and natural joy for living, provided a balance for those humans wracked by stress. He advised, "Dogs are an antidote to the machine-shop precision and the speeding machinery of our present day tempo of living."[23]

At a time when many dogs were regularly employed in useful activities such as hunting and guarding, busily being primped and groomed for showing purposes or merely relegated to the backyards of suburban homes, Judy urged dog owners to just enjoy the companionship of their dogs.

For the overworked, overtaxed human, Judy prescribed time spent simply enjoying the company of dogs, be it a romp on the beach, in the surf, a walk in the field or at the very least a walk around the block.[24]

Of those accused of regarding their dogs as furry children, the childless Judy offered a few words of advice. To those he referred to as, "mossbackers," individuals who ignorantly quipped, "Them wimmen oughter have kids instead of dogs," Judy admonished that many women who owned dogs did have children and that many childless women with dogs would prefer to have their own children, but fate had prevented it. Judy also observed that some of the latter group were incapable of bearing children and some did not have husbands. In Judy's time, society did not favor those who opted for single parenthood.

As he had in the columns of *Dog World* throughout the years, Judy crammed *Don't Call a Man a Dog* with an abundance of information that he organized in typical Judy fashion. The volume was divided into a "General Section One with Five Parts," and a "General Section Two" titled "Will Judy's Scrapbook on Dogs," which was divided into two parts.

Part 1 of the second section consisted of poems and other material about dogs composed by the author himself, as well as "Other Selected Writings on the Dog," a presentation of Judy's personal favorite passages and poems.

But the exuberance of Judy's writing often trumped his attempts at writing in a detailed and orderly fashion and often resulted in the curious repetition of his most fervent points. In some ways Judy molded the mindset and the behavior of his readers using similar methods he employed to train dogs: repetition and the activation of memory.

Section 1 contained five parts that appeared under the headings of "Man as the Dog's Greatest Conquest," "The Dog's Use of His Five Senses," "The Mind of the Dog," "Dogs as Teachers" and "Unfairness to the Dog."

Section 2 presented written works created by the author, which included poems titled "My Dog Is Dead," "The Old Dog" and "Be Not So Cruel." Under the section "Prose Compositions" were listed other writings by Judy that included "Why the World Likes Dogs," "A Dog's Prayer for His Master," "No Room in Heaven," "A Dozen Dog Care Do's and Don'ts" and "An Apology for the Dog Catcher."

Among selections of writings by other authors were Senator Vest's "Tribute to a Dog," "The Power of the Dog" by Rudyard Kipling, "Little Dog Angel" by Norah M. Holland, "The Little Black Dog of Christ's" by Elizabeth Gardner Reynolds and an assortment of "Proverbs and Bits of Wisdom About Dogs."

Judy began part 1 with the line, "Introducing myself as the author of this book, I am happy to have gone to the dogs."[25] With these words the impassioned author prepared his readers for a different kind of dog book. In the following paragraphs he explained how he had been educated for the ministry but chose another path when he pursued his law degree and ultimately became the publisher of *Dog World* magazine. Judy additionally confided that "my friends assure me that each change was a step upwards."[26]

He also noted that he wasn't alone in his devotion to the canine, for many of his fellow–Americans, regardless of reigning political powers, had joined him. Judy extolled, "The more America goes to the dogs, the better I like it."[27]

By the time *Don't Call a Man a Dog* was published, businesses based on the care and maintenance of dogs had significantly benefitted from America's growing fascination with dogs. That the nation's growing obsession for all things dog had "gotten a substantial niche in our life sentimentally, usefully and economically" bode well for the future of the industry and Will Judy.[28]

By 1949, Judy noted that there were approximately 240 pedigree dogs mingled with what he called, "a vast host of just-dog," that made up a worldwide canine population he estimated at 190 million.[29] He exuberantly declared that "the dog has cast his lot with the human,"[30] and that no other species was so widely dispersed on the planet, with possibly the exception of the common brown rat.

In general section 1, Judy printed the word for dog in ten international languages along with a poem he had written titled "How the Dog was Named." In its eight stanzas, Judy presented a scenario where God gathered all the species on earth to seek assistance from the animal kingdom.[31]

In the last stanza, the sound of barking encompasses the throngs of animals and God is aware of the traits of the dog that make it a perfect candidate. He beckons to the dog to come to his side and invites him to serve with the words: "I backward gladly spell and call you DOG."[32]

Judy also used the pages of *Don't Call a Man a Dog* to promote the last full week in September as a special time put aside to honor the dogs of America. He noted that he had personally established National Dog Week in 1928 and credited the National Dog Welfare Guild for seeing that it was observed for those seven days as well as in spirit year-round.[33]

By the time *Don't Call a Man a Dog* was published, Will Judy's National Dog Week had been observed 21 times and was widely embraced by the 15 million dogs of the nation or one of every ten persons who now owned dogs in America.[34]

The book provided some telling statistics of the heightened status of the canine in America. Of the nation's estimated dog population, Judy noted that approximately 20 percent were purebred with the remaining 80 percent comprised of what Judy termed "just dog—mongrel, mixed-bred, mutt, but all-dog. One hundred percent man's best friend."[35]

Americans increasingly spent larger sums of money on the care of those dogs and by 1948 Judy estimated that the nation's dog-owning citizens spent nearly $229 million on items related to the care and feeding of their pets.[36]

Of these expenditures it was noted that the retail sales of commercial dog food was nearly $145 million with $2 million invested in medicines and soap, $5 million for collars, with fees for veterinarians totaling approximately $12.5 million dispersed among 1,800 practicing veterinarians in 1,400 small animal hospitals.[37]

The world of breeding and dog showing also represented a large outlay of cash with $3 million spent on the arranging of champion and match shows and field trials as well as the purchase by Americans of 600,000 purebred puppies representing a cost of $24 million. Additional items such as licensing fees and personal property taxes (dogs were considered chattel, therefore taxable) accounted for the remainder of total expenditures.[38]

But Judy looked beyond the facts and figures of the dog business and explored in depth the spiritual value of dogs. In a chapter titled, "Every Dog has His Day," he shrewdly observed that throughout history, referring to a man as a dog had been intended as a form of insult or reproach. Judy found this unacceptable and undeserved, noting, "Just what the dog, could he talk, would call some human beings, is a matter of interest."[39]

Judy pointed out that even in the realm of religion the dog did not receive the respect it deserved. Well versed in the teachings of the Bible, the author presented several references from the good book that devalued a dog's worth. Among these: "Give not that which is holy unto the dogs," Matthew 7:6; "For without are dogs and sorcerers and whoremongers," and "His watchmen are all dumb dogs, they cannot bark; sleeping, lying down, loving to slumber," Isaiah 56: 10.[40]

He wrote that in ancient times the dog was generally regarded as, "low and worthless."[41] Despite the fact that they served man by protecting their homes, children, and property, dogs were frequently mistreated, forced to sleep in gutters and fed from the "swill barrel," in reward for their service to man.[42] In a segment titled, "In Praise of the Word Bitch," Judy discussed his displeasure at the debasement of the technical term for a female dog.

Judy noted that just as the word dog was frequently used by one man to offend another, the phrase, "son of a bitch" was often hurled in anger with the intent to insult a man *and* his mother. He sternly reproached those individuals who allowed the word "bitch" to roll off their "malicious tongues" in anger and advised humans to use the word in reference to a female dog only as it was "a word as fit, as logical for the speech of children and of men and women, as any other word in a book of holy wisdom."[43]

Despite these prejudices, Judy maintained that the quality of life for dogs had slowly improved as the world became more civilized. However, he maintained that humans regarded the traits of courtesy and kindness as signs of physical inferiority and emotional weakness.

In minster-like fashion, Judy reminded readers that it took more courage to speak up for others and to defend the oppressed than to courageously traipse across a battlefield to receive a medal of honor.[44]

In chapter 3 of general section 2, Judy got to the crux of his beliefs as to why dogs deserved to be exonerated by man when he expounded on the interpretation of the term, "Every dog has his day."

He explained that the old adage used to mean that it was acceptable to kick a dog around and allow him to fend for himself except for the one day of his life when kindness and honor were graciously bestowed on him.[45]

In contrast, Judy wrote that the "world of dogs have progressed,"[46] to a point that every day of the year was the dog's day and a more advanced and evolved society could wisely choose to properly train, feed and treat dogs in a humane manner.

Judy also maintained that while humans had benefitted from inventions and discoveries,[47] members of the animal kingdom, including canines, lacked the conveniences we had grown accustomed to. While we had evolved and progressed over the course of 2,000 plus years, dogs still only had their limited physical abilities and instincts to aid them in their daily quest for survival.

Judy wrote that despite their lack of evolution from their primary form, dogs had "become the greatest achievement and victory of man over the animal kingdom."[48] Dogs were the selfless visitors that emerged from the woods and fields and purposefully chose to live in the yards and homes of man until they were eventually considered members of the human family.

It was Judy's unmitigated belief that the only thing that had prevented the species of dog from rising above the level of beast was its lack of a thumb and an "alfabet."[49] He set forth that man's greatest achievement was the invention of "the alfabet" which he described as, something humans took for granted.

With the development of an alphabet, man had obtained the ability to form words and sentences that enabled them to exchange thoughts and ideas in written and oral form and to preserve thoughts, words and actions.[50] He drolly observed that without words the book in the reader's hands would not exist and they would not be able to issue commands to their dogs!

Despite their inability to speak, dogs had come close to breaking down "this speech barrier," bringing the dog to almost a human level.[51] To those who claimed that they conversed regularly with their dogs, Judy confided that he regularly talked to his own pack.

Through vocalization and movement of its body and tail, the dog communicated with amazing success by talking from both sides of its body.[52] However, Judy reminded readers that without an alphabet and hands, dogs were still ruled by the laws of the jungle much as they had been 50 centuries before. He implored readers, "Have you ever stopt to consider that every door is a prison to a dog—because he has not hands with which to turn knobs and keys?"[53]

In a section titled, "The Dog's Use of His Five Senses," Judy discussed how dogs had come to uniquely employ the senses of touch, taste, sight, hearing and scent. He ranked the importance of each sense to the dog, with smell as the most important to a dog, followed by hearing, sight, taste and touch.

The dog's sense of taste was said to be about 20 percent as effective as that of a man's. The sight of the dog was ranked as third in significance and was considered about 80 percent as effective as man's, with hearing 140 percent as keen and smell as 300 percent "as usual as in the human."[54]

The dog's lack of vocal and manual ability may have served to keep it dependent on man, but its senses of taste, touch, sight, hearing and olfactory skills had evolved together in ways that compensated for other short comings. When these five senses, combined with what Judy termed a "group of mental activities" or "Thinking Faculties," the dog became distinguished from all other creatures in the animal kingdom.[55]

Judy wrote that the sense of taste is of little concern to dogs since most of them consume food without benefit of careful chewing. Food is broken down by an abundance of gastric juices found in the stomach of the dog. Judy explained that through ancestral memory dogs learned that those who gulped their foods survived another day. He advised that even a good dog should be forgiven the occasion when it growled at those who approached its food. It was just practicing a survival technique.[56]

But Judy warned that as dogs came to share their homes with those of humans, they had become overindulged and lazy. He blamed many of their illnesses and diseases on improper diet, overfeeding and lack of exercise.[57]

The sense of touch in canines is irrelevant according to Judy, who noted that the dog's wavy or wiry coat covers its thick skin and offers protection from the elements.[58]

Even a dog's paw is not readily engaged in a useful or meaningful manner, although Judy observed that on occasion dogs with high levels of intelligence and varied experience learned that a well-placed touch of a paw often yielded desirable results.[59]

The dog's vision is not as important as it is for a human. Dogs see less acutely than humans. A dog's physical limitations of navigating the world in a horizontal position held close to the ground ultimately compromises its scope. When Judy asked readers to imagine the world as a dog, he likened this vista to a "forest mainly [seen] as short trunks and without branches."[60] In general the dog's sight is keener at greater distances, where they are able to discern moving objects more quickly than men.[61]

On the topic of canine vision Judy noted that in 1928 he had been the first in his field to declare publicly that dogs were color-blind.[62] Judy wrote that in canines, color blindness affected both males and females of the species, unlike in humans where the condition occurs five times more frequently in males.

He noted that dogs viewed the world monochromatically. They detected "color" in single shades and tones and saw objects in terms of general shape and form. Only those dogs carefully trained to do so could see in detail.[63]

The ears of a dog were placed high on the head and presented in two types, low hanging flaps or erect and batlike (the latter often being the result of a surgical procedure called docking). Dogs cocked their heads in order to "catch" sounds, and although the hearing of a dog was finely tuned, they also "heard" through vibrations that even enabled a blind dog to be a reliable sentinel.[64]

In 1931 while hosting his own radio show, Judy recalled how his guest, Lee Duncan, the handler of the famous German shepherd, Rin-Tin-Tin, coaxed a low growling sound from the dog in response to Duncan's command to speak.[65]

At home Judy's Doberman, General, had been in a room where

Judy's show was being broadcast. Upon hearing "Rinty's" growl, Judy was informed that General had leapt up and went to search for the source of the threatening dog while dispatching a few growls of his own.[66]

Judy wrote that the original dogs of the wild did not bark. The bark of the modern dog was teased out, shaped and encouraged by the hunters of long ago. He also noted that the undomesticated members of the Canidae family that include foxes and wolves did not bark and were only capable of howls and whines.[67] With humans, dogs reacted to tones and inflections and were made curious by the cries of children and anxious by angry voices. Judy noted that these "throat sounds" emitted by canines were more varied than any other animals on earth. With over a dozen specific inflections, the vocalizations of each dog were unique and contained a specific purpose. A perceptive dog owner could identify a particular dog by the sound of its bark and discern pain, joy, pleading, fear, fighting and sounds of warning.[68]

Of all its sensing abilities, Judy wrote that a dog's sense of smell was its most vital, observing, "A dog without keen scenting ability is like a cook without fire."[69]

Smell was the most imperative to a dog's survival from the very first moments of its life. Born without sight, the first nine days of a puppy's life are guided by its sense of smell. A dog's keen olfactory abilities help it to locate objects, meet up with other dogs and allow it to develop a type of canine code that keeps a pack safe from danger.[70]

Judy regarded the canine nose as a true wonder of nature. Like in humans, the dog's nose projects directly above its mouth and is literally a dog's first contact with the world. But unlike the nose of humans, the canine nose is designed with a large area of membrane on the upper inside area that allow nasal nerve endings to be engaged more readily. The upper sides of a dog's nose are "slitted" in a way that allows the nostrils to fan the air to increase sensation.[71]

In Judy's estimation, the sense of smell worked double-time for a dog because it was as important as taste was for humans, noting, "he's [a dog] a gourmand of the nasal variety."[72]

Dogs recalled the history of an object most readily through scent. The dog concerned itself with the "useful" smell of stinky fish and rotting meat, since these odors were associated with a source of sustenance.[73]

Dogs "of good nose or strong scenting ability" were the most loyal and expressed more affection toward their owners. These dogs became more attached to the scent of their master's family. Of this, Judy wrote that all humans possessed a unique "aura of odor." Tiny particles of something he termed effluvia had nothing to do with cleanliness, but could be disagreeable to a dog. A dog put off by the odor of a particular individual was in all probability recalling an unpleasantness or danger associated with someone's effluvia, causing the dog to growl or behave strangely or aggressively.[74]

The sense of smell in sightless humans rivals the olfactory sense of a dog, becoming stronger over time, which allows them to identify people, locality and objects.

It was the dog's acute sense of smell that forged its enduring bond with humans so long ago when its incomparable scenting capability made it an indispensable hunting aid to the hunter. Despite changing weather conditions and other environmental factors, dogs adapted and made themselves useful by hunting all types of game throughout the world.

To those not familiar with the specifics characteristics of each breed, Judy wrote about the groups of sporting dogs that included setters, pointers and bird dogs. He explained that these "sighting" breeds keep their nose to the ground and follow the scent of prey. Once the prey is located in the woods or grass, the dog freezes. Its tail is held rigid with a front foot upraised as it goes "on point." This posture is held until the human hunter flushes the prey into the air.[75]

Continuing his discourse on the dog's invaluable olfactory sense, Judy also presented the hound group, which were used as trail hunters in the field, and gun dogs, which were categorized as breeds that tracked the "foot scent as it was deposited on the ground."[76]

Judy also extolled the capabilities of military dogs that were of great assistance to soldiers due to their well-developed sense of smell. He described those dogs relegated to sentry duty as having, "an extra eye, one which could pierce the darkness or like the radio wave, go thru objects instantly."[77] A trap, an attack about to get underway, a nearing sniper or weaponry—not much could escape the detection of these highly trained canines.

Although he referred to the canine's unequalled scenting ability as "nature's marvel,"[78] he warned that this innate quality would be diminished or even lost when dogs became coddled and overindulged. A lazy dog kept indoors and the puppies it produced were in danger of losing their innate sensing abilities. "Environment lessens heredity," admonished Judy.[79]

He urged dog owners to take their dogs, no matter what breeds, out into the natural environment as often as possible. "Let them run to heart's and nose's content."[80] Even breeds that were not regarded as "hunting dogs," such as Pomeranians, Pekingese, and all terriers, were capable of picking up and pursuing a scent for fun and exercise.

By instilling an understanding of how a dog utilized its senses, Judy used the pages of *Don't Call a Man a Dog* to explore the "mind of the dog." He began with what he called a dog's "thinking faculties."[81]

Like many of his colleagues, Judy pondered the reasoning capacity of canines. He believed that the dog used a constellation of mental activities driven by natural instincts, which included memory and identification, pride, humiliation, awareness of right and wrong and imagination. Judy wrote that these mental activities were separate from instinct but based on a dog's "ability to function just a little short of reasoning in the pure sense."[82]

With his observations on the "thinking faculties of the dog," Judy presented his conclusion that although dogs could think in a limited capacity, they relied on instinct and could not "jump from the known to the unknown." The actions of dogs were the product of memory and repetition.[83]

To illustrate this point Judy offered the story of a dog left alone in a room with a slab of meat hanging from the ceiling by a string. Although a chair is readily available, Judy asserted that most dogs would starve before being able to "think" of moving that chair to gain access to the food source.[84]

Many of Judy's readers wrote to him to tell him that their dog was an exception to the rule. They believed that their dogs were capable of deliberate thought and reason. But Judy responded that in most cases, dogs did not "reason in the sense that they uses logic, syllogisms, conceptions and new ideas."[85]

Judy presented another example of a boxer named Kitty. Kitty was a comfort-loving dog with a fondness for lying on the expensive sofa and pillows of its master. To break Kitty of this habit, a mouse trap was set and strategically, but safely, planted near Kitty's favorite resting places. When the dog set off the trap she was startled.

Through the process of association and memory, just seeing her owner go through the motions of setting a trap now acted as a deterrent for the boxer. But Judy did admit that there were exceptions where a more independent or less obedient dog *might* figure a way to use its paws to set the trap off in a way that would render it useless as a scare tactic.[86]

This supported Will Judy's discourse on the astute memory of the dog set forth in chapter 10, "Memory and Identification by the Dog."

Judy stated that "memory is the chief mental ability of the dog's mind." Through a collaboration of sight, scent, the sound of a voice and recognition of mannerisms a dog would always remember an old master, even after years of prolonged absence.

Judy relayed a story that took place at a dog show event in 1930. A breeder of Sealyham terriers had sold a dog to an American buyer eight months earlier. As the breeder walked about the aisles of a dog show, she heard a dog whine and strain to catch her attention. It turned out to be one of the pups she had bred. Remarkably, she had had no contact with the pup since its 3,000 mile journey to its new home in the United States.[87]

Identification was a strong component of the dog's ability to memorize, as illustrated in the case of Kitty the boxer, who assessed the potential danger of a mousetrap just by watching its owner go through the motions of setting the trap. In a similar manner, the dog of a hunter knows what is to follow when its master merely reaches for the shotgun on the wall.[88]

The simple importance of a dog's ability to recognize its owner was briefly covered at this point. Judy warned of the dangers of approaching a sleeping dog and advised readers not to surprise a slumbering dog, even if it was a familiar one. "Let sleeping dogs lie," he wrote, because a dog's first impulse when rudely awakened will be to act in a self-protective manner.

Most of what was classified as bad behavior was just a dog's way of coping with unfamiliar or threatening situations. To illustrate the point, Judy asked dog owners to understand that a dog that "made off" with articles of its owner's clothing, such as a shoe or sock in their absence, was only trying to keep a part of his beloved human nearby it until the return of its master.

In a section titled "The Dog's Pride and Humiliation," Judy urged readers to have respect for the self esteem of dogs. He reminded them that a dog could be humiliated and its feelings easily wounded by a thoughtless owner, especially when it was in the presence of other canines.

He recommended letting a dog play the role of "dashing knight," no matter its size or stature. By letting a dog present a posture of bravery when protecting against a human or another dog, it derived a sense of purpose.

In terms of individuality, Judy asked readers to "concede to him [the dog] all the rights and privileges a dog claims for himself ... let him live a dog's life."

Under the heading, "The Dog's Awareness of Right and Wrong," Judy noted, "All reactive life, even that of vegetation, acquires a sense of right and wrong," which was based upon the principal of pain and pleasure. A dog was primarily motivated to please its master and most would suffer greatly in order to carry out its master's commands.[89]

In the training of dogs, Judy wrote that pain serves as the negative motivator with hunger representing positive motivation and reinforcement. The former was recommended when a puppy was housebroken. Judy noted that a puppy could quickly learn that relieving itself outdoors was pleasing to its owner and avoided punishment.[90]

To illustrate the dog's ability to differentiate between right and wrong, Judy offered a story about two dachshunds, a breed he described as clownish, loyal, colorful and alert. These dogs were told by "word, gesture and reenacting" to stay off a new couch. But upon his return home the dog owner found the two dogs curled up fast asleep on the forbidden sofa. The dogs were punished and the warning was issued again.

On the second day, arriving home from work, the owner was pleased to see the dogs resting on the floor. But upon further inspection, he found the couch to be suspiciously warm in spots.

Day three revealed the cleverness of these dachshunds. This time, the owner made his way up the stairway, quickly and quietly, giving no advanced warning, only to find the two dogs on the sofa "hastily blowing their breath to cool it off."[91]

In writing on "The Quality of Imagination in the Dog," Judy stated that dogs formed mental pictures and demonstrated the ability to anticipate and enter into situations that required it to transform "illusions and delusions into actualities."[92]

Judy cited examples of dogs that played with stuffed animals with the same enthusiasm and purpose as if they were playing with the real item and dogs that joyfully pretended to race their masters or track a thrown ball as if they were retrieving prey.

But even in play, Judy understood that the dog aimed to please his master and observed that when a dog owner challenged his dog to race, the dog would enthusiastically keep up, but never go too far ahead lest the human be the loser.[93]

This enduring quality of imagination allowed the dog to enter "whole-soul" into a make believe world and served to keep a dog spirited and youthful to its final days.

While a great deal of time and energy was expended in the training of dogs, Judy proposed that although many humans regarded the dog as a "dumb creation," dogs actually taught humans basic lessons of morality and "good living."[94]

Dogs taught lessons of loyalty, patience, forgiveness, unselfishness, concentration, a "general and practical" philosophical approach to life, the power of curiosity and the benefits of living life in the moment.

Judy wrote extensively on the virtues of the dog because he believed that "there are so many facets to the dog's diamond of happy living." He understood that a dog's owner was the most important person in its entire world; his god and ruler. He went so far as to declare that a psychic exchange occurred when dog and master gazed into each other's eyes. For Judy the energy was almost palpable.[95]

The loyalty of a dog set it apart from all other animals and Judy regarded the dog as a loyal soldier that put aside its own needs while placing complete trust in its master. He advised the dog owner, "You are the world's ruler insofar as this worshipper of yours is concerned."[96]

It did not matter to the dog if its owner was a congressman or an ex-convict, penniless or worth millions, dressed to the nines or in rags, or resided in a tenement or a castle. To the dog all that mattered was that at the end of the day its limitless patience would be rewarded when it was reunited with his master.

To illustrate this point Judy recounted the story of Shep, a dog that had spent countless hours waiting for his injured master on the steps of St. Anthony's hospital in Rock Island, Illinois, in 1942.

Shep's owner had fractured his skull and had been rushed to the hospital. Shep followed closely behind. Before the dog's owner was admitted for medical treatment he uttered the words, "Wait here, Shep; I'll be back." But the man never recovered and his obedient dog loyally carried out his master's last command. Each day Shep remained posted near the spot where he had last seen his master.

The Franciscan nurses at the hospital grew aware of Shep's sad vigil and became his caretakers. He kept up this daily routine until he suffered a fractured spine when he was hit by a truck while out for some exercise.

Judy suggested that if Shep's owner had had any way of knowing about his dog's undying loyalty and could speak from beyond, he would have whispered in his dog's ear, "Good boy, Shep—I am waiting for you."[97]

In discussing the patience of a dog Judy asserted that humans suffered from what people in foreign lands dubbed "Americanitis."[98] The symptoms of this particular disease included rushing about, fuming and ranting.

Judy recommended that frazzled humans could take a lesson from their four-legged teachers. In capital letters he proclaimed, "THE MOST PATIENT THING IN THE WORLD IS YOUR DOG."[99] On this topic Judy waxed poetically about the dog's legendary patience in a poem he wrote titled, "Waiting for Master."

Loyalty and patience were virtues Judy valued in dogs, but it was the trait of forgiveness that truly set them apart from man. Judy proclaimed that forgiveness was seldom sincerely exhibited in humans, but was the one most readily practiced by canines.

He observed that the popular maxim "forgive and forget" was frequently uttered by men and women, but most humans carried grudges and nursed "smoldering resentment" while awaiting the day when they could get even with those they believed had wronged them.[100]

In stark contrast, Judy wrote that dogs practiced forgiveness in a saintlike manner. A dog owner who beat or whipped a dog without provocation was readily forgiven by the dog, for that dog lived only to receive its master's approval at any cost of comfort or dignity.

Throughout all his writings Judy maintained that if a dog disobeyed its master it was most likely caused by the human's inability to effectively communicate his intention to the animal. If words and commands were spoken too quickly or shouted, the dog became confused. Judy instructed dog owners to speak to their dogs in a slow, concise and "ordinary" tone of voice.[101]

On the topic of corporal punishment Judy warned dog owners to refrain from using their hands to strike a dog. He recommended instead that a sound whack be delivered to the dog's backside with a rolled up newspaper only when absolutely necessary. The dog's "backbone, the tender ears or the loins," were never to be assaulted to avoid permanent injury.[102]

After the disobedient animal received this necessary correction Judy implored the punisher to consider the repentant dog lying in the corner of the room. It sighed while placing its head strategically on its front paws while trying to garner sympathy from its master. When the desired result was not quickly obtained, the determined dog moved stealthily across the room to its target and once there pressed its sensitive and moist nose against the hand that held the newspaper that had been used just moments earlier in its discipline.[103]

To those dog owners who were quick to resort to physical punishment of dogs Judy offered this condemnation: "You strike your dog, you whip him, you even lower yourself and debase your soul to kick at him and you really kick your own dignity into the ditch."[104]

After loyalty, patience and forgiveness, Judy listed unselfishness as one of the dog's outstanding traits of character. Of this he concluded that while men were the most selfish beings, dogs were the most unselfish living things on earth.[105]

The dog lived in the moment, happy to give 100 percent of its time and effort to its master with its only "payment" being what Judy called "dog coin," a reward administered in the form of praise, a pat on the head and of course, the master's companionship.[106]

Judy noted that out of the more than 60,000 species known to man at the time, the dog was the only animal that without any physical coercion came by choice to man's side to offer companionship.[107]

The ability to concentrate wholeheartedly on the task at hand was another virtue of canines.[108] Judy presented the image of a dog on the hunt as an example of absolute concentration. In this instance, the dog's complete mental and physical activities were absorbed to the extent that it was oblivious to danger.

Judy listed actual words and phrases in the English language that contained the word dog to define persistence and endurance. People were described as dog-tired, working like dogs, doggedly determined, dogging issues and trouble, or actively hounding opportunities. Judy maintained that even when ill, the dog outdid humans, as suggested in the phrase "as sick as a dog."[109]

Judy suggested that humans emulate the work ethic of the dog and went as far to offer this tool-inspired definition for the canine. "Dog: any of various devices for holding, gripping or fastening something."[110]

In presenting the sixth of the dog's seven natural teaching abilities, Judy regarded the dog as a natural "filosopfer." He proposed that in its relaxed approach to life a dog offered an excellent example of how to live in the moment. Humans could learn from watching puppies play amongst themselves and older dogs taking a good stretch followed by a long nap in the sun after a large meal.[111]

Judy added the dog's sense of curiosity as the seventh mode in which a dog enlightened humans. He stated that whereas curiosity may kill a cat, it kept a dog alive. Curiosity remained part of the dog's mental activity from the moment it opened its eyes near the tenth day of its life to when it reached ten years of age, which Judy likened to a 70-year-old human.[112]

"The dog is the supreme example of the practice of joie de vivre," Judy declared in his inclusion of a dog's teaching capabilities. The sound of its master's laugh, the rustling of leaves on a sidewalk or a crawling insect never lost its magical ability to entertain and engage; a reminder for humans to preserve an eternal fascination with ordinary events.

In its inability to age intellectually or emotionally, Judy viewed the dog as a "practical filosofer."[113] He asked readers if they had ever seen a dog that was old at heart. Despite its graying muzzle, stiff quarters and watery eyes, there was an undying spirit of the young pup maintained in an older dog. The dog never forgot how to play; it grew older, but not old.[114]

Judy concluded his discourse on the ways dogs taught humans about living life to the fullest by advising readers that they need not be concerned about leading a dog's life, for it was the inhumane way in which many humans treated dogs that created misery in a dog's existence.[115] He further suggested that men should in actuality lead a dog's life in an effort to live life to its fullest.

The educational powers of a canine were even more effective when presented early in a human's development, as explored in the section titled, "Dogs as Teachers of Character-Building in Children." Judy held the view that children possessed a natural fascination with animals and that those who were reared with animals received an education in character that would last a lifetime.[116]

Judy unabashedly declared that every child should have a dog and that he pitied the child who grew up not having one. He regarded a dog as a home-based teacher and spiritual guide and wrote, "The dog is a daily, living sermon, without offense."[117] He proposed that among other things, a dog imparted lessons of responsibility, obedience and reasonableness, orderliness, kindness and caring.

Children raised with pets learned that another living being relied on them for care. A dog needed to be fed, brushed, walked and trained. In the acceptance of these responsibilities young people received an early lesson on successful parenting techniques. Judy declared this process as one that would occur only after years of classroom learning.[118]

Through dog ownership a young person learned why rules were important as they saw them applied to others. This positive association reinforced the importance and logic of order and fairness in the household and other situations in which one found themselves later in life. Through the use of reasonable discipline Judy believed children learned to be gentle *and* firm guardians. Through this process the young person gained awareness that "a good parent is a tyrant but an understanding one."[119]

Judy believed that kindness was not inborn in humans and that the development of a kind heart was "an index of true civilization."[120] Children raised with a household pet received a master's course in kindness and compassion. He urged parents who included pets in their homes to assign to their children duties that promoted the care of those animals.

As he had in the pages of *Dog World* in promoting National Dog Week, Judy used the pages of *Don't Call a Man a Dog* as an opportunity to remind readers that "every good home may not suitably have a dog; but every dog should have a good home."[121] He also restated that he did not necessarily want to see "more or better dogs," in the nation, but for more humans to be better dog owners.

He also noted that children raised in the homes of those who bred dogs learned the process of conception, or what Judy termed the "seed planting and of harvest or birth."[122]

This natural exposure offered children a wholesome education on a subject that was often regarded as taboo. Consequently, Judy believed that these enlightened young people learned to regard reproduction as natural and wholesome.[123]

In the completion of the first half of *Don't Call a Man a Dog,* Judy imparted his enduring conviction that above all, "The dog is superior to the human in all the cardinal moral virtues." After clarifying all the key points, he concludes that if humans were as good as dogs, most of the former would be closer to enjoying the eternal glory of heaven.[124]

In presenting all canines as loyal, patient, forgiving, focused, selfless, eternally youthful, and possessing the ability to impart these divine qualities to others; Judy ecstatically proclaimed that dogs were "the nearest approach on earth to the actual living of the teaching of Jesus of Nazareth."[125] With attributes like that, Judy once again advised it would be truly unfair to call a man a dog.

In the section titled, "Will Judy's Scrapbook on Dogs," the author presented a collection of poems and essays that he had personally composed over the years. These items presented Judy's unique perspective on matters of the dog, placing a spiritual component on the breeding, showing and training of dogs.

On these pages the author delved the more soulful and sentimental issues of dog ownership. He offered moving accounts of extraordinarily dedicated dogs, wrote about the respect he held for the elderly dog and reconfirmed his belief that dogs did go to heaven and expressed his disdain for those who believed otherwise. He shared his personal recommendations of where dogs should be buried and even expressed his reasons why he believed purebred dogs made better pets than those of mixed lineage and raged against cruel and irresponsible dog owners.

In an essay titled, "Why the World Likes Dogs," Judy wrote that "the world likes dogs because dogs are nearest to moral perfection of all living things."[126] In Judy's opinion dogs were the most unselfish, patient, grateful, friendly, forgiving and loyal "things" in the world.

The first line of Judy's "A Dog's Prayer for His Master" presented a dog asking the Lord of humans to "make my master faithful to his fellowmen as I am to him."[127]

This loving dog prayed that his master be cheerful, grateful, without deceit and as patient, uncomplaining and as courageous as he.[128]

In "Be Not So Cruel," Judy wrote as a dog pleading not to be struck in anger. The loyal dog points out the wrongfulness of his master's misplaced ire, reminding him to be thankful for all the times the dog had protected the household and family members and remained a loyal friend during the hardest times, stating, "My mind recalls your grief and lonesome want." The dog's plaintive plea, "Then be not so cruel with your blows!" repeats four times throughout the essay.[129]

In "An Apology to the Dog Catcher," Judy revealed his personal and private torment at not being able to rescue and protect all dogs. In this essay Judy wrote about an occasion when he and his colleagues stood by as a vehicle dispatched by the Chicago Municipal Animal Shelter screeched to a stop on the busy streets of Chicago. Judy watched helplessly as a large black and white terrier mix shrieked in terror as it ran from three dog catchers.[130]

The dog eluded the net of its pursuers and Judy and his colleagues found themselves cheering for the dog's successful escape. While Judy knew that it was wrong for dogs to run free in the city, the use of a dog catcher's net was not the solution he envisioned when he campaigned for the elimination of stray dogs from the streets of America. Writing about this incident Judy unabashedly proclaimed, "We almost shouted out, 'Ha, Ha, he got away.'"[131]

This dog had successfully avoided capture, but Judy's pleasure was short-lived. As the dog catcher's truck drove past him again, he observed in its window nearly a half dozen dogs peering out at him with eyes filled with fright and wondering.[132]

Judy, who had dedicated so many years of his life to improving the welfare of dogs, understandably found this image disturbing. In his anger he wrote that he wished he could change the lettering of the dog catcher's truck so it read, "Municipal Animal MURDERING."[133]

But Judy did not blame the dog catcher. He noted that these men, in their occupations, were just decent employees and citizens doing the necessary but distasteful job for which they had been hired. Judy placed the problem directly on irresponsible dog owners, stating that having a license to own a dog did not give a dog owner the right to allow his dog to roam about unattended.[134]

He suggested that dog owners, not their dogs, be licensed and only after a thorough assessment of their merit would an individual be allowed the privilege of becoming a licensed dog owner.

In his emotional writings on the dog catcher Judy relayed that 95 percent of all dog-related problems were the result of stray dogs and that these unsupervised canines accounted for almost all cases of rabies. He sympathized with these dogs for he understood it was only natural for them to move about from place to place as they explored the sources of all kinds of tantalizing scents.[135]

Of those innocent dogs Judy explained that only one of every eight stray dogs that ended up in the dog pound were reclaimed, and the rest were murdered, "not thru any wrongdoing on their part."[136]

Judy lashed out at the negligent owners of those six incarcerated dogs on their way to the pound. He wrote that these irresponsible humans were the ones that should be sitting in the back of the dog catcher's truck like criminals. He asked his readers to join him in condemning the millions of careless individuals that made it necessary for the position of the dog catcher to exist in the first place and declared these individuals outright murderers.[137]

While Judy held all dogs in high regard, his personal experience led him to favor the purebred female dog as the most desirable pet. This was candidly revealed in two items found in *Don't Call a Man a Dog*: "The Seven Advantages of Owning a Pedigreed Dog," and "In Praise of the Female."

"It is true that a dog is a dog the world around and the dogs themselves know nothing about pedigrees," Judy wrote, but he ultimately placed the blame for the problems of rabies, dog pounds and "nabors' complaints" on the actions of mixed breeds.[138]

Judy's logic followed that those who paid good money for a purebred puppy, which at the time cost from $25 to $75, made a financial commitment and would take good care of their "investment."[139]

Judy further reasoned that individuals who purchased a purebred dog did so because they truly desired one, unlike individuals who acquired a puppy only to help those that needed to place a litter of unwanted pups.[140]

"The pedigreed dog has a distinct individuality,"[141] wrote Judy, arguing that breed knowledge and responsible dog ownership were inseparable. The dog owners who understood the instincts and traits associated with individual breeds were better suited as guardians of their dogs. This knowledge also allowed dog owners to better assess the health and temperament issues of their pets.

As a seasoned breeder and trainer of dogs, Judy described the pedigreed dog as "a trademark, brand-stamped in disposition and manners as stated."[142] From a business standpoint, a breeder of sound and healthy pups could sell a litter in advance, since the breeder was able to "bank" on the health and temperament of the parents of the purebred puppy.

Additional income could also be derived from those involved in providing breeding services. Judy also pointed out that it cost the same to train and care for a pedigreed puppy as a mixed-breed dog.

On the subject of the responsible dog breeding, Judy presented ten items under the heading of "Breeder's Code,"[143] which required all breeders to be held to the highest of standards.

Among the items listed were his mandates that conscientious breeders must study the bitch as well as the sire, examine the grandparents of the dogs involved, ignore breeding superstitions, emphasize the facts of breeding over names and titles, and keep and maintain proper breeding records.[144]

To ensure future generations of healthy dogs, Judy further advised that deformed and weak offspring be "put away," and dogs deemed shy or nervous should not be bred. He recommended honoring the "bred-by-exhibitor dog," and to only breed dogs with "good temperament and strong nerves."[145]

In the segment titled, "In Praise of the Female," Judy extolled the value of the female canine. He stated, "NOTWITHSTANDING that prejudice often prefers her brother, the female dog has all the virtues of her species and fewer of the vices."[146]

Among these virtues Judy listed companionship, protection, and a deep sense of duty, which the female carried out with more gentleness and gracefulness than her male counterpart. Judy noted the female of the species sensed danger more quickly, was a better watch dog, discriminated more acutely between stranger and friend, assumed a motherly interest in children, and was more protective of babies.[147]

Judy observed that the female possessed better manners and consumed their food with more finesse. They were easier to housebreak, eliminated less frequently, and confined their elimination process to smaller areas. In addition, he found females tended to be less destructive around the house and in the garden, and less likely to wander from home.[148]

Judy asserted that dog obedience trainers preferred to work with females because bitches learned more quickly and were more eager to please than males. He noted, "Her [the bitch's] conscience is more sensitive to disobedience," and observed they were more focused in the field when on the hunt and were easier to train as guide dogs for the blind.[149]

Judy reminded readers that while the male is in season each day of the year, females were in heat for a scant 40 days of the calendar year. But it disturbed Judy that this fact often caused the female to be "shunned, almost cursed as tho her sex were a plague."[150]

Most importantly, through her ability to reproduce, the female added to the family income by "presenting her owner with duplicates of herself to carry on in other homes."[151]

On the opposite spectrum Judy explored the emotions surrounding the passing of a cherished dog. In "My Dog Is Dead," he examined the sacred rituals between human and dog and the void that occurred when a beloved dog passed. "The house is dreadful still, until I wish I heard four feet come pitpat down the hall,"[152] he wrote.

Judy accessed the reader's senses with his use of descriptive words that recalled all the sensations associated with a beloved dog; its moist nose, the demanding paw, pleading eyes and plaintive bark, all deemed by the author as, "sweet annoyances," often taken for granted but now no longer to be enjoyed.[153]

In "The Old Dog," Judy paid tribute to the senior dog, gently guiding the reader through twelve heart-wrenching stanzas that tell the story of a devoted dog owner as he watches his dog surrender to age and eventually death.

But the story did not end here. Much like his "Purgatory for Dogs," Judy wrote glowingly of a time in the future when dog and owner would reunite in the presence of God.

Judy expanded on this theme in another essay titled, "No Room in Heaven for Dogs," subtitled, "An Answer by the Editor of *Dog World* to a Letter from a 12-Year-Old School Boy."[154]

In this moving item Judy addressed a young boy's distress after being told by his Sunday school teacher that there was no room in heaven for dogs. Judy gently consoled the young man by explaining that heaven was a big place filled with millions of good souls.

He assured the boy that without the company of dogs these people would be very lonely. Heaven was a soothing place that offered shade trees and flowers with bubbling fountains and filled with dogs of all kinds that happily napped in the "sunshine of celestial spaces."[155]

Judy assured the boy that he believed that Christ himself had been the guardian of a little black dog and that this dog had crossed the Sea of Galilee and loyally followed Christ through the streets of Jerusalem and licked his master's bleeding hands.[156]

He ended his heartfelt reply by expressing his sorrow that someone had told the young man that dogs could not be found in heaven.

Judy genuinely believed that although dogs went to heaven, many of the grieving dog owners left behind were desirous of a physical location where they could pay their respects to and honor their dearly departed dog. Judy touched on that subject in his essays, "Where to Bury a Dog," and "The Most Unusual Dog Cemetery in the World."

In the former, Judy reprinted a piece written by Ben Hur Lampman from Lampman's book *How Could I Be Forgetting?*, published by Binfords & Mort in 1926.

Lampman was a newspaper editor and writer who served as poet laureate for the state of Oregon from 1951 to his death in 1954.[157]

The essay "Where to Bury a Dog" was based on a question Lampman had received from a reader in Ontario, Canada, who inquired, "Where shall I bury my dog?"[158]

With a flair for picturesque prose Lampman began his essay by writing about a setter he once knew that was buried beneath a cherry tree, and how in the springtime petals from the tree decorated the green lawn above the dog's burial spot.[159]

Lampman suggested that a resting place beneath any flowering tree or shrub was as good a place for a dog in death as it had been in life.[160] He also recommended windy hilltops, a familiar stream, or a field where nearby herds of cattle grazed as other ideal final resting places.

Ultimately Lampman concluded that there was a special place where man's best friend remained forever alive in spirit in the minds of its grieving owners, and that place was "in the heart of his master."[161]

In his essay, "The Most Unusual Dog Cemetery in the World," Judy described a visit to Edinburgh Castle in Scotland. He had stopped at a war memorial set high up on a hill and there among several statues and markers Judy spotted one dedicated to a German shepherd dog of war for its service during battle.[162]

As Judy surveyed the valley that spread before him, he was surprised and deeply moved to see a sign that read, "Cemetery for Soldiers' Dogs." Each grave marking was inscribed with the name of each dog and the year of its passing, ranging from 1866 to 1947. Among the names were "Flora, Canteen Pet," "Yum Yum," "Billie Tinker," and "Little Tim." Judy and his colleagues counted 23 such graves, which Judy regarded as a "tribute to the soldiers who owned these dogs and to the dogs themselves."[163]

The second part of "Will Judy's Scrapbook on Dogs" opened with four pages dedicated to Senator George Graham Vest's "Tribute to a Dog." In an item titled, "The Story of a Great Literary Gem," Judy printed the full version of the famous tribute and presented some of the lesser known details of the case and made note that his version of the story was carefully researched and authentic.[164] Judy retold the story of Old Drum, a dog owned by a man named Charles Burden. While out trailing through the backwoods of Missouri, Old Drum was shot by Burden's neighbor, a man named Lon Hornsby. Hornsby was a livestock rancher who had recently lost more than 100 sheep, which he attributed to attacks made by dogs. On October 28, 1869, it was discovered that Hornsby had asked a man by the name of Richard Ferguson to shoot Old Drum.[165]

Burden filed a suit before the County of Madison Township's Justice of the Peace and the case went before a jury on November 25, 1869. A jury failed to reach a decision and the case was scheduled for retrial the following month.[166]

This event was attended by an emotional crowd of "farmers, cattle raisers and hunters," and others who had a professional stake in the outcome of the case. For his loss Burden was awarded a mere $25.[167]

But Hornsby successfully appealed to the Johnson County Court of Common Pleas and was granted another trial the following March. This, featuring two attorneys for each side, resulted in a favorable outcome for the killer of Old Drum.[168]

When Burden was awarded a fourth trial the case received such widespread public interest and resulted in so much sympathy for the dog's owner that the courthouse could not accommodate all those who came to watch.[169]

Both sides presented strong cases until George Graham Vest of the law firm Phillips and Vest of Sedalia, Missouri, approached the bench. Vest represented the grieved Burden and was about to advocate for canines in a way that had never been done before.[170]

Vest only spoke for a brief time, but his words were so powerful and evoked so much emotion they would impact dogs and their owners for years to come. Burden was promptly awarded $300 for his suffering.[171]

Judy wrote that ultimately nine trial lawyers were involved in the case surrounding Old Drum and many of them were noteworthy. Judy reported that one of the attorneys was a man named David Nation, the husband of Carrie Nation, a radical figure in the women's temperance movement. A lawyer by the last name of Elliott became the judge of the Court of Common Pleas of Johnson County, another lawyer named T. Crittenden went on to become the governor of Missouri and another by the last name of Cockrell served on the Missouri senate for 30 years. John F. Phillips was appointed a commissioner of the United States Supreme Court for the state of Missouri and Vest went on to serve as a Missouri senator for 24 years.[172]

The remaining pages of "Will Judy's Scrapbook on Dogs" were sprinkled with Judy's favorite poems and quotes regarding man's best friend. Some, with titles such as "Now I Have a Friend"[173] and "Doggy Advice in Doggerel,"[174] were credited to mysterious writers.

These items were followed by cryptic comments in parentheses that appeared after the credit "ANONYMOUS," and included phrases such as "but clever and 'realistic?'" and "if it ever had an author."[175]

Following the rhyming verse titled, "Doggerel,"[176] after the "Anonymous" credit there appeared the comment, "an author who has written many things about dogs,"[177] leading readers to believe it had been penned by Judy himself.

"The Dog in the Library," by Ethel King, was reprinted by Judy as a discourse on the simple occasion of a dog and child at the library. King wrote a touching poem about a little, "brown-patched, clean-white, devoted and content"[178] dog that accompanied its youthful master to the library and sat quietly by and watched wistfully as children made their literary choices and then fled away to play elsewhere, leaving the uncomplaining dog alone.[179]

"Dogs as Companions" offered an essay from *Thoughts of an Idle Fellow* by Jerome K., where the author gave a literary opinion as to why he believed that dogs were superior to his fellow man. He wrote, "And they never ask a young author with 14 tragedies, 16 comedies, several farces, and a couple of burlesques in his desk, why he doesn't write a play."[180]

Jerome went on to list the qualities he found so comforting in dogs; dogs were imprudent, never critical or judgmental and always there for their masters, to comfort, guard or to sacrifice their own lives for them if necessary. But Judy might have taken issue with the author's closing thoughts when describing man's best friend as "foolish, brainless, soulless dog!"[181]

Other essays and poems included "The Faith of a Dog," written by blind poetess Margaret Nickerson Martin, whose poem celebrated the love offered by an older dog.[182] In "The Little Black Dog,"[183] Elizabeth Gardner Reynolds pondered if Christ had a dog. On an interesting note, Reynold's views on that topic differed from Judy's: he had written earlier in "No Room in Heaven for Dogs" that he believed Christ did have a very loyal black dog. But Reynolds believed otherwise,[184] suggesting that Christ wouldn't have prayed in the Garden alone, if he had a dog.

"Constancy," by Fred B. Mann, praised the dog's ignorance of wealth[185]; "Pals," by Susie H. Best, captured the special bond between a boy and his dog[186]; and John Galsworthy's "When the Dog's Soul Comes thru His Eyes" fully captured the essence of what Judy had tried to impress upon his readers from the first page of *Don't Call a Man a Dog*.

Galsworthy wrote, "If a man does not soon pass beyond the

thought, 'by what shall this dog profit me?' into the state of simple glad-
ness to be with dog, he shall never know the very essence of the companionship which depends not on the points of dog, but on some strange
and subtle mingling of mute spirits."[187] The last image contained in *Don't
Call a Man a Dog* featured a drawing of a blind man accompanied by
his guide dog with the caption, "Eyes for the Blind."

With its quirky sentimentality and gentleness, *Don't Call a Man a
Dog* is a classic that combines all of its author's strengths and experience
in the world of dogs. Judy's words and passages resonate with truth and
carry a timeless message that celebrates the bond between human and
dog.

3

Will Judy's Writing on Dog Obedience Training

A world of pleasure and usefulness can be gotten from the trained dog.

—Will Judy, *Training the Dog*[1]

From 1932 to 1953 Will Judy wrote extensively on the topic of dog obedience training. As dogs were increasingly utilized to guard, protect, guide, assist, sooth and entertain, a diverse field developed around the specific training requirements for each of these tasks.

Today's dog owners have a myriad of choices and sources when it comes to educating themselves about dog obedience training. There are hundreds of books and numerous television shows and videos that present dog training information on demand.

The field of dog training has evolved over time to adjust to the dog's more intimate role in the daily lives of humans. Training philosophies and methods differed, but Judy's natural approach to dog training focused on his belief that "To train a dog is not to place something new into his mind, but to draw out of his mind all the possibilities within."[2]

Judy entered the publishing field with his own books on dog obedience training to educate an eager audience of training novitiates. He had some stern words for his competitors. "There are many books on training," he wrote. "Some are excellent. Others good, still others a waste of pulp trees in the forest."[3]

To modern day professionals in the dog obedience field, most of Judy's material may appear simplistic in its basic principles, but from the period of 1927 to the late 1940s American dog owners were in dire need of professional guidance delivered in an easy-to-read format. Judy's straightforward delivery infused with spiritualism and a psychological approach to dog behavior was well received by those who already pre-scribed to his popular *Dog World* magazine.

In the ninth edition of his *Training the Dog*, published in 1953, Judy noted that since its first printing in 1927, 60,000 copies had been sold.[4] That particular edition was dedicated to the South African dogs that Judy had judged in conformation and obedience trials in Johannesburg at the Kimberley Kennel Club in October of the previous year. His obser-vations recorded during that event were also included in a section titled, "DeBeers Alsatians in South Africa Have Won World Renown."[5]

Judy's feelings for the beloved dogs that had been part of his life were evident from the book's first pages. Like he had in previous print-ings of *Training the Dog*, Judy listed all of them that had graced his life along with their quirks and special gifts.

The first edition of *Training the Dog* was dedicated to Judge Judy, a smooth fox terrier who was a "clown, guard, companion and friend,"[6] with the second dedicated to Colonel Judy, another smooth fox terrier that Judy described as a dog that "considered me the chief thing of importance in the world."[7]

Printing number three was written for a chow named Foo Foo that had lost its life for the love of his master. Edition four was dedicated to three friends, Freckles Judy, an English setter, Fritz Judy (also known as Sigal von Judy-guard), a Doberman Judy claimed owned him, and Brazen Bozo, a bull terrier that the author described as an "Epicurean sensualist, who passed contentedly at age sixteen."[8] The book's fifth edi-tion was published in honor of Duchess Judy of Dogwood, a cocker spaniel Judy described as "a blond beauty, who is personality personi-fied."[9]

Training the Dog, edition six, was written for General Judy, a Dober-man the prolific publisher claimed "thinks that life isn't worth living unless it is lived with me." This edition was sprinkled with numerous antics of this intelligent canine.[10]

The value of military dogs was evident in Judy's dedication of the seventh edition of *Training the Dog* to the 13,815 war dogs that had served in the United States military during World War II, "on the home front and on far-flung battlefronts throughout the world."[11]

The honor of dedication for edition number eight went to Baron the boxer, whom Judy described as "eighty-two pounds of canine lusti-ness and affection," and to Colonel Judy the second, whom Judy wrote was of the harlequin variety of great dane, "as interesting as the harlequin of the stage."[12]

The table of contents of the ninth edition of *Training the Dog* set Judy's volumes on this subject apart from other books in its category. These books appeared to be just like any other standard entry on dog obedience. They were filled with the requisite topics of advice on how to teach a dog to come, sit, stay, tips on housebreaking a dog, and the specialized training of dogs used in hunting, dog racing and pulling sleds.

But what differentiated Judy's writings on dog training from its competition was the author's impassioned messages contained in its foreword and introduction, where Judy's early experience in the ministry was evident from the very first pages.

In the foreword of the ninth edition, Judy addressed his audience more like a minister delivering a Sunday morning sermon than a professional trainer of dogs. He preached to his followers who were increasingly interested in learning how to raise mannerly dogs that posed no threat or danger to other living beings.

Judy reached out to his fellowship, boldly declaring that "the Almighty created us as humans with the possibilities within ourselves of becoming godlike."[13]

He appealed to readers not to regard animals as "the dumb creation," which he stated was a man-made term that implied man's superiority over members of the animal kingdom. He stated that humans had an obligation to do for other living beings what they could not do for themselves.[14] This included man's duty to keep animals free from pain and suffering.

In bestowing kindness to creatures so dependent on man, Judy likened humans to "vicars of God."[15] He shared his belief that by demonstrating this respect toward those living entities that were considered by many to be without souls, man's own soul would climb higher.

"The trainer must be fearless, must pretend indifference and must make himself a kind and understanding despot over his dog."[16]

In the book's introduction Judy explained how no other species of animal had so successfully made the "leap from savagery to civilization." Obedience training was necessary; however, he cautioned humans not to make the mistake of applying the rules and viewpoints of man when dogs were "brot into a routine of obedience to his human master."[17]

At the time of the third printing of *Training the Dog* in 1932, America's landscape was rapidly changing. The suburbs of large cities presented a new social frontier for dogs and the humans who cared for them. Judy recognized that these changes might test the bond between man and dog and not always in a positive manner.

Judy understood that it was more important than ever for dog owners to respect the rights of those who did not have dogs and those who did not regard them as man's best friend. Better dogs and better care for them was the underlying theme of all of his writing on how to improve the relationships between people and dogs through training.

In the early 1930s Judy's lessons on dog handling and training for the average American dog owner was already having an impact on the nation's dog owners. The busy streets of American cities presented dogs with an environment far different from the farms and fields to which they had become accustomed. Dogs now had to navigate the challenges of dense urban populations, frequent encounters with strange members of their own species and packs, automobiles and the busy thoroughfares and sidewalks they now all shared.

By 1932 dogs had become a major presence in rural, urban and suburban centers, and this constituted a greater, almost urgent need for dog obedience training to aid in the control and socialization of dogs. Judy viewed this training as a life-saving and peacekeeping measure.

From a psychological approach the author noted that the foundation of his pedagogy, or body of training knowledge, directed that dog owners be constantly aware of their surroundings, diligently anticipate dangerous situations and be at the ready to issue appropriate commands.

As to how dog owners could gain such control of their dogs was Judy's primary objective. In a section titled, "The Dog on the Street," Judy advised dog owners that "The dog on the street offers many problems, but most of these are solved already if the dog is steeped in obedience."[18]

In the asphalt-covered city environment the dog could no longer rely on its sense of smell or hearing to guard it from harm. "The dog learns to adjust himself and that is why changing conditions and their demands upon him do not find him losing out."[19]

But Judy also recognized that the very nature of canines made this adjustment a challenging one, since they were social and curious creatures. He reminded would-be dog handlers that the dog's sociability made them anxious to mingle with others of their kind as well as the humans that shared their streets.

His recommendations to dog owners were simple and straightforward. All urban dogs must be leashed, or muzzled if not leashed, and all dogs were to be fitted with collars that bore identification and licenses.

But Judy chastised the officials of his beloved city of Chicago for taking this process too far. Dogs on the streets of that city were required to be muzzled *and* leashed, a practice Judy considered excessive, even for a city of Chicago's size.[20]

The proud dog-loving citizen of the Windy City issued his own thoughts on the matter, advising that in the absence of a rabies quarantine, "dog lovers should have such rules revoked."[21]

Judy suggested that a more reasonable ordinance would merely require that a dog be located within 50 feet of its owner, allowing for the dog to be under its master's control. He wrote that a dog that could not be controlled in that situation did not belong on any street.[22]

Leashed, muzzled or running free, by their very nature a dog would inevitably meet another dog, and the dog owners needed to be prepared for any outcome. Judy noted, "Dogs are politicians, and therefore bluff every other dog they can."[23]

Judy asked his readers to take into consideration the pride of a dog when they observed dogs relating to each other and sizing up new circumstances. He pointed out that a small dog barked ferociously behind tall fences and barked even louder as the "intruder" on the other side of this barrier grew more distant. The small dog was only trying to prove his worth to its master and the world.[24]

When a dog was about to venture out to greet or meet another dog, Judy recommended that its owner not call it back too quickly as this marked their dog as a coward in the eyes of the other. He explained that dog-on-dog interactions were inherently filled with anxiety experienced by both of the engaged dogs. In most cases dogs were frightened of each other and each waited for signs of weakness and cowardice. Mild aggression was a manifestation of a dog's innate behavior, "and in this dogs are little different from you and me and other humans," he noted.[25]

Fear displayed on the part of the dog owner only served to accelerate aggression in a dog and brought out its natural instinct to protect. A trained and educated dog owner possessed the ability to remain calm and to refrain from striking or kicking an agitated dog or dragging a dog by the tail or hind legs.

To avoid hostile exchanges between dogs, Judy advised that the dog owner maintain eye contact with his own dog and to deliver the appropriate commands in a calm manner. As a last resort, Judy suggested that cold water be poured on the heads of the fighting dogs or the use of "spirits or pepper," carefully administered to the nose. If this failed, a finger inserted in the rectum of the dog worked wonders; however, dog owners who were bitten in the course of these activities were advised not to blame their dogs, since this was a natural reaction.[26]

Cats were also a major source of distraction for dogs in urbanized areas. Judy recommended that dogs be allowed to encounter cats at an early stage of their development to keep them from the chase. "One humiliation and some scratches are enuf to teach a dog that cats are furry dynamite," he noted with humor.[27]

Automobile traffic posed another serious distraction and danger to dogs on, in, and around busy roadways. With more and more cars on the nation's roadways, it was now a common practice for dogs to accompany their owners as automobile passengers.

Judy noted that dogs adapted very well to travel and had mastered the art of riding in an automobile: "The dog refuses to become old fashioned. He fits himself quickly into man's latest modes of living."[28]

On this matter Judy invited readers to consider the dog's view of car transport, where the dog experienced the sensation that it was in motion although its legs were not. Although Judy's recommendations for canine car passengers appear quaint and simplistic by modern standards, they illustrate how man's relationship with dogs was evolving with new technology and social interactions.

Judy advised drivers not to allow a dog to put its face to the wind to avoid harm to the eyes and chided those dog owners who placed protective goggles on the faces of their dogs. He cautioned that dogs were not to be placed on the running board, fenders, or hoods of an automobile, to prevent them from being assaulted by wind, dust or the threat of being brushed off by "a passing machine," or knocked to the ground with a sudden stop or turn.[29]

Dogs were not to sit in the front seat, to prevent them from lurching against the driver or steering wheel. Owners of dogs that had recently consumed food were advised that their pets should avoid car travel to prevent gastric troubles and vomiting.[30]

Today most dog owners are warned not to leave a dog in the car unattended and in many states it is unlawful to do so, but at a time when car alarms were not available Judy took another approach, saying that a dog left in a car served as "a reliable auto lock and the dread of car thieves."[31]

He also warned that dogs were not discriminatory and often had acquired new homes after not being able to resist the open door of a stranger's automobile.[32]

The breed of a dog also influenced its adaption to city life. To provide a personal example, Judy referenced one of his own dogs named Colonel Judy, described as a typically willful fox terrier. Colonel Judy, like most of his breed, was quick to learn if he wished, but was also willful and often chose to disobey. Taking breed characteristics into consideration, the author understood that a harsh command was required to stop the curious and innately stubborn little terrier from running out onto the street, chasing a cat or meeting another dog.[33]

With proper training Judy had observed that dogs trained to stop with their owners at street corners naturally proceeded to move with the flow of pedestrians when the traffic light turned green. A street-savvy dog that wandered into traffic was even capable of assessing the danger of an oncoming car and retreated to the safety of a curb to wait for a better opportunity to cross. Judy claimed to have witnessed dogs that actually looked both ways before crossing a busy road.[34]

Judy emphasized that consistency was key in this type of advanced training and warned would-be dog trainers to "make either no rules in training or no exceptions to the rules," to avoid regression.[35]

Through repeated experiences dogs had adjusted to urbanized environments and were increasingly streetwise. As with any negative "reinforcement training," a dog struck by an automobile or knocked down by a car's "projecting board" would learn to fear them and avoid another painful encounter.[36]

Dogs that actively chased cars presented another danger. Judy warned irresponsible dog owners that it was just a matter of time before their dog slipped under the tire of an automobile or distracted a driver.

In writing on this topic in 1941, Judy suggested the introduction of a mild shock administered to dissuade a dog that is prone to chase cars or run in traffic. Judy admitted that many readers had expressed displeasure with him at this technique, describing it as inhumane. To these critics Judy responded that many of them had never had the task of training a "perverse, maliciously stubborn, semi-criminal dog." He wrote that his detractors must assume responsibility for the needless deaths of poorly trained dogs and noted, "Mistaken kindness can be bitter and unneeded cruelty."[37]

Judy advised that most dogs readily responded to the sound of their own names and that every dog deserved a good and reasonable name. Furthermore it was important for the dog to take pride in its name. Judy recommended that the dog's given name contain some special connection to the looks, personality or even origin of the specific dog.[38]

He suggested that the name of a dog be no longer than two syllables, containing only one or two vowels, and advised that the dog owner not overuse their dog's name so as to more readily engage its attention in matters of obedience and training.[39]

In the sixth edition of *Training the Dog*, published in 1941, Judy fielded questions from readers who often sought what Judy called "magic formulas, secret words or charms," to be used to make a dog understand and obey.[40]

Judy believed some individuals possessed a natural ability to train dogs, even if they lacked a formal schooling in the field. Nonetheless, he saw the value in educating the masses of novice dog owners who had no understanding of canine behavior. From a business point of view, Judy saw the potential for this expanding market; it was an advantageous time to be considered an expert on the subject of dogs.[41]

In developing the mental abilities of dogs, Judy stated that they could take better care of themselves if allowed to develop their natural instincts and learn new skills in any situation they encountered.

Judy was fascinated with a dog's potential to communicate. For him, the only thing that differentiated a dog from a man was the former's lack of an "alfabet" and thumbs. He reveled in the manner in which a dog could communicate with just a shake of its tail. For Judy, there was "nothing in this world more expressive than a dog's tail—except a woman's smile."[42]

Through their expressive eyes, stance and inflections in their "voices," dogs "spoke" to man like no other animal. Judy boldly suggested the possibility that in time, dogs might develop speech. Through the training of the "most apt," this teaching of speech could be passed on to its puppies and so on. This ability to speak would be followed by the dog's ability to reason.[43]

Judy shared the story of his correspondence with a woman who wrote that she had taught her cocker spaniels how to "utter" certain words. The reader claimed that her cockers spoke in "full, deep voices, although their tones and themselves are all different." Judy relayed that she had explained while some of her dogs spoke quickly, others did so with pauses. Her youngest dog, named Seal, spoke with a southern drawl, but pronounced his words in "true northern manner."[44]

This woman was certain that these dogs truly understood the meaning of the words they used. "Wanna ge' down," for when they wanted out of her arms; "Ha-wo" for hello; and for more food or treats, "ah wan m-more" were among the phrases and words she claimed they purposely used.[45]

Judy himself was inclined to believe that some dogs were capable of understanding as many as 300 words or commands.[46] Of his own Doberman named General, for whom the book was dedicated, Judy wrote that the dog had come to understand over 40 words and phrases, among them "frog," a favorite plaything; "Vaseline," a command that allowed Judy to rub the gel around the dogs mouth as a form of laxative; "Where's Buster?," the name of the dog next door; "hamburger," denoting a trip to the meat market; and his own name, as well as such commands as come, heel, sit and down.[47]

A basic tenet of Judy's training approach stressed that "sound and object should be associated to eye and ear of the dog," to avoid confusion and strengthen association. Judy suggested most dogs could reach their potential to recognize over 200 objects. By showing an object to a dog and then repeating the object's name several times, the association is successfully and correctly made.

Judy taught that the psychology behind successful obedience training was based on cause and effect. A sound or movement made by the master had to be followed by action on the part of the dog. Association followed by imitation: concise phrases repeated consistently in the same order. Repeated phrases like "Buster, ball, fetch-ball" would promote successful teamwork, the cornerstone of successful training.

For Judy, speech and the printed word were to the development of a human's communication skills as hearing and seeing were to that of the dog's. But he was quick to caution his students that dogs did not understand "words as words." There had to be a strong link between a command issued in a consistent tone of voice and deliberate actions to promote successful teamwork.

The underlying component of developing a dog's true potential rested in the canine's natural desire to please its master. For a dog it was important only to know if its owner was pleased or displeased with its behavior. The assumption was that in most cases a loyal dog would endure pain and suffering to carry out the commands of its master. Judy further believed that the mind of the dog had untapped potential and only through the process of proper obedience training would "the understanding between man and his dog be deeper and more soulful."[48]

He proposed that the full abilities of the dog were not yet fully comprehended by those who studied them. Through proper and enlightened training dogs were capable of hundreds of tasks not yet witnessed by man. He additionally noted that cats suffered greatly due to the fact that most people never thought to spend time or energy on their training.[49]

Judy was unwavering in his belief that a dog must have complete faith in his trainer, and there was no room for doubt. He wrote, "One half of his [the dog's] training is not training but confidence in his master to the utmost."[50] The dog must trust that the proper consequence will follow if he has pleased his master. Good teamwork is paramount for successful training, and the dog must not lose faith in his trainer's ability to gain the goal mutually.[51]

Along with this condition of faith, the elements of pain, humiliation, and pride entered into what Judy referred to as "principles of pedagogy." But Judy cautioned the trainer that the dog looks at the world as only a dog could and advised dog owners to think as a dog would, and not try to humanize him.[52]

A competent trainer tapped into the specific motivational zones of a dog, be it an empty stomach, a desire to be outside or a need to be in a calm environment. Pain and hunger are the strongest motivation when training dogs; pain represents the negative and hunger the positive enforcements. This approach called into play the dog's use of its senses, which Judy listed in this order of importance: smell, hearing, sight, touch and taste.[53]

Judy noted that dogs perceive the world in tones of black and gray. He also stated that dogs could not see as far in the distance as humans, but are able to detect moving objects more quickly than man. Because of the dog's height, it also see less of an object at close range.[54]

A dog navigates its world with its sense of smell that develops in the suckling puppy during the first nine days of life, when its eyes are still closed. Through this highly developed sense, dogs recall if objects or living things are friendly or dangerous and also bond with their human caretakers and were more loyal and affectionate with them.

Hearing is also crucial to a dog's well-being. Judy cited an experiment conducted by a Dr. Elmer Culler, a professor of psychology at the

University of Illinois, in which Dr. Culler concluded that the hearing ability of a dog was about 40 percent superior to that of a human.[55]

Judy noted that dogs hear in large part through vibrations picked up through the body, which allow even dogs that are deaf to "hear." A dog with impaired sensory capabilities was as good a candidate for training as dogs with intact sensory capacities. In an item he titled, "Case Study #3: Deffie the Deaf Dalmatian," he wrote about his training of a dog that had been born deaf and came to live with Judy.[56]

Judy named the Dalmatian Deffie and trained the dog by engaging its sense of sight and human signaling. The command of "come" was performed through the motion of clapping hands. "Stop" was accomplished by arms outstretched horizontally, as were other commands employed very specifically. For example, to indicate disapproval Judy waved his left arm in a circle.[57]

Outside on lead Deffie was also carefully guided. By not pulling on the lead the dog became sensitized to the subtle nuances of the leash holder and could be directed to go left or right and stopped with a very slight tug of the leash. Deffie's off-lead training could also be adeptly handled. To achieve positive results Judy used a long cane to tap on the dog, which caused Deffie to slow and look back at his master for a direction.[58]

On the topic of training dogs that could not hear, Judy referenced a story of a reader who wrote to him and explained that she had trained her deaf three-year-old Boston terrier by the switching off and on of house and porch lights. This was something even the experienced author admitted to not having thought of himself.[59]

In "Case Study #4: Lissen the Blind Scottie," Judy's gentle humor and tolerance was again evident in his choice of dog names. He relayed the story of Lissen, a Scottish terrier that was born sightless. Upon receiving the Scottie, Judy recalled how the little dog presented such a pathetic image when it stood motionless with unseeing eyes opened wide upon leaving her crate.[60]

Judy understood that Lissen was acting instinctually and from experience. He imagined Lissen's former life, where other dogs that were unaware of Lissen's lack of sight most likely tried to engage the terrier in the typical rough and tumble activities of canine play and competitiveness. In Lissen's cautious and rigid posture, Judy noted "the patience, the quietness, the motionlessness so characteristic of the blind, was hers and by necessity."[61]

How to train such a dog became Judy's personal challenge. He focused on Lissen's keen ability to listen. With gentle petting, some food and milk, Judy gained the trust of the terrier and got to work.

At *Dog World* headquarters Lissen was allowed the run of the house and was free to roam about on the four floors of the building occupied by the publishing house. Judy and his staff observed Lissen's adaptations on a daily basis.[62]

Judy observed that the dog's sense of direction was strong. "Soon or late, her aimless wandering brot her back each time to the spot where we first had given food to her."[63] Her food plate became her home plate. With nose to the ground she navigated the room slowly and safely and never stumbled into furniture or the wall.[64]

Unlike Deffie, Lissen had a slight advantage because she was easily trained off leash and was able to respond to the verbal commands of "come" or "heel."

As Lissen had come to Judy late in her life, surrendered by her owner, Judy believed the dog had missed out on the delights of a "normal" dog's life. He feared that Lissen was always just one step away from harm, such as an attack by another dog or the crush of automobile tires.

But Judy was practical when it came to quality of life issues. Not wanting the dog to come to such a brutal end, he believed it was more humane to end the dog's life in a painless manner that would put a gentle stop to the dog's "constant night of darkness."

Judy believed that dogs had different intelligence levels. He bluntly stated that some dogs were dumb while others were smart and quick to learn. He estimated that about 80 percent of all dogs were capable of being trained to utilize their unique intelligence and adaptability to situations, resulting in very different outcomes.[65]

Under the heading of "Shy, Nervous, Cowardly and Vicious Dogs," Judy covered the handling and care of dogs with special emotional needs. Judy noted that dogs displaying any of the four traits or a combination of any required a special master.

Of the first condition Judy wrote, "A shy dog is an abomination." These dogs were born shy and doomed to die shy. The trait of shyness in a pup manifested by the age of eight weeks and was easy to detect. Unlike its littermates, a shy pup hid in corners and did not rush to greet strangers. Despite kind treatment they "give the impression of having been badly treated previously."[66]

Judy wrote that shy puppies often proved to be dangerous and advised that these pups be humanely "put out of the way, for their own sake, the safety of others, and for the sake of the breed."[67]

If this could not be done, Judy advised that shy dogs never be used for breeding purposes and must be treated kindly and retained by the same owner for life. He noted, "A new master after six months of [the dog's] age can not cause a change." He also recommended that a shy puppy be kept away from other pups with the same condition and should be played with "roughly" but gently.[68]

Judy explained that unlike its shy cousin, the nervous dog could be cured with the introduction of a proper diet and "sympathetic handling." The nervous dog was not to be overfed and was to receive plenty of exercise. An implicit trust in its handler was also a necessary component.[69]

Cowardly dogs were "disgusting to humans and likely to other dogs," and were despised by humans and their own kind. Judy classified cowardly dogs as dangerous because they were prone to pounce on, chase or bite smaller dogs as they snarled and growled menacingly, only to turn and run if their victim confronted them. Cowardly dogs might cringe in the presence of older dogs and adults and snap at children, seizing upon what they sense as helplessness.[70]

Judy advised that cowardice in a dog could be lessened but not cured. But he warned humans not to judge these dogs too harshly and sympathetically observed, "Many humans are cowards but are able to conceal the cowardice. The dog is forced to reveal cowardice" when placed in threatening situations.[71] If a large dog suffered from cowardice, Judy suggested letting it gain confidence by allowing it to fight a dog of equal size.

A vicious dog, on the other hand, was often the product of an abusive master; the dog had probably endured a history of mistreatment. Judy advised, "A dog is not to be judged according to his master so much as his master is to be judged by the nature of his dog." Viciousness was remedied by the dog's acquisition of a kind but firm master. If this failed, Judy advised that the dog must be fitted with a muzzle when "brot" outside.[72]

For Judy the manner in which a dog was commanded to act and behave was equally important to what the dog had been trained to do. He sternly admonished those who lost control of themselves and punished a dog in anger.[73]

Judy's training philosophy contained elements of both negative and positive reinforcement, but at no time was cruelty to be part of the former. He further stated that in most cases the punishment administered to dogs was unjustified and noted, "I think it to be true that in nine cases of ten where dogs are punisht, they are punisht too much."[74]

When the situation warranted it, Judy suggested that "The dog is to be punisht with dignity by the master in natural normal condition."[75] He advised that a quick slap with an open hand or a newspaper delivered with reasonable force as not to cause the dog permanent physical harm was sufficient. He warned dog owners not to hit a dog on or near its muzzle, head, ears, paws, or its backbone. The dog owner was advised to target the dog's upper thigh area, the tail region and sides as many dogs had perished from kidney failure as the result of severe blows and kicks.[76]

Never was the dog owner to command a dog to come in a friendly manner only to whip him when he obeyed. "If a dog is to be whipt, he should be come upon openly and promptly and in act of his misdeed."[77]

As an experienced trainer educating other trainers of dogs, Judy's ultimate goal was to cultivate fairness and reasonableness in his students. If the dog owner had any doubt that a dog should be punished they were to refrain from punitive actions and if there was any question that a dog deserved praise, then praise was in order.[78]

Judy wrote that small acts and gestures were valued by the dog. Soft words of approval as well as "a dainty morsel, a bit of meat, or a sweetened crust,"[79] would suffice. But he urged owners not to overdo rewards, "or else the dog will understand that he is doing the work for the reward and not because he is commanded to do it."[80]

As in the case of negative reinforcement, timing was important with the employment of positive reinforcement. It was to be administered quickly by the trainer so the dog associated the "treat" with his obedient response to a command.[81]

The traits of aggression and viciousness were never desirable qualities of any family pet. But Judy informed readers that there were certain professions where these attributes could be carefully channeled for the good of humans. He was among the first in his field to see the true potential of dogs used in police and military operations and had definitive thoughts on the topic.

Judy was troubled that the terms German shepherd and police dog had become synonymous in many parts of the world and that this breed's association with police work had damaged its reputation.[82]

He clarified that "the term police dog does not denote breed but the use to which a dog is put."[83] Judy noted that almost 90 percent of the dogs used in police work were actually shepherds, but that only a small percentage of shepherds were used as police dogs. These medium-sized dogs were described as "active, alert, hardy, strong, fearless, not grouchy," characteristics that made them ideally suited for police work. Their highly developed sense of smell and inherent distrust of strangers also made them strong candidates for this work.[84]

Judy wrote that only shepherd dogs possessing the degree "P.H., polizeihund," or police dog, were officially termed police dogs. This title was bestowed on the dog by specialty clubs only after the dog had passed rigorous testing.[85]

Other breeds, including Doberman pinschers, Airedales, Belgian sheepdogs and great Danes were also adaptable to training for police work.[86] However, bloodhounds, a breed that excelled in tracking work, were deemed "too sluggish" for general field work.[87]

By 1902 German police forces regularly used shepherds for the duties of guarding and protection. Judy credited a man by the name of Lieutenant Most and his work with the Doberman pinscher for pioneering and advancing this effort. By 1912 400 German police branches employed 1,300 police dogs and of those, 360 were Doberman pinschers. All told, it was noted that "every sixth police officer had a trained dog."[88]

Germany was so advanced in its implementation of police dogs that it had established a school devoted to the training of these dogs. Located in Gruenheide, Germany, the institute offered two courses each year and graduated approximately 100 dogs per course. Upon the completion of their training, these dogs were purchased by the German police force.[89]

It was also noted that Germany continued to employ these highly trained dogs on a scale that had not been nearly matched by the United States 30 years later.[90]

Judy's supposition that a dog's ability to assist if not altogether replace humans in the role of guarding and protection was pioneering. "A policeman and one dog can do the work of two policemen," he wrote.[91]

Police dogs warned of the presence of criminals and prevented ambush and attacks on police personnel. These canines were capable of exploring dark and hidden places that were difficult to access and locations that posed a great risk to humans. They could also corner suspects and detain them until their capture.[92]

Judy recommended that every American police car be equipped

with a police dog and that every prison employ a number of them. He reported that in 1932 New Eastern State Penitentiary located in Graterford, Pennsylvania, had employed four dogs for guarding and protection purposes and that the program had proven so successful that one dog had already replaced one human member of a patrolling pair.[93]

The training of dogs for police work presented no magical technique, but could be broken down into three categories: obedience, protection and detection. They could be trained to detain a suspect before capture, prevent a prisoner from escaping, retrieve objects a suspect unloaded and to have no fear of bullets or blows delivered by the detainee. Canines employed in detective work were also capable of trailing and tracking skills.

A staunch supporter of the use of police dogs, Judy also faulted the manner in which some of these dogs were trained and the long term ramifications thereof. In particular he disagreed with the process of training referred to as "man attack" or "man work," a practice where dogs attacked trainers wearing padded suits. On this matter Judy wrote, "I must take issue with practically the entire system of police training,"[94] and stated that his views on this type of training were "contrary to those held by practically all German and American trainers."[95]

Judy was specifically concerned that dogs trained in "man work" techniques were permitted to become household pets upon their retirement from police work.

The dog's breed was not at issue, since Judy adamantly proclaimed that any dog trained for this type of intense work "should not be owned as a pet or in the household or by private parties," because they were aggressive and inclined to attack.[96] He believed that due to the intensity of this type of training, the reputation of the German shepherd dog had suffered.

Judy was in agreement that it was "well for the training prisoner to be in a box or up a tree," as this taught the dog to bark when warranted. He also agreed that in certain situations it was useful for this "prisoner" to wear a padded suit for protection from the dog-in-training as a method to teach it not to bite the body of a human in the field. But Judy saw a down side to this method that was detrimental to the dog's future.[97]

Judy despised the exhibitions performed at shows where the playacting criminal was "padded and swelled until he looks like a constipated frog,"[98] while being attacked and bitten by a police dog. He believed that these scenes were overdramatized for entertainment value and ultimately caused spectators to be fearful of dogs in all situations. Judy decried much of the training of police dogs as "a farce," and concluded that these dogs would not be able to recognize an actual criminal in the field.[99]

Judy thought it would be more desirable to have police dogs trained to bark loudly and circle the criminal they pursued, with the ultimate goal of detaining them without physical contact. He stated that there was only one condition when a police dog should actually attack, and that was when a gun was fired. In that event, Judy wrote that the dog be trained to jump upon the perpetrator and hold them by their clothing.[100]

Judy pointed out that a well-trained dog also had the ability to partake in the duties of locating and protecting the more innocent victims in the field, such as "the lost, wounded, drunken, apoplectic, or fainting persons."[101]

In 1932 America also lagged behind their European counterparts in tapping the potential of dogs on the battlefield. In the third volume of *Training the Dog*, Judy extensively covered the topic of dogs of war. Although much had been printed about the role of war dogs in the First World War, he wrote that "much had been glorified until to separate fact and fiction, truth and legend is difficult."[102]

Judy acknowledged that dogs had been "used on the field of battle almost since the beginning of wars," but noted that the first organized and intelligent use of war dogs occurred during the "World War," an event Judy had experienced in a very personal way.[103]

The dogs of World War I were used in three categories—sentry, messenger and guarding—and with the tasks of carrying messages, guarding prisoners of war, locating the wounded, and warning of intruders.

Judy extolled the war dog's ability to recognize "human distress," to distinguish the dead from the wounded and to differentiate between the uniforms of enemy forces and those of their own.[104]

Dogs were used to search for the wounded on the battlefields of France as early in 1895, when the National Society for the Sanitary Dog was established by that nation with the purpose of training dogs to search for victims hidden from view and to retrieve articles from a victim or a body.[105]

Judy believed that the specific training of military dogs was based on the foundation of general obedience training. He wrote that dogs that were able to understand and respond to the commands of heel and sit, remain in the down position in the absence of handler, and jump free over a 40-inch barrier were capable of military maneuvers.[106]

The teaching of a dog to search and locate wounded soldiers provided an example of this. Judy explained that in training dogs of war, German forces attached a sausage or "bringsel" to the dog's collar. The dog was trained to return with the bringsel in its mouth when a wounded man was located.[107]

Judy shared that the Dutch Society for Red Cross Dogs held annual trials where dogs were awarded diplomas after meeting specific requirements. With the command of "seek," which was delivered with a directional by its handler, a dog was activated to "beat or range" at a distance of approximately 300 yards without pausing to urinate, sniff or bark.[108]

Dogs were also trained to locate a wounded person and to retrieve any object that it could carry in its mouth. Upon returning to its handler, the object was to be dropped at the "let go" command. The dog was then placed on a long lead and issued the "where" command. The dog was trained to lead its handler to the victim without further command and without being distracted or misled by extraneous activity in the field.[109]

In 1902 Germany began to officially train dogs for use in the military. Dogs were divided into three categories: medical department dogs, messenger dogs and sentinel dogs. By the advent of the First World War, Germany had already amassed a highly prepared force of war dogs furnished by a network of organized societies.[110]

The Belgium War Office had also established a war dog training kennel by 1910. The popular dog of choice in this case was the innately qualified Belgian sheepdog of the Malinois and Groenendael varieties. In the early phase of the war, each company of the Belgian forces possessed "twelve dogs and six small wagons," on which machine guns and other combat material were transported.[111]

Three years later the French War Office had established a war dog training kennel located at Chalons. By 1914 this facility had successfully trained over 600 dogs for military use. Soon after, the office established an official war dog service that was successfully reorganized and renamed the "Service des Chien de Guerre" in 1917.[112]

British forces utilized messenger dogs, and the Italians used military dogs only to transport food to the front lines in mountainous terrain, but despite all the success European nations had demonstrated with their employment of war dogs, it dismayed Judy that the United States did not officially employ any dogs of war during World War I.[113]

The British eventually established training centers for military dogs. Located in Shuburyness, England, the dogs underwent an intensive six week training period. Judy noted that the British dogs were trained to "go to" one keeper, while those trained in Germany worked between two handlers.[114]

Each European nation favored particular breeds for their military canine forces. While the Germans favored the German shepherd, Doberman pinschers, Airedales and rottweilers in that order, Judy wrote that the English favored "Airedales, and some collies, retrievers and lurchers."[115]

The German military seriously considered the poodle for military work for a time. Although an extremely intelligent breed, Judy wrote that they were ultimately deemed "shortsighted and unable to withstand the sun." The collie breed fared no better.[116]

By 1928 Germany had established a plan that allotted one dozen dogs to each artillery regiment, with 24 appointed to each infantry regiment. Judy made note that German military personnel now focused on training dogs of war to work with one handler and to "go to destinations not before traveled by them."[117]

The care and consideration afforded dogs of war was of utmost concern to Judy, who noted their special needs. For instance, the harnesses designed for war dogs were not suitable for dogs, since a dog's back was described as "floating and weak."[118] Judy advised that a well-designed harness device for military dogs must exploit the strength of a dog's neck, because unlike horses, a war dog was only capable of completing a daily journey of approximately 35 miles and was only able to carry a load of about 30 pounds.[119]

But war dogs did offer unique advantages. When lined up single-file in groups of six to eight and under the direction of only one handler, military dogs could "cover ground which horse, mule, man or even tank could not reach."[120]

Judy concluded that in military operations these "work and liaison dogs were especially successful, more so than sentinel, patrol, auxiliary and medical dogs,"[121] and stated that the German and Belgian forces had experienced more overall success in their utilization of war dogs than the British and the French.[122]

The fact that many war dogs often fell victim to the ravages of battle troubled Judy. He cited an event at Verdun, France, where 17 human couriers lost their lives. A courier dog was subsequently used in successfully completing its task, only to lose its life when a shell exploded shortly afterward.[123]

Despite the danger placed on war dogs, Judy understood their value in this emerging role and remained puzzled as to why his own country refused to officially include them in their military forces.

In the fifth edition of *Training the Dog*, published in 1941, Judy reported that although earlier editions of his books on dog training had included detailed sections on the subject of war dogs, one had not been included in this edition. Of this omission he wrote that his query to the United States Army Chief of Staff in November 1940 "brot the reply that the United States Army has not any provision for the use of dogs in war operations."[124]

While some dogs found work on the battlefield, others were increasingly employed in the entertainment industry. By 1932 Judy reported that "dogs have won their place in the sun in the cinema or moving pictures."[125]

By 1941 dogs had become a familiar feature of many major motion pictures. Dogs such as Strongheart, Peter the Great, Rin Tin Tin and Lightning and Flash had already made their mark in Hollywood, starring in silent films. But Judy proudly acknowledged that the appeal of the dog on the silver screen had endured and the dog had "won his way in the talkies or barkies."[126]

Hollywood executives quickly came to understand that an adorable and clever dog on the screen translated to greater revenues for a movie studio. "With the exception of a beautiful woman, a dog most readily adds a human interest touch and liveliness to any picture," wrote Judy.[127]

The dog's role in the movie industry also highlighted the adaptability of the canine. The film industry was growing at so rapid a pace that it presented new challenges for both dog and handler. Commands administered verbally on the set of silent films had to be delivered in an alternate manner as films were increasingly produced with sound.

To elicit the desired result, the dog was required to focus on its trainer at every moment. Commanding a dog to perform yawns or to open and close its mouth called for new techniques. To induce a yawn, for example, the trainer used motions such as massaging their own facial muscles.[128]

Judy also noted that to prevent boredom or fatigue in the canine actor, stand-ins or "models" were placed in position for the camera while the cameramen prepared to shoot a scene.[129]

Judy recounted a meeting that had taken place the day he had performed a "read proof" for the chapter on training the dogs for the cinema in 1941. He wrote of how he had dined with Carl Spitz, a personal friend and renowned Hollywood dog trainer, before taking in Spitz's act at the Chicago Theater. Spitz had successfully trained the cairn terrier, Toto, for its role in the *Wizard of Oz*, a Scottie in *The Light That Failed,* Promise the pointer for *The Biscuit Eater* and Mustie the mastiff for his role in *Swiss Family Robinson*.[130]

During Spitz's show, the talented trainer demonstrated how dogs sat, moved backward, barked, rolled over and looked left and right by the administration of commands delivered silently with the motions of his hand, arms, leg and feet.[131]

Judy embraced all the ways the trained dog served man, but he also understood that their value went well beyond the military, police work and the entertainment industry.

He stated that within the last quarter century nothing the dog had done was as important as the way the dog served as a guide for the blind. Of this he wrote, "Here is work so worthy that it clearly makes the dog an invaluable part of society."[132]

Judy was quick to point out that not all guide dogs were "seeing eye" dogs and that only those that had been trained at the Seeing Eye in Morristown, New Jersey, officially earned that title.[133]

Judy wrote that it had been his privilege to visit the Seeing Eye school in May of 1939. He explained that although the school was located in Whippany, New Jersey, most of the dogs and their future handlers were trained in a facility in Morristown, four miles away. In that community the dogs learned and practiced their skills in the real world, on the town's busy intersections and sidewalks with the special permissions and cooperation of local authorities.[134]

Individuals eligible for the program were required to be between the ages of 16 and 50 and to pay a fee of $150, which Judy noted was intended to "create in the blind person a spirit of confidence and learning ability."[135]

Male and female dogs were eligible for training as guide dogs, but were required to be older than 14 months. All dogs, regardless of their sex, were referred to as "she" and their blind handlers of either sex were addressed as "he" to avoid confusion when notes were taken during training sessions. It was noted that in 1939 approximately 60 percent of the working Seeing Eye dogs were female.[136]

Dogs were carefully matched with their human partner; "dogs of short steps" were selected for women and for a tall man it was found that a taller dog worked best.[137]

Dogs with extra long coats were not suitable for this role because they were perpetually damp and muddied easily in rain-prone regions. Qualified dogs possessed "good feet, sturdiness and intelligence." To test their tolerance to sudden and loud noise each dog safely experienced the exploding of a torpedo.[138]

Those who trained Seeing Eye dogs were required to train for a period of three to four years. The trainee spent the first month of the program wearing a blindfold and lived as a blind person did. The training sessions for the Seeing Eye dogs ran for three months. The blind person acquiring the dog underwent a one month training period and also had to have full confidence in their dog to avoid miscommunications that could endanger both.[139]

Judy noted that the breeds of shepherds, boxers and Dobermans were the dogs most often used for the Seeing Eye dog training program, with the shepherds employed most frequently. The pedigree papers of each dog remained at the school to discourage the unauthorized breeding of these dogs.[140] The working life of a guide dog was estimated at eight years.[141]

Basic training for this program required dogs to be taught to walk quickly to "give contrast to a warning stop."[142] The sightless handler was trained to issue four basic commands to their dogs: forward, right, left and down.[143]

When turns were made, the handler remained still, allowing the dog to initiate the turn. The handler used a taut, long U-shaped handle that ran from the breast of the dog to the handler's left hand.[144]

At the completion of their training, the dogs were isolated for a period of three weeks to guard against possible disease and were not allowed to run together, to curb aggression.[145]

Judy relayed that the pairing of a dog and a blind handler was not always successful. He observed that due to the difference in the life spans of man and dog, the institution that trained these pairs "must concern itself with dogs for a short time and then with human character for many years."[146]

Despite the unique relationship that bonded them, not every individual privileged to receive the services of a trained Seeing Eye dog turned out to be the best dog owner. In his writings on the ongoing training of these dogs, Judy commented that "an increasing part of the work is the checkup on graduates, not the dogs but the blind persons."[147]

He further noted that the difficulties that arose between the blind individual and their guide dog were more often than not the result of the former and often necessitated a "heart-to-heart talk with the blind person."[148]

Many of the chapters of the 1953 edition of *Training the Dog* remained unchanged from previous versions. In this edition, however, the chapter dedicated to war dogs presented a shift in the policies dictating the nation's use of military dogs, which Judy happily noted had been significantly revised from a decade earlier, due to the events of World War II.[149]

Judy reported that in 1942 it was proposed by a "group of dog people" that the United States Army begin to recruit dogs for active war services. As a result, five war dog reception and training camps were established under the supervision of the Remount Service Quartermaster General's department.[150]

The program was a great success. Within three years a total of 19,400 dogs had been recruited for military training. Of these dogs, 18,000 were offered to the government by their owners and another 1,400 were purchased or obtained otherwise by the United States Army.[151]

To help with this "grand patriotic service,"[152] the Dogs for Defense group was organized by civilians, with the sole purpose of supervising the collection and delivery of selected canines to their training centers. By the end of World War II 15 war dog platoons "were on active duty in the theatres, five more had completed training ... and another five were ready for specialized training."[153]

It was noted that the 25th and 26th canine platoon units had fought with the "6th Army from New Guinea to Okinawa."[154] The former had been engaged in continuous combat for 13 months and had been successful in leading over 800 patrols against enemy forces.[155]

Judy also cited the contributions of the "Quartermaster-trained" sled dogs that had assisted the Air Transport Command and had rescued stranded fliers in the "bleak Aleutians."[156]

Additional dogs made up a part of a contingent of 209 dogs that were flown to Belgium in February 1945. These dogs assisted in the evacuation of the wounded through the Northwestern Front, navigating snow that often measured more than four feet.[157]

At the cessation of World War II, most of these war dogs were sold or given to "suitable persons" and some were returned to their original owners. But Judy also noted that 4,446 "were destroyed on the basis of type or temperament," physical disability, or were classified as unsafe for civilian life.[158]

These dogs met the requirement of being "well-boned, sound in mind and body." The average dog weighed between 70 to 90 pounds and measured 24 to 26 inches in height. The dogs were in excellent physical condition and possessed strong backs and deep chests. Their well-formed feet and legs and exceptional jaw power made them perfect for military service.[159]

Temperament was also a key factor in their fitness for military service. Judy wrote that these shepherds met stringent requirements that called for them to be "alert, full of energy, of even disposition, willing to listen, learn and obey, and be free from variable or unpredictable reactions."[160]

The establishment of training centers in the United States for dogs of war created a great need for those who could properly train them. Judy identified seven qualities of candidates for this work:

1. Friendly attitude toward dogs
2. Intelligence
3. Patience and perseverance
4. Mental and physical coordination
5. Physical endurance
6. Resourcefulness
7. Dependability

Most importantly, Judy advised that "the general instruction to the trainer is to work with a firm hand and without abuse."[161]

War dogs received basic training at these facilities, where they mastered the commands of heel-sit, down, stay-come, jump and drop on and off lead, as the situation dictated. Dogs were also acclimated to riding in cars and to the intense sound of gunfire.[162]

Dogs that displayed excessive nervousness faced early rejection from the program. Judy reported that over a period of just ten months, 801 dogs recruited from just one state by the Dogs for Defense group were turned away for that reason. Another 142 were deemed "not fit" for service and 112 were marked as having "no guts." Of the last group Judy wrote that these dogs were too shy, good natured, or slinked at or feared gun fire.[163]

The most important factor in selecting dogs for military service was that of "aggressiveness," officially defined as "the degree to which the dog asserts himself or is inclined to attack."[164]

Some dogs were naturally more aggressive than others, but Judy wrote that aggression could be developed in most dogs through a training technique called "soft agitation." This method called for the dog to be pushed by its trainer, who taunted the dog with his hands or a gunny sack. This technique was introduced during the third week of training.[165]

The next progression was to introduce "rough agitation." This involved the inclusion of a second man who played the role of "attack victim." Judy noted that in this type of training a padded suit was required to be worn by the victim.[166]

Dogs were required to trail a man across "broken ground, briar fields, thru old buildings, thru conduits, across swamps," in daylight and at night, and under conditions that presented loud noises and distractions. Most importantly, a dog must be "alert" and able to detect and discern a potential enemy in "natural night light" at a distance of 200 yards.[167]

By the end of a dog's six-week training program, a successful trainer had readied his student to be a capable four-legged soldier. The properly trained dog now was able to patrol the coast, guard factories and prisons, protect shipyards, detect scents in the jungle, transport ammunition, deliver messages and be prepared to search for concealed enemies and wounded soldiers.[168]

Judy was satisfied that the United States military had finally grasped the true potential of properly trained war dogs and provided accounts of their achievements on the battlefield. He cited a bulletin issued by the Office of Technical Information dated May 29, 1945, in which the Quartermaster General reported, "No unit employing war dogs suffered casualty from ambush or sniper." The remainder of the bulletin praised the dogs of the 26th QM War Dog Platoon, who assisted in clearing out hidden Japanese forces on Morotai Island.[169]

The efforts of these dogs of war were also lauded in a report presented by Colonel Walter J. Hanna, C. O. office, 155th Infantry of the War Department. The colonel commended the scout dogs that had located hidden Japanese positions and noted that these dogs had completed over 100 successful patrols with infantry troops.[170] It was also noted that during that period, "not a unit suffered a casualty from enemy ambushes or snipers."[171]

Those who professionally trained dogs for military service had found a niche for their skills. However, Judy also understood that the average pet owner now required competent individuals to help them to train their pets.

In the ninth volume of *Training the Dog*, Judy wrote about career potential for aspiring dog obedience trainers in a chapter titled, "Dog Training as a Profession." Judy knew that with the increased popularity of dogs in America an emphasis was placed on the value of well-behaved pets. In the opening sentences of this chapter Judy stated, "The public demands control of a dog when on the streets or in public places." In his trademark style Judy noted that "nabors" needed protection from the nuisance of barking dogs, biting and other bad behavior.[172]

Dog obedience training promoted qualities in an animal that reaped the rewards of "pleasure and usefulness," and offered a sense of satisfaction and pleasure to the trainee.[173]

Judy encouraged those who had an interest and the aptitude for training dogs to regard obedience training as a viable career option. "The demand for dog training likely will increase steadily for many years," he correctly predicted. He envisioned training classes offered in every community in the nation.[174]

Judy identified four essential qualities required for those who wanted a career in dog obedience training. First and foremost, he set forth that the candidate must possess "a basic knowledge of the psychology of the dog's mind" and a strong grasp of the way dogs viewed the world.[175]

Second in order of importance was the candidate's understanding of what Judy termed pedagogy, or a general knowledge of teaching methods. This knowledge was to be combined with the qualities of patience and "thoroness," which were key factors in the molding of a dog's mind.[176]

The fourth quality was one that Judy valued in himself: the aspiring trainer had to display a true and abiding love for dogs and all the qualities they possessed.[177]

Judy divided training instruction into basic groups: formal obedience for dog shows and obedience trials, specialized training for hunting and field work, training for "home and companionship," and intensive training for the purposes of police work, guiding for the blind, and for stage and "trick work."[178]

The first category pertained to the programs established by the American Kennel Club in 1936. This course offered training in various degrees with methods and techniques dictated through official bulletins issued by the American Kennel Club. Judy noted that in obtaining these degrees, both the dog and the owner were trained as a unit.[179]

Of all these training categories Judy stated that the training of dogs for "home and companionship" presented the greatest opportunity for aspiring obedience trainers and offered general advice for the management of this type of business.[180]

Judy offered suggestions for the private training and boarding of dogs. A two- to four-month-long session was recommended when a private course of training was prescribed. It was advised that the trainer request a fee of $70 to cover all training expenses and boarding. Daily training sessions were to be comprised of a one hour session in the morning and an hour in the afternoon for a period of six days a week.[181]

It was noted that there were no permissions, licensing or fees required in any state, governing office or even the American Kennel Club to set up a dog training business or facility. Judy advised, however, that the owners and trainers at these facilities had several legal aspects to consider when operating a dog training facility and recommended the use of boarding contracts to protect both dog owner and professional.[182]

According to Judy, the best canine students were purebred dogs organized in groups of no more than 20 dogs. For maximum effectiveness, formal group training sessions should occur once a week. A one-hour class conducted over the course of ten weeks was sufficient for the typical dog owner, at a of rate $1 per session. Judy recommended that all fees be collected in advance.[183]

Judy presented a set of governing rules for dogs participating in public training classes. For example, dogs in training should be older than eight months of age and were not to be fed within six hours or offered water within three hours of a session. Bitches in heat were excluded from all sessions and all dogs were to wear collars, but not of the choker type, and be held on a lead no longer than six feet.[184]

No handler under 12 years of age was to be allowed to participate in these group training sessions, and each trainee was allowed only one dog per session. Dogs were to be kept under full control at all times during sessions and handlers were to clean up any "nuisance or accident" caused by the dog.[185]

Above all else Judy urged that during all training sessions, all handlers were to exercise consideration for other handlers and their dogs.[186]

In his extensive body of written works on the topic of dog obedience training, Judy's personal lifetime experience in the ministry, military service, legal profession and publishing was always evident. For Judy the socialization and channeling of the dog's natural abilities in the show ring, on the battlefield, on city streets and in the back yards of America rested on his unwavering belief that a well-trained dog was a "companion worthy to walk by the side of man, the only god he knows."[187]

4

The Handy
Dog Booklet Series:
Advice on Every
Aspect of the Canine

In 1950 Judy published the seventh edition of a series titled *Handy Dog Booklets Series*. These booklets, compiled in one hardcover volume, showcased Judy's personal experience and knowledge pertaining to every conceivable issue affecting American dogs and their owners.

Thirteen booklets in all presented an eager audience of dog owners with a detailed education on every aspect of the canine. Each booklet contained a wealth of information on the intimate details of the dog's anatomy, reproduction, the proper development of breed lines, the whelping of puppies and how to care for man's best friend to ensure that their natural life on earth was as happy, comfortable and healthful as possible.

Judy used these booklets to reminded readers how all the hard work and sacrifice that went into raising a good dog was rewarded many times over by the love and affection that was received in return.

Writing on the section titled, "Anatomy of the Dog," Judy boldly asserted that "a dog is not greatly different from the human animal," with the exception of its walking on four legs.[1]

Although this booklet was designed for the layman, it was in no way meant to encourage the average dog owner to assume the role of a trained veterinarian. As for those who bred dogs professionally, Judy expressed his astonishment about their lack of knowledge on the anatomy of the very champions they bred. He claimed most dog breeders could not identify the location of a dog's major organs.[2]

Judy divided this booklet on the dog's anatomy into ten detailed sections that commenced with "The Skeleton or Bone Structure," and ended with the "Sensual System or Organs of Sense." An eleventh segment presented a "Glossary of Terms Useful to the Dog Breeder and Dog Show Judge."[3]

In the glossary readers learned that "fiddle-front" meant bandy legged, and "flew" referred to the overhanging upper lip of a dog, which was not to be confused with "dew lap," the loose flabby skin that hung from a dog's throat.[4]

Related to the segment on the anatomy of the dog were booklets titled "Handling the Mating," "Stud Dog's Care and Management," and "Whelping of Puppies."

The first two titles dealt with the important matter of producing champions among all breeds. In the topic that dealt with the mating of dogs, Judy began with the assertion that it was odd that so much had been written about the breeding of dogs, but little was "said about the actual mating and the care and handling of the stud and the matron," before, during and after the event. He expressed that this lack of knowledge had unfortunately lead to the psychological and physical harm of the animals involved.[5]

Judy advised dog breeders on the optimum conditions that would result in the creation of, "good type offspring"[6] in a planned and thought-out process. He discussed this topic in specific sections, such as the "Day of Heat" for optimal mating, planned down to the actual time of day.[7] He offered feeding instructions for the bitch and stud and described the manner in which the humans involved in the conjoining of dogs were to safely handle the manual manipulation of the mating pair to achieve success.[8]

On a final note on this subject, Judy observed that human intervention was often not necessary, since the dogs involved decided "most of these matters and it is often just as well."[9]

In discussing the significance of the all-important stud dog, Judy set forth that just one strong stud was capable of passing on a breed's best qualities and could cause change within a breed within a period of ten years.[10]

As evidence of this he offered the case of a bull terrier stud that around the time of 1860 "threw all-white puppies," with the result that within just a few years all-white bull terriers were the only "allowable" color for that specific breed.[11]

To further underscore the importance of the stud dog's role in shaping breed standards, Judy noted that within a 20-year period as many as 162,000 dogs could be traced to just one male ancestor if the stud was allowed to mate once a week for a period of seven years.[12]

In comparison, it was noted that on average, a female dog produced no more than five litters in her lifetime, or approximately only 30 puppies, and that over a period of many years one female dog could alter a breed type through her male offspring.[13]

Judy recommended that dogs between the ages of 12 months and seven years be used for stud purposes. Factors that influenced this were the size of the breed and the dog's general health.[14]

In four out of five cases when a mating was not successful, Judy placed "blame" on the female. He warned against spreading rumor of a stud dog's lack of productivity, because this was ruinous to the reputation of a breeder and the stud dog. He was aware that jealousy ran rampant among the owners of rival stud dogs, and on this matter Judy once again called for the display of good sportsmanship.[15]

The role of the "stud personality" was also important. Judy wrote that a successful stud dog "must be preeminently maleish in temperament" and possess qualities of fearlessness and be aggressive and courageous. His general health must be robust, with a "toughness of body and stamina" to match his personal qualities.[16]

In a section titled "Feeding the Dog," Judy relayed dietary information for all classes of dog owners in a manner that was described as "correct scientifically above all other things"[17] and covered all phases of the feeding process in a style that was easy to read and follow.

On the topic of dogs and food, Judy astutely observed, "Half a dog's pleasure in life is in eating and half his health lies in his eating." Judy warned dog owners that too much food, the wrong kind of food, and food that was improperly prepared resulted in a sick or generally unhealthy animal.[18]

Judy acknowledged that those looking for guidance on how to properly maintain their dog's diet were often confused by the myriad of choices that befell them, and the contradictory advice by so-called experts confused many well-meaning dog owners.[19]

To these befuddled individuals, Judy wrote that despite all the expert dietary advice available, most dog owners would improve their dog's health by simply providing adequate exercise, housing them in a dry and ventilated environment and not overfeeding them.[20]

Judy offered recommendations on the kinds of foods that were most beneficial for dogs. He admitted that in the past, table scraps had accounted for the diets of many an American dog since most dog owners thought these scraps were good enough for a dog. But Judy believed otherwise and pointed out that manufactured dog foods were "evenly balanced, scientifically prepared," easy to obtain, traveled well and did not spoil too quickly.[21]

In addressing those in the business of dog breeding, Judy referred to something called the "generation test," in which the diet for female dogs was proven to aid in the production of milk and the development of other reproductive functions. Good food value was the ultimate goal in maintaining the stamina of a mother dog charged with nursing a large litter.[22]

Judy specifically recommended that a dog's diet be comprised of approximately "70 percent carbohydrate (starches), 22 percent protein, 5 percent fat, 2.5 percent ash, 0.5 percent fiber."[23] It was noted that while dogs were at one time primarily carnivorous and that meat continued to be a central part of the canine diet, certain changes in their environment had made them omnivorous.[24]

Judy was a product of his time and influenced by his rural upbringing. He suggested that horse meat, raw or cooked, was a good source of nutrition for all breeds of dogs, but cautioned that horse meat was not governmentally inspected. While pork was to be fed only occasionally, mutton, beef and veal were good sources of essential minerals and vitamins.[25]

Judy believed that dogs preferred raw meat and it had more nutritional value for them, but he recommended all meat be slightly cooked to kill germs: broiled, roasted or boiled, but never fried. As a dog matured, the proportion of meat in its diet was to be lessened.[26]

Pasta products such as macaroni and spaghetti with a touch of celery or tomato were recommended to fatten a dog during cold periods. Vegetables could be included in the dog's diet as a way for them to receive adequate vitamins and were cited as a good source of roughage. Cow and goat milk and cottage cheese were also good choices.[27]

On the topic of commercial-grade dog foods, Judy informed readers that up until approximately the year 1920 most manufactured dog food was of the "dog biscuit" variety, which was now called dry food.[28] The use of dry foods, or "biscuit," originated in Great Britain around 1870 and was originally derived from the hardtack remains of a journey at sea. The term biscuit derived from the fact that this type of food was comprised of mainly flour and other cereals. Judy preferred the term "dry food" to biscuit. Large biscuits broken into smaller pieces became food known as "kibble biscuit."[29]

Judy called a dog that initially refused to eat dry food "a wise being."[30] A dog hoping for a more robust meal would patiently wait and ignore the dry food in hopes of obtaining a juicy bit of meat instead. When this occurred Judy advised dog owners to show no mercy, as with most certainty a hungry dog would break down and eventually savor the dry food.[31]

To those who wished to make their own dry food, he recommended leaving the task to commercial manufacturers, but advised those who did choose to make their own kibble not to use cracklings or waste tissue of animals. The best commercial dry foods were "stripped of all vague or mysterious terminology," and were comprised of meat, bone, and scraps, as well as oatmeal, wheaties, and other ingredients such as dried buttermilk, barley malt, wheat germ and cod liver oil among others.[32]

Cod liver oil was recommended as an established part of the diet; it could be mixed with food or delivered by the spoonful. It was noted that cod liver oil promoted bone growth, lessened the chance of the development of rickets and helped boost the stamina of a dog. The substance was to be administered to puppies as young as two months of age, however, Judy advised that most dogs enjoyed it so immensely that care was to be taken not to overprovide.[33]

When canned dog food was introduced to an enthusiastic population of dog owners sometime after, Judy reported that most, but not all, standard brands of moist dog food were well prepared and provided adequate nutrition.[34]

In 1946 the United States Department of Agriculture issued the first regulations on wet dog food, requiring ingredients to be listed in "order of predominance." Although inspection was optional, many cans displayed a government inspection mark. Such a mark informed consumers that the contents of the can was deemed a "normal maintenance food," which was comprised of a minimum of "10 percent protein, 0.3 percent each calcium and phosphorous, 0.15 milligram of thiamin. At least 30 percent of product must be meat or meat by-products." Vegetables and grains were to be of the finest quality, "sound and clean."[35]

Judy warned that at no time should dogs be allowed to eat sweets (with the exception of ice cream), chocolate or any candy, puddings, the bones of chicken, fish or rabbits, or pastry items.[36]

Judy advised on the diets for adult dogs, nursing bitches and puppies, and how much to feed dogs and how often. He even discussed topics such as "feeding equipment," which included well-designed food and water dishes and "kennel feeding routine," where he offered suggestions on how kennels could economically fortify commercial food.[37]

He informed readers that food lodged in the stomach of a dog required 15 to 28 hours to completely pass. Based on his studies on how a dog's food was digested, he recommended that an adult dog be fed one meal per day to avoid digestive ailments.[38]

Judy wrote that half of a dog's weight is comprised of water and provided guidelines for its proper consumption. As it is for humans, water is essential for carrying nutriments throughout the digestive system and in the disposing of waste cells. It was recommended that puppies be limited in their water consumption because so much of their diet provided the necessary moisture, and they tended to overindulge when it was readily available. For puppies up to six months, water was to be provided four times a day. A full-grown dog was to be given fresh water three times daily.[39]

Judy disagreed with those dog experts who advised that dogs have constant access to water. He wrote that dogs drank too much and too often when allowed to drink at will, which often resulted in a variety of digestive ills.[40]

For dogs suffering from gastric troubles, broth or milk was suggested as an alternative to water. Judy also advised that medicines were not to be mixed with food in the dog's bowl because this might foster distrust during feeding times and lead to permanent hesitation at the feeding bowl.[41]

On a final note on the subject of dogs and feeding, Judy informed his readers that to feed the domesticated dog the same diet as the one he was accustomed to as a wild animal of the woods was illogical. He left the choice of a raw food diet or a prepared one to the individual dog owner.[42]

Judy also wrote on the topic of canine waste management, or more specifically, how to successfully housebreak a puppy, which was a topic that was directly related to the feeding process. Reflecting the shift in the way dogs were cohabitating with humans, Judy noted that American families were more often than not welcoming dogs into the homes and increasingly regarding them as family members. It was therefore necessary to humanely and gently educate the dog to the nuances of "etiquette as practiced by human society" when it came to the dog's urination and bowel movements.[43]

Unlike cats that were practically born housebroken, dogs had to be taught that the residence which they shared with their humans was not a bathroom. Judy called for patience in the housebreaking process and reminded puppy trainers that it would take four to six weeks to successfully achieve the desired results, with occasional lapses to follow.

To achieve success he recommended regularity in the puppy's feeding schedule, "to the minute." Within ten to fifteen minutes after its feeding, the puppy was to be taken for a walk outside the home on a familiar route, with consistent markers where it had eliminated on past occasions.[44]

Judy was acutely cognizant of the psychological factors that played on the dog's process of elimination. He observed that a dog may be walked for over an hour only to relieve itself once it was back in its home. He advised allowing a dog to run loose and unmindful of being watched so that "the association between relieving himself and punishment is not in his mind."

Judy reminded dog owners that a puppy did not know the difference between an expensive imported carpet and a "ragrug." He advised dog owners, "Do your daily duty to your dog and he will do his," and assured that with regular feeding and walking schedules all dogs were eventually housebroken.[45]

He also reminded frustrated dog owners that all the affection and loyalty they would receive from their dog for the next eight to twelve years more than made up for all the ruined rugs and foul odors.[46]

Judy cautioned that the memory of a puppy was approximately only 30 seconds long and made additional punishment futile.[47] When it came to housebreaking a dog, Judy advised owners that "nature, regularity, and your watchfulness are the three teachers."[48]

If a dog owner caught his dog in the act of urinating or defecating in the home, Judy's advice was to react quickly. While shouting and acting decisively, the dog owner was to seize the dog by the neck and place its nose close to the spot, "where the deed was done." The owner would then deliver a few whacks with a folded newspaper or open hand. The dog was then to be quickly taken outside.[49]

He also offered harsh words for those who refused to clean up after their dogs on the streets of an increasingly urbanized America, stating, "Few things are as offensive to the public and to true dog lovers as the soiling of pavements by dogs."[50]

Judy placed the blame for this unsanitary and inconsiderate practice squarely on those careless dog owners who had created what he deemed "coddled spoiled dogs." He strongly embraced the motto "Curb your dog" as a way to promote the importance of dog obedience training and good dog citizenship.[51]

In the booklet titled *Puppies and Their Care,* Judy noted that he was writing for two "classes of dog owners." The first was comprised of dog breeders and the second class something he deemed "all those persons who are dog owners and lovers of dogs."[52]

In this booklet's introduction Judy wrote on the topic of National Dog Week. He wrote that one of the slogans of this observance was "Every dog needs a good home." However, Judy suggested a good corresponding message would be "Better dog care and better dog owners."[53]

Judy wrote that individuals who did not invest the time, energy and provide adequate care for their puppies and dogs were the people who created the need for a dog pound and should be picked up and thrown in the pound instead of their dogs.[54]

To those who held the belief that Judy only cared about the welfare of purebred dogs, he made it known that he believed "Every breed is a good breed. The world around, a dog is a dog, whether purebred or mongrel."[55]

With the boom in America's canine population, Judy correctly foresaw the need for increased legal protection for the nation's dogs and their owners. He shared that as early as 1932 he had authored the only publication in the nation that informed dog owners on the important legal issues that affected them.[56] In the booklet titled *Laws on Dogs,* Judy wrote, "The increasing part dogs occupy in our life today has necessitated growing attention to 'canine jurisprudence.'"[57]

According to Judy dogs had progressed from being regarded as the "beast of the field" with no rights at all to a status of having many of the same rights enjoyed by humans.[58]

Judy reminded readers to remain logical and to understand that dogs could not be held accountable for the troubles they encountered or caused if their natural and "irrepressible interest in living" led them, and subsequently their masters, into legal problems.[59]

Contained in the chapters of *Laws on Dogs* were Judy's writing on the history and source of canine law, title of ownership, licenses and taxes, justifiable killing of dogs, restraint, quarantine, examination and inoculations, protection of rights of dog owners, liability of dog owner for acts of his dog, laws against cruelty, laws particularly affecting breeders, kennelmen, exhibitors, dealers and veterinarians. At the end of this section Judy offered templates of "model dog laws" proposed for use in municipalities across the nation.

Judy noted that in some courts dogs were regarded as personal property and appointed the same value as cars, stocks and homes. In other cases, dogs were viewed as a "necessary evil" and a public nuisance and faced the penalty of immediate death when found to have engaged in unlawful or destructive activity.[60]

Judy attributed the inequality of laws pertaining to canines to English law, since that country had developed much of what made up modern dog law. He specifically placed blame on Sir William Blackstone, an eighteenth century English lawyer and judge. Judy stated that Blackstone had designated dogs as personal property.[61]

Blackstone set forth that dogs were considered animals of no value as they were not a source of food. He stated that dogs were animals kept for "whim and pleasure," and although a man was allowed to "maintain a civil action for the loss of them," their theft was not considered larceny.[62]

But there were inconsistencies in the laws regarding dogs and by contrast, the statute 10 George III c. 18[qm] mandated that those who imprisoned, knowingly harbored a stolen dog, or the skin of a stolen dog, could be whipped by two Justices of the Peace.[63]

Frustrated by the lack of uniformity in the legal system pertaining to canines, Judy protested that in one court in one region of America the dog was honored and deemed sacred property in the same manner as cars, houses and stocks. However, in other regional districts dogs were viewed as a "necessary evil," and faced immediate death when they were suspected or accused of damaging or reckless behavior.[64]

This inconsistency that dictated the legal system and its harmful impact on the welfare of dogs distressed Judy. Blackstone's legacy had created a dangerous situation for the treatment of dogs in that it "originated the dual doctrine that dogs are property in the civil court but not in the criminal court."[65]

Judy was scornful of Blackstone's logic and proclaimed that a dog was "as useful as he was a thing of pleasure."[66] He invited those who disagreed to consider the dog's value in roles as an aid to hunters and as a herder of livestock, transporter, guard, messenger and protector of man.

Judy asserted that the Blackstonian Doctrine as it pertained to canines had to be discarded to make way for a more modern view on the dog's status in America and elsewhere. Judy understood that as more people professionally bred purebred dogs, the laws concerning these investments were in need of major revision.[67]

It was reported that by 1950 dog breeding was a thriving industry in the United States and in other parts of the world, with nearly $50 million regularly invested in the manufacturing of "remedies and supplies for man's best friend, the dog."[68]

However, the lingering damages of Blackstone's legal decisions regarding canines continued to pique Judy's ire. He cited a ruling made in the state of Missouri as an example of the harmfulness of Blackstone's influence. In that case of 1869, Judy observed that the dog was unquestionably regarded as property in the state of Missouri and that while it was determined that civil damages could be recovered for injuries inflicted on them, it was not "an offense at common law to kill a dog, and in that respect the common law is still in force in this state."[69]

Judy noted that even by the year 1950 the United States government had passed no uniform laws concerning canines. He wrote, "The registration of dogs as purebred animals is not any concern of the government."[70]

It was noted that the only dog-related subject the federal government had concerned itself with was through the Food and Drugs Act, the Insecticide Act and the U.S. Public Health Service, with Provision 11–54, requiring rabies vaccinations and health certificates for dogs entering the country from certain foreign nations.[71]

Judy faulted the use of the term "common law," and suggested a better term might be "law as determined by court decision," in accordance with "generally accepted principles of jurisprudence."[72] He also noted that dogs fared better in those states that enacted their own specific laws regulating the fate of canines.[73]

Judy called for uniformity in dog laws at the state and local level. He condemned those provisions he described as "rigid and extreme," carried out by those who did not especially appreciate dogs, and urged those who cared for canine welfare to focus their efforts on enacting model state and local ordinances.[74]

For Judy the topic of canines and the law went beyond matters of "property rights." For him this matter centered on "the unwritten code of chivalry toward all living things high or low." Judy wrote that there was no need for apologies or hesitation in battling for the lawful rights of animals. "For those who can not speak for themselves, we must cry out when pain, whether physical or mental, is inflicted upon them," he rallied his readers.[75]

Calling on his training in the ministry, Judy reminded his fellow man that they must "carry out the mandate the Creator has placed upon us." This dictated that humans give the "lower kingdom" its due.[76]

Judy reported that most, but not all states had established humane laws against cruelty to animals. Fines ranged from $3 to $200 for various forms of cruelty, including the beating, torture, mutilation or killing of a dog. Other laws punished those who withheld shelter, food, water or the abandonment of older, infirm, injured sick or disabled animals and those who participated indirectly or directly in dog fighting operations.[77]

In his handy booklet on *How to Sell Dogs,* Judy made it clear from the opening sentences he believed that "Good faith and full honesty mark almost all dog sales."[78]

The sale of pedigree dogs and the advertisements for these transactions were responsible in large part for the success of the publisher of *Dog World* magazine, which presented countless display and classified advertisements paid for by a multitude of kennels and breeders each month. The guidelines affecting "Sales Guarantees" was of utmost import to Judy.[79]

In the early 1950s Judy reported that there were approximately 70,000 active breeders of pedigree dogs in the United States and 6,000 in Canada. He strongly advised that all those involved in the sale of dogs, from hobbyists to professionals, must conduct their business within a code of conduct that benefitted man and animal.[80]

Judy expressed concern for the future welfare of saleable purebred dogs. He wrote that "an active market has been created for the sale of the dog as companion, guard, and useful aid," as well as the market for those who bred dogs for "easy money," without much regard for their [dog's] physical or emotional lives.[81]

The requirements for success in dog breeding included a sincere love for man's best friend, a solid understanding of laws involved in the heredity and bloodlines of particular breeds, the necessary time and expenditure of effort required to study those bloodlines and the patience to withstand the lengthy trial and error process that was necessary for conscientious breeding.[82]

Judy noted that responsible dog breeders must also possess "the spirit of sportsmanship," the thrill of breeding prospective "winners," the ability to promote an attitude of good sportsmanship at dog shows and the ability to be a gracious loser on the dog show circuit.[83]

In listing these requirements, Judy's goal was to discourage those who went into the breeding of purebred dogs in search of a quick profit. Those who did not heed the author's advice would resort to griping and complaining while adding no value to the dog breeding community and would be considered "just another cull."[84]

Breeders were advised to reach out to prospects. Judy commented that although dogs could not sell themselves, no other item offered for sale had "the appeal which is possest naturally by a little tailwagger who wags his way into the heart."[85]

Judy set forth eight principles of successful puppy selling that included the constellation of casual contacts; the use of signage; opportunities presented at dog shows and related events; sales produced through "good will"; leads garnered through advertising in dog magazines, general publications, and printed literature; and the use of mailing lists.[86]

At a time when Americans were enjoying the newfound freedom provided by automobile travel, Judy suggested that breeders of pedigree dogs post promotional signage along the roadside to attract customers. He suggested that breeders paint signs with attractive colors and place them "in V-shape or at right angles," to enable two-way exposure to drivers.[87]

Judy assured that these signs would attract many casual callers whom he referred to as mere "curiosity seekers." These visitors were to be promptly sent on their way, as well as those who were merely seeking pets, not show dogs, and expected to pay lower prices for a purebred dog.[88]

On the topic of promoting the business of breeding through dog magazines, Judy noted that only those publications with "bona fide circulations delivered a message to those who were fully invested in the 'prospect-buying field.'" Judy also shrewdly recommended that breeders set aside a set amount of funding for advertising in dog-related publications—"one-eighth of all gross income," to be exact.[89]

Financial aspects notwithstanding, Judy stated that "sales thru good will" ultimately resulted in the satisfactory sales of healthy and happy dogs. "Old customers, satisfied customers" were the mark of a professional and legitimate breeder.[90]

Those who wisely advertised consistently in the proper venues induced confidence in those who viewed those advertisements, and those whose advertisements were most frequently posted were the most likely to benefit from increased sales.

Judy shared with his colleagues in the industry that only those breeders who presented the clearest message to potential dog owners would win the battle of the patrons. He asserted that good sportsmanship combined with a sincere love of dogs was essential in the promotion of selling methods that encouraged humanitarian practices in the field.

As final selling points offered for the successful sales of pedigree dogs, Judy recommended that the breeder state the major wins of their dogs, properly price their puppies, provide images of their dogs to increase "drawing power," offer a catchy logo for their kennels, avoid humor in their ad copy, change copy every few months, capitalize on seasonal advertising opportunities, take larger advertising space to allow for frequent revision of ad copy and promptly respond to prospects. Judy summarized, "The more you tell, the more you sell."[91]

In a section subtitled "Status of Pet Shops," Judy wrote that these outlets were "not fully nor properly developed." He noted that dogs should not be sold like items at the corner grocery store, and many of the pups sold at retail outlets suffered from ill health. Although he noted that the conditions at these outlets had improved over time, he predicted that most sales of dogs would occur between a breeding kennel and a client. Of this he wrote, "The dog is a living breathing thing rather than a piece of fixed merchandise."[92]

In 1949 Judy reported that approximately 500,000 purebred puppies were satisfactorily sold in the nation and that only a few of these customers actually saw the dogs before their purchase.[93]

Once the sale was successfully negotiated, the next step was to guarantee the safe delivery of the puppy to the anxious new owner. This was often completed by way of air transport and express railway.

By the late 1940s most air carriers were accepting dogs as cargo shipped in the baggage area. This development greatly increased the sales of pedigree puppies. Judy advised that shipments of dogs made by air must take place on planes that were pressurized, ventilated and heated and only on flights traveling at the equivalent of 9,000 feet. Crates were not to be placed in the nose of the plane or its rear as these areas were not usually ventilated or heated.[94]

Flights at altitudes above 12,000 feet were harmful to dogs because it caused difficulty in breathing and could cause their collapse.[95]

He reminded breeders to procure the necessary paperwork and records required for a successful shipping process that ensured the sound physical condition of the shipping crate, instructions on how the dogs should receive food and water and the proper labeling of the containers.

Judy wrote that the well-being of the puppies being transported via air was insured by the kindness provided by what he called the express agents. Under the heading "The Puppy's Plea," Judy offered an example of a label used in the shipping of 701 puppies to the winners of the Liberty Magazine Free Puppy Contest in 1924.[96]

The label introduced the puppy by name and reminded the "expressman" that this precious cargo was dependent on him for all its care until safely delivered to its new master. The message imparted the poignant message, "Mr. Expressman: Have a heart. I'm only a lonesome puppy, away from mother and family, a stranger far from home. I am not vicious; do not be afraid of me."[97]

Judy also recommended that transported dogs always wear a collar and that a lead be attached to the dog to make it easier to walk the dog and to prevent a spooked dog from running away. For the crate's bedding he advised the loose layering of material such as excelsior or sawdust covered with straw.[98]

In the Handy Booklets titled *The Show Dog in the Ring* and *Dog Shows and Rules,* Judy's direct and truthful approach served to at the same time encourage and discourage many new dog owners who wished to own a champion show dog. Judy made it clear to readers that not every purebred dog was destined to become a champion. With brilliant insight he wrote, "Not all that glitters is gold, however, gold must glitter, else it is not noticed."[99]

In a brief discussion of the history of dog showing in America, Judy reported that the first formal dog shows in the world were actually held in New Castle, England, around 1859 and in the United States approximately two decades later. He noted that there had been 557 "point of championship shows" held in the United States by the year 1949.[100]

In his trademark style Judy began the section on *Dog Shows and Rules* with some humor in sharing his personal experiences that took readers inside the frenetic world of a dog show. Grouped under the title of "Dog Show Impressions," the segment started with the word "barking" and ended with the phrase, "final bark—final final bark."[101]

He described the women at these events as beautiful, well-groomed and glamorous. Among these colorful impressions Judy interjected a "dog magazine solicitor extolling his publication at so much per year."[102]

Judy explained to the uninitiated that organized dog shows were established to theoretically aid in the better breeding of dogs. A winning dog simply met a "certain agreed standard of perfection," for a particular breed.[103]

Each breed had its own standard based solely on the physical qualities of a dog, such as its height, weight, the shape of the head and body proportions. While no dog met with perfection, those closest to the established standard were the ones that became champions.[104]

In what read like a virtual Dog Show 101 lecture, Judy guided hopefuls through the ins and outs of this tight circle of dog showing. He offered tips that ranged from how to get started to the basic principles of showing techniques, as well as providing sound advice on the good sportsmanship that was desirous of all participants in and around the ring.

In addressing novices who wished to become active in the dog show community, Judy reminded them that the key to winning in the show ring was not about rubbing elbows with the judges or wooing them with gifts, dinner or flattery. Dogs won when their handlers presented them before a judge in a manner that showed the dog to its best advantage.

Judy conceded that some show dogs possessed something he referred to as "it." According to him, a dog that had "it" showed well and exhibited a personality that begged for a blue ribbon and could beat a "slightly better dog."[105]

"If all the world's a stage," Judy borrowed from Shakespeare, "a dog show ring is the center of the stage where able acting and good showmanship are desired."[106]

Judy recommended that dogs commence training for the ring as early as four months of age and noted that some dogs were natural show dogs that required very little training for this purpose. It was advised that pet dogs in general did not fare well in the show ring and that dog owners who handled their own dogs in the ring did not typically win.[107]

Professional dog handlers were preferred over owner handlers in the show ring. Those individuals who collected fees for their handling

Lindale's Fortune Cookie receives award for best puppy in the show from Judge Will Judy, at the Amphitheater in Chicago, 1967 (courtesy of Carol [Cloud] Vondrak).

services were required to be licensed by the American Kennel Club and were to earn and keep all prize money, with ribbons and cups going to the owner of the dog.[108]

Judy described the complex point system used in judging dogs and those accrued by show dogs on the road to becoming champion. It was noted that only purebred dogs were allowed to register for sanctioned dog show events. Dogs that were blind in both eyes, deaf, permanently lame, under the age of six months, or had been altered were not permitted in the show ring. Those dogs whose appearance had been "faked" through artificial means or had the color of their coats enhanced with dye were also not permitted to compete in the show ring.[109]

In *Dog Shows and Rules*, Judy explained how dogs were shown in "classes," with each breed judged separately and the males of the breed judged first. The classes were divided into five distinct groups: Puppy, Novice, Bred-by-Exhibitor, American-bred and Open.

The Puppy Class was comprised of dogs six to twelve months of age that were whelped in the United States or Canada or were a product of a breeding that took place in America or "possessions."[110]

The Novice Class was designated for dogs age six months or older that had never won first place in any category except the Puppy Class. As its title implied, the American-bred Class included only those pups that had been whelped in the United States.[111]

The Bred-by-Exhibitor Class was established in 1949 and allowed those dogs that were not champions to be shown by their owners. Any dog over six months of age that was not a champion was permitted to compete in what was called the Open Class.[112]

A potential dog show champion was a dog of either sex that had gained a total of 15 points as "winners male or winners bitch at AKC point shows," with a number of intricate considerations that factored in the regional wins of the dog and the number of dogs competing in its class, as well as points awarded to each sex of a specific breed.[113]

Judy wrote about the importance of a club's preparation for a dog show and the publicity necessary to make it a successful event. To maximize attendance and exposure, clubs were advised to work with dog magazines and local newspapers and radio stations and suggested the press rep for each dog club to contact the "Dog Writers' Assn.," which at the time was headquartered in Newark, New Jersey. Reporters were to be extended invitations to the event and offered press passes.

As a dog show judge Judy was sensitive to the fact that the average dog owner regarded their dog as a champion. He addressed these individuals about the pitfall of what he termed "kennel blindness." He warned that once the "pet dog" entered the ring to be scrutinized by a multitude of critics and compared to other dogs, their faults became blatantly apparent. The egos of many dog owners had been deflated under these circumstances.[114]

The subject of learning how to show a dog was also introduced. Judy recommended that the handler not be too gentle when training a dog for the show ring, to discourage the dog from regarding this activity as play. He suggested a "quick slap" with an open hand be delivered under the dog's jaw to encourage the dog to hold up its head. The handler was also instructed to be firm when positioning the dog's legs in the desired showing pose.[115]

The use of commands such as "Hold it," or "Stay," were important to master when coaching a dog to hold a judging pose in the ring. "Steady" was used to prevent the dog from moving out of pose, with "OK," or "Let's Go," used to coax the dog to quicken its pace. Judy confided that there were expert handlers who used only hand motions to lead dogs through their paces.[116]

The "condition" of a dog was also very important. Condition was a term that connoted "the state of health which gives spirit, normal appearance and harmonious movement to the dog."[117] On the day prior to the showing event, a dog was to be bathed, have the tartar removed from its teeth, its toe nails were to be manicured and whiskers trimmed. Each dog was to be officially registered in advance for show participation and be suited with a proper shipping crate.[118]

Desired equipment for professional presentation at the event included a brush and comb for grooming, a rounded collar, and a flat show lead with a bench chain for securing a dog in the stall. An identification ticket and exhibitor pass rounded out the list of recommended tools for professional showing.[119]

For those particular about their dog's feeding habits, Judy suggested affixing a sign on the dog's crate that advised caregivers, "Do not feed or water." It was also recommended that the handler or owner make available the dog's regular food.[120]

Judy suggested that on the day of the show, dogs were to be fed only after their presentation, noting that "a hungry dog is an alert dog."[121] This would also prevent stomach ailments in the dog that might become upset during the excitement and uncertainty of travel. He recommended that dog owners and handlers or a familiar human remain with the dog as much as possible when being transported to any event.[122]

Handlers also received advice on personal grooming and presentation. Women handlers were advised to avoid wearing outfits with "frills and banners," or anything that flopped about that might distract or frighten a dog. Men were not to wear a hat into the ring.[123]

Clothing was not to be flashy or gaudy, so as not to detract from the dog. Judy went into detail on what breeders of certain dogs might wear. He wrote of a female poodle breeder and handler who wore gloves the same hue as that of the dog being shown and humorously suggested that those showing "dals" might wear a polka dot tie or dress in the ring.[124] Women judges were reminded that "all eyes are on you from all sides," and that they should not squat, but stoop when examining a dog.[125] It was further advised that neither gender wear "tight under things," and recommended all wear heavy-soled shoes. Handlers with "hot" feet conditions were advised to rub their feet with vaseline or cold cream on the day of the show.[126]

During the event it was recommended that a dog not be tied "too short or too long" during its time on "the Bench."[127] The handler was to be ready and positioned near the entrance of the ring when their dog's class was called. The dog was to be led calmly into the ring once the previous class was dismissed. Upon entering the show ring the handler was to be in control of their dog and aware of their surroundings at all times.[128] It was suggested that the handler try to be the first into the ring, since this provided a "psychological advantage." For those showing smaller breeds he advised that the handler carry the dog through the loitering crowd at the entrance of the ring.[129]

The dog was always to be kept to the left side of the handler so as not to obstruct the judge's view of the dog and of the handler's left arm, on which their registration number was clearly displayed.[130]

Judy did not approve of the use of judging blocks or platforms in the show ring. He preferred that dogs be exhibited in a more natural condition that allowed all breeds to have their paws planted firmly on the floor. Upon striking a pose, the handler used hand motions, a ball, squeaky toy or a morsel of food to keep the dog alert. It was noted, however, that the best handlers did not employ any of these methods.[131] Handlers were advised to keep their dogs in the best lighting conditions, because the artificial lighting of the show ring created pockets of shadows that were detrimental to viewing.[132]

Despite his promotion of good sportsmanship, Judy warned of "unscrupulous exhibitors" who might resort to trickery in the ring. To avoid the problems this might present, he advised novice handlers to keep their dogs three feet away from others to avoid confrontation and not to allow a competitor to stoop or stand too close to their dog.[133]

This process must have presented a daunting task as all of the above and more was to be accomplished while the handler astutely sized up the preferences of each judge and tried to stand out. But Judy reminded handlers that this did not mean one was to "monopolize the eye of the judge."[134]

Upon entering the ring, all dogs were paraded in view of the judge until the "halt" command was delivered. Dogs judged "clearly out of the competition" were quickly waved out of the ring. Those remaining were to be allowed to stand at rest so as to be relaxed and ready when it was their time to be scrutinized. All dogs were to remain in pose until ribbons were awarded.[135]

In another take on the otherwise serious subject of showing dogs, Judy finished *Dog Shows and Rules* with two humorous items. The first titled, "The Author at Last Finds the Perfect Dog Show," offered a tongue-in-cheek account of Judy attending a dog showing event that bought out the best in man and dog.[136]

Judy wrote that he envisioned a pleasant scenario where a dog show provided enough ringside seats for everyone, a sign that indicated the presence of a show veterinarian, an information booth, reasonably priced food and refreshments, a welcome committee for new exhibitors and a loudspeaker system that informed the audience of ongoing events. Added to this wish list was the changing of the sawdust on the show ring floor midway through the event and washrooms that were still clean at the end of the show.[137]

In this "perfect dog show," the sardonic author also conjured up images of a disgruntled exhibitor who, after daring to toss a less desirable yellow ribbon to the floor in disgust, was called before the judges to apologize. He also pictured that just inside the show ring stood a table set aside exclusively for the press.[138]

In his parting notes Judy also offered an item on "The Spirit of Sportsmanship," where he reminded readers that he had judged championship dog shows all over the world and that the process was no easy task. He wrote that at all times dog show judges were to be shown "due courtesy and sportsmanship in the show ring," and that exhibitors were required to pay their entry fees well in advance, with the knowledge of which judge would be judging their breed. The judge's opinion of a particular dog was to be taken in stride, whether the owner or handler agreed with it or not. Failure to win was never an excuse to abuse or berate a judge.[139]

For those who did not wish to embrace this behavior, Judy advised the exhibitor that it might be wise "not to show under this or any other judge whose ability is doubted."[140]

Judy reminded America's growing population of dog enthusiasts that although these events were competitive and fascinating, they should be regarded as a friendly occasion that allowed "sportsmen to gather from all sections of America."[141]

5

Will Judy's Writing on the Nature of Mankind

Although Will Judy is best known for his writing on the topic of dogs, his lifelong interest in the nature of men and women were by-products of his youthful training for the ministry and his time spent traveling the world.

Judy understood the importance of appealing to the intelligence and humanity of those who stood at the other end of the leash, although he often indicated his belief that dogs were of much higher character. Judy never lost sight of the fact that it took a thoughtful, enlightened human to raise a good dog, and his thoughts and words also translated into action when it came to enlightening humans and serving mankind.

At the age of 36, Will Judy published a book that presented revised versions of personal essays he had originally composed when he was between the ages of 23 and 25 and then again from age 31 to 35.[1] The depth and insight contained in these essays belied the mature and reflective nature of a young man only in his mid-twenties.

Men and Things, subtitled *Fifty Essays About Human Nature, the Ways of Men, and Their Private and Public Conduct*, featured a bright yellow cover with the image of a monkey holding two balls labeled "Wisdom" and "Folly." Writing credit went to the "Editor of Judy's Magazine and Author of *Dog Encyclopedia*."[2]

A list titled, "Other Books by Will Judy to Be Published Later" belied the scope of the young author's writing ambitions. Each title was presented with suggested "probable prices" that averaged $2 a copy.[3]

The proposed titles included *Battlefield Essays*, filled with items Judy had penned while serving in France during the World War, *Myself*, described as a "Spiritual Autobiography"; *My Son and I*, based on "letters to a youth at school"; *The Diary of a Peace-Loving Soldier*; *Lydonia*, a work about a "land beyond the South Pole"; and *Scrap Book*, to be comprised of the author's "miscellaneous and random thots."[4]

Men and Things was dedicated to a man named Edmund B. Chaffee, whom Judy described as a friend who had inspired the author to "look at life in thotful moods and with an amused smile."[5]

Chaffee was a Michigan native who abruptly dropped out of law school to become an ordained Presbyterian minister. He later became a syndicated columnist and editor of the *Presbyterian Tribune*. He dedicated his life and work to what he called the "masses of men and women who have to work for their living."[6]

Under the heading "Massage Your Mind," which appeared on the back dust jacket of the book, Judy explained that the 50 essays contained in the book would open "new vistas of ideas," and could be appreciated in solitude when the tired reader needed a remedy for weariness.[7]

Reviews for *Men and Things* were derived from diverse sources and were all very positive. "*Men and Things* is thought-provoking," proclaimed the *Boston Globe*. The *Detroit Free Press* described the essays as "snappy" and "sincere." Alfreda Page of the Camp Fire Girls Organization of New York City called *Men and Things* "delightfully refreshing." I. H. Brumbaugh, former president of Judy's beloved Juniata College, declared that the noted graduate's essays possessed the elusive quality of "personality."[8]

Perhaps the most poignant review was one written by Henry N. Jordan, the chaplain at the Battle Creek Sanitarium in Michigan. The chaplain described each of Judy's 50 essays as "a gem." Jordan wrote that Judy's works contained wit while being "so full of such helpful spiritual sense," that each one resembled a sermon. The chaplain revealed he shared the essays with patients while making his rounds.[9]

In the book's introduction Judy discussed how he felt compelled to write essays and the challenges presented in their composition. Of this genre he wrote, "Truly the essay is a hard way to glory," noting that it was human nature to preach, but not to invite the preaching of others.[10]

He wrote that "most geniuses are fools and the world is fearful of fools," and stated that the content of a notable essay transcended its author. A truly great essay "builded upon a message which commands a hearing in all centuries and all tongues," and never lost its impact upon the entirety of its retelling.[11]

Judy declared that grammar, syntax and quality of writing were unimportant in the creation of a superb essay. He wrote essays because it gave him pleasure to cull impressions from his personal experience in a truthful manner, and then "to fashion it with a new birth," a process Judy likened to "the first Creation," that made the writer almost god-like.[12]

Judy explained that he wrote his essays to make him an equal of all men and to bring him a lasting measure of fame throughout time. He observed that paintings, landscapes and architecture contained truth and beauty, but "words are the fountain of youth for ideas, and who writes words well and nobly will live with all the posterities, and beyond them until the soul of man shall be no more."[13]

The first essay of the series began with a dissertation on "Thinking." On this topic he wrote that "the brain sweats to think; wherefore, few think."[14] The subjects of criticism, principle, prejudice, wealth and ambition were all examined and dissected by Judy's sharp insight and wit. Lighter essay topics included in the collection were those written on youth, wooing, woman, travel and jokes.

Of "Woman" Judy wrote, "Three things have not nationality—the dog, death, and a beautiful woman." He warned against the dangerous qualities of what he termed "coquets" and "bad women." In the choosing of a wife, Judy observed, "choose wearing qualities and beware of her who is as a dish of cooking, admired chiefly for the dressing."[15]

On the subject of wooing Judy advised caution and penned, "All the world has been or hopes to be a lover." He cautioned, "Beauty of body is enemy to Faithfulness and dwells too much with her cousins Haughtiness and Vanity."[16]

On the keeping of diaries Judy wrote that one was mature enough to maintain one by age 16 and that "the rewards for the labor of maintaining a diary are not small." According to Judy, those who maintained diaries learned the importance of regularity, achieved practice in self expression through words, were able to polish their ideas and benefited from the soothing act of self-reflection. Last, but not least, he astutely noted, a diary "tickles vanity harmlessly."[17]

Judy's fiftieth essay extolled the virtue of planning and the tendency for humans to disregard its importance.[18]

The final pages of *Men and Things* highlighted Judy's appreciation and respect for the printing industry. In place of the words "finis" or "The End," the number 30 was used as the "Period of the Printer."[19]

Judy explained that those in the printing trade used this numerical notation to mark the end of a book. He referenced President Warren Harding, who had been a member of the printing industry at one time. On the occasion of his funeral, Harding's casket was followed by a group of fellow tradesmen who carried a floral design crafted in the figure 30.[20]

Judy took the opportunity to promote other books offered by the Judy Publishing Company on the back pages of *Men and Things*. There a full-page promotion appeared for a book titled *All about Naturalization,* authored by a Jacob Legion Tenny, recognized as a former United States naturalization examiner. Tenny's book was described as a helpful source of information that filled "a long-felt want," and answered 247 inquiries regarding the acquisition of United States citizenship and the workings of the American government.[21]

Another full page advertisement presented "The Jack and Starlight Series of Sentiment Cards," which were postal cards that featured excerpts of Judy's personal writings. They were advertised as printed on quality cardboard and priced at ten cents apiece. Described as decorative and "suitable for framing," it was suggested that a minimum of five should be ordered.[22]

Judy had already served as the head of *Dog World* for a period of four years by the time *Men and Things* was published, and in this presentation of these 50 essays he took advantage of that fact. A full page was dedicated to promoting the books Judy had written about dogs. Listed were breed specialty volumes on the Bulldog, Doberman pinscher, chow chow, dachshund and the Boston terrier, in addition to his practical guides such as his *Training the Dog, Kennel Building and Plans* and *Training the Police Dog*. For those who preferred more spiritual offerings, *A Dog's Prayer* and *Tribute to a Dog* were suggested.[23]

Another Judy book titled *Dog Encyclopedia* was also promoted, which was described as the "most complete and meaty reference work on dogs." *Dog Encyclopedia* was proclaimed the standard work of reference on dogs to be utilized by schools, libraries and dog-related organizations and clubs. It was also noted that no other book on dogs offered so many images of dog breeds.[24]

Many of the books published by the Judy Publishing Company included drawings and cartoons. Judy used the opportunity to advertise a book written by the "Famous Cartoonist" Charles Lederer, titled *Cartooning Made Easy*, which offered 30 entertaining lessons with 413 illustrations to help budding cartoonists.[25]

Several other books offered by Judy Publishing were also promoted, including one written by Leon F. Whitney titled *The Basis of Breeding,* which was touted as a good selection for those interested in fostering "better stock in animals or humans." For health conscious readers there was an offering titled *Blood Pressure and its Treatment,* by Doctor Walter E. Simmonds, presented as a "way to relief by modes of living and adjusting ones habits of life."[26] For those wishing to improve their presentation skills, Judy presented *Public Speaking and Voice Culture* by E. L. Beshore.[27]

In his poignant work, *A Soldier's Diary,* Judy wrote about how his 22 months serving in the United States Army had taught him many things and that he would not trade these experiences "for any ten years of my life." He wrote of how he simultaneously liked and hated the army and how over time, it was the "spirit of the uniform" that had instilled in him a pride to cause him to salute "promptly and snappily."[28]

Judy credited his respect for women and the elderly to his military service. But he observed that he was first a citizen, and a soldier second. He shared that as a man of peace he hated war and describe it as "a painted woman, more attractive at some distance."[29]

Judy's affection for his adopted city of Chicago was also manifested in the written word. In 1953 he wrote and published a book titled *Chicago the Pagan* under the assumed name of Weimar Port, a name derived from a dog breed. This book was dedicated to James J. Ley, who was described by Port as a "fellow wanderer in and about Chicago."

This book was touted as "a mind guide to Chicago's soul," and offered the reader a "3-D, Cinerama, cinemascope" guide to the sights and scenes of the Windy City. Port described the book as his own personal manner of informing visitors of the "thing to be seen," along with some "personal aura of whether it is worth seeing."[30] This book offered 65 chapters graced with 32 illustrations, comprised of woodblock, pen and ink sketches, etchings and some of Judy's own handiwork.

It was stated that the author's purpose was to educate and inform readers who planned to visit Chicago—those who were long-term residents of the city and even those who had no plans to visit Chicago—about the sights, landmarks and unique history that made the city special. The book's pages were designed to provide a sense of that city's "paganism of pleasure, its warmth of welcome, its lustiness of life, its sincerity of soul."[31]

In 1962 Judy wrote a book under another pseudonym, Wymar Port, titled *Sayings of Rammikar.* This book was described as the author's effort to decipher and bring into the present the writing of Rammikar, "the Last of the Mayan Wise Men."[32]

In a special publisher's note, Judy addressed the uncertainty of the publishing industry. He referred to the book publisher as an odd combination of "educator, financier and gambler." He shared that the publishing world maintained an air of glamour but it also presented the unglamorous possibility of failure.[33]

Judy warily informed readers that every two books out of three went into "red ink," yet each book published brought a great promise of success. He wryly observed that while humankind readily spent money on cake and alcoholic beverages, most were hesitant to expend the cash or mental effort to purchase and read a good book, despite the fact that these items cost about the same amount of money. He noted that only the book remained a steadfast and enduring companion over time.[34]

Each new book presented a monetary gamble for even the most experienced publisher. But for "Wymar Port" it was well worth the risk for a book's enduring value. He wrote, "A good book is a continuing university within its field—a university which even the lowest in finances can attend."[35]

Writing as Port, Judy was a worldwide traveler fascinated with the history of the Mayan civilization and in particular Rammikar, a ruler who inhabited North America well before the visitation by Christopher Columbus. Port regaled him as "the last of the really great Mayan writers and thinkers."[36]

He reported that evidence suggested Rammikar was not entirely of Mayan ancestry. A description of the ruler called him "fair in complexion, eyes not dark, hair sandy rather than black." This supported a theory that Rammikar, also known as the "White God from Heaven," and his people were possible descendants of Norsemen who migrated to America between AD 1,000 and AD 1300.[37]

It was reported that this coincided with the discovery of the Kensington Rune Stone that was uncovered in Minnesota and attributed to the period of AD 1300. It was also noted that some members of the Native tribes that inhabited the shores of the Mississippi and Missouri rivers were paler in skin tone than members of neighboring tribes.[38]

Port imparted that Spanish friars believed that the "Christian doctrine" had been introduced in Mexico at a time that preceded Columbus by centuries. More specifically, it was speculated that St. Thomas the Apostle, in a state of remorse, had followed Christ's command to "Go ye therefore, and teach all nations," and had arrived in North America.[39]

Port supported this possibility by reminding readers that many historians believed that Christianity was introduced to the Toltecs in the Mayan peninsula during the tenth century.[40]

The author clarified that *Sayings of Rammikar* was not intended to be a comprehensive study of Mayan civilization, and it was stated that the goal in writing the book was to give credit to the "exotic wisdom" of Rammikar, whom Port dubbed "the Confucius of the Mayans," an important figure who was seldom referenced in the works on the Mayan culture.[41]

The book's table of contents underscored Judy's fascination with all aspects of the mysterious Mayan civilization. There were chapters that discussed the importance of maize to the Mayans, provided material on the history of Chichen Itza and discussed the enemies of the Mayans.

In the chapter titled, "State of Illinois Shows Itself Germane to the Mayans," it was again maintained that "Columbus was a latecomer," and that a variety of explorers had visited North America long before the year 1492.[42]

Port referred to news items from the early part of 1960 that reported on the remains of a Native American village in Collinsville, Illinois, not far from St. Louis, Missouri.[43]

It was estimated that this village was active from approximately AD 900 to AD 1500. Comprised of ten dwellings, fire pits and storage holes, the village was located not far from Cahokia Park where a pyramid stood 105 feet high and covered 16 acres of land. It was written that this pyramid was the work of mound builders who "may have been preceded by a half-dozen civilizations." This suggested that "early America may date as far back as 2000 BC."[44]

While the historical research was important to Port, it was the philosophical and spiritual approach of Rammikar that intrigued the author. Rammikar's saying number 461 stated, "Walk with God," which Judy interpreted as "the priest can not look inside your head." Port wrote that this was just the right saying to conclude this book, as Rammikar "walks into the western twilight."

Judy's summation on the *Sayings of Rammikar* was to advise men to agree with their religious leaders when in their presence, but to think for themselves when alone. Judy's individualistic and idealistic nature was evident when he wrote, "Walk with God and keep in step with him;

talk with God but in your own language. He is chief of interpreters, he alone can see inside your head; be one with God and there is no death."[45]

Judy's contribution to the betterment of civilization extended well beyond the written word. In 1958, he endowed his alma mater, Juniata College, with a generous donation to its lectureship program. The Will Judy Lectureship provided the college with annual visits from leaders in government, education, the arts, natural sciences, and business. In setting up the lectureship, Judy specified that "the detection of fallacies in reasoning" be a feature of at least one lecture, and required that lecturers remain on campus "long enough to enter into the discussion generated by his or her remarks."[46]

In 1959, Henry Margenau, a physicist-philosopher, became the program's first speaker. Since that time, other notables making appearances have included African-American comedian and civil rights activist Dick Gregory (1969–70), biochemist and writer Isaac Asimov (1971–72), and political activist and presidential candidate Ralph Nader (2002–03), with the final lecture presented by creativity expert, Sir Ken Robinson (2008–09).[47]

6

Will Judy's World of the Dog

The cover of the February 1925 issue of *Dog World* magazine featured a plain white background upon which the entire transcript of Senator Graham Vest's *Tribute to a Dog* in plain black lettering was printed. While the layout appeared unremarkable, the message was. A personal notation by Will Judy stated that the publisher considered Vest's words to be "the most eloquent and appealing of all the many tributes to the dog."[1]

In 1870, George Graham Vest, a lawyer and future senator from Missouri, penned that notable phrase as part of a speech he made during the trial of a man who sued a neighbor for deliberately shooting and killing the man's beloved foxhound, Old Drum.[2]

Vest's emotional oration brought everyone in the courtroom to tears. He won his case without any reference to previous testimony or facts of the trial, choosing to base his argument on the universal connection between a beloved dog and its owner. He stated, "The one absolutely unselfish friend that a man can have in this selfish world, the one that never deserts him and the one that never proves ungrateful or treacherous is his dog."[3]

At the time of this issue's publication, Vest's tribute had stirred the souls of dog lovers for 55 years and was more relevant than ever due to the growing popularity of the American dog. As a fledgling publisher in 1925, Judy understood the benefit of exploiting the emotional content of Vest's tribute, a literary item that would personally inspire him throughout his long publishing career.

In this February 28 issue of *Dog World*, Judy invited guest contributors to write an article that focused on a specific breed that answered the universal question, "Why I like the [breed inserted here]."[4]

DOG WORLD

FEBRUARY 1-9-2-5   **Twenty cents**

Senator Vest's Tribute To a Dog

A dog had been killed in a small town in Missouri. The owner accused a neighbor of the act and brot him into court.

After the witnesses had been heard on both sides, a young attorney, George Graham Vest by name, later to become a United States Senator, arose and in a soft voice, addrest the jury in behalf of

the owner of the dog. The jury deliberated only a few minutes and returned a verdict of guilty against the killer.

The address of Senator Vest on this occasion was as follows and may be considered the most eloquent and appealing of all the many tributes to the dog. —DOG WORLD MAGAZINE

THE BEST FRIEND a man has in the world may turn against him and become his enemy. His son or his daughter that he has reared with loving care may prove ungrateful. Those who are nearest and dearest to us, those whom we trust with our happiness and our good name, may become traitors to their faith. The money a man has he may lose. It flies away from him when he needs it most. A man's reputation may be sacrificed in a moment of ill-considered action. The people who are prone to fall on their knees to do us honor when success is with us may be the first to throw stones of malice when failure settles its clouds upon our heads. The one absolutely unselfish friend that a man can have in this selfish world, the one that never deserts him, the one that never proves ungrateful or treacherous, is his dog.

A MAN'S DOG stands by him in prosperity and in poverty, in health and in sickness. He will sleep on the cold ground where the wintry winds blow and the snow drives fiercely if only he may be near his master's side. He will kiss the hand that has no food to offer, he will lick the sores and wounds that come in encounter with the roughness of the world. He guards the sleep of his pauper master as if he were a prince. When all other friends desert, he remains. When riches take wings and reputation falls to pieces he is as constant in his love as the sun in its journey through the heavens.

IF MISFORTUNE drives the master forth an outcast in the world, friendless and homeless, the faithful dog asks no higher privilege than that of accompanying him to guard against danger, to fight against his enemies. And when the last scene of all comes, and death takes the master in its embrace, and his body is laid away in the cold ground, no matter if all other friends pursue their way, there by the graveside will the noble dog be found, his head between his paws, his eyes sad, but open in alert watchfulness, faithful and true, even in death.

Cover of February 1925 issue of *Dog World* with the entire "Tribute to a Dog" by Graham Vest, a personal favorite of Will Judy's.

A writer by the name of F. D. Hart of Colorado proclaimed that he believed that the Newfoundland was "the brightest star in the world of dogs, the Honest Abe of the canine race."[5] In his essay titled "The Newfoundland—The Dog with a Soul," the breed that accompanied Lewis and Clark on their expedition was glorified. Hart wrote, "I like the Newfoundland because I could almost believe that he is a dog with a soul."[6]

Hart wrote that the Newfoundland was an excellent protector of its master's home and a sturdy and tireless worker, noting how the breed's ability to haul water and fetch wood had received the notice and admiration of royalty in England.[7]

Under the heading "Bert Finch's Ideas" appeared a series of random items. Submitted by a man described as "one of the leading writers in America on dog topics," the column was filled with gossipy dog news items that offered the contributor's observations on trends in the world of dogs.[8]

One such item titled, "An Excellent Suggestion," addressed the *English Daily Press* and their diligent quest to obtain photographs of small dogs participating in dog shows. Finch claimed these photographers wished to present these dogs wearing ridiculous costumes in an attempt to ridicule dog owners who treated their dogs like children.[9]

Finch wondered why these dogs were so harshly criticized and posed the question, "Are not horses gaily decorated at horse shows?" He cautioned those who showed their dogs not to make themselves targets of this jaded press and to be alert to these opportunists who endeavored to have the public view small dogs as "useless, brainless and silly."[10]

Finch additionally offered critiques on the modern versions of dachshunds, cocker spaniels and bulldogs. Of the first, he noted that in years gone by, this breed was more substantial, and that the cocker spaniel was bred much too small for showing purposes and needed "more leg and substance." Of bulldogs, Finch wrote that in past years they had not been so "piggy looking, fat and useless."[11]

He had more positive things to say about Airedales and fox terriers, writing that these breeds had shown great improvement over the course of 20 years. In closing, Finch wrote under the subheading "Bert is Patriotic," and suggested that Dobermans and shepherds deserved more simple and short American names instead of the names used in foreign markets, which he thought too long, unwise and ridiculous.[12]

In regard to another breed of dog, an item titled "The Airedale Slump" informed readers of the Airedale's current unpopularity. Judy disclosed that a breeder had written to him stating that he was going to stop breeding them because "he would rather drown his puppies than sell them at ten dollars each," the amount that he was currently being offered for his dogs.[13]

Judy was aware that the dog-loving public was fickle and that certain breeds had enjoyed varying degrees of popularity at different points in history. In his role as a responsible and humanitarian judge of dogs, Judy responded to the writer by stating that the Airedale was just as desirable and lively as it had been 20 years ago at the height of its popularity.[14]

Judy further wrote that "perhaps the airedale has been betrayed by his frinds [friends]," explaining that cause and effect could bring about the demise of any breed. He ended the article by rousing breeders in typical Judy style, stating that the breeders of Airedales should abandon their dreams "in which they see a black hearse going by, an airedale in it, and drawn by a team of shepherds and wire-hairs," referring to the breeds that were currently enjoying popularity.[15]

The airedale was not the only dog that was experiencing unpopularity at that time. In a feature designated as "Barks: The Livest Page of Dog News in America," the German shepherd dog also appeared to be out of public favor. In a letter addressed to Mr. William Lewis Judy, Editor, and titled "The Man-Eating Shepherd Dog," a reader implored of Judy, "Why do breeders continue to make the prospective police dog buyer think that they are man-eating dogs?"[16]

The frustrated writer from Olean, New York, was disturbed by the public's perception of the breed and cited a newspaper article that served to solidify the public's distrust of the breed. He went on to propose that many feared the German shepherd as they mistakenly believed they were more wolflike than other dogs.

The writer ended his letter by stating that he wanted the public to understand that when raised like any other breed, the German shepherd proved to be an excellent companion, was good with children and were protective of and loyal to their owners.[17]

Judy responded and stated that it was more important than ever for the dog fancy "to fight the propaganda against dogs." The publisher called for an organized national effort to circumvent the public's increasing opposition to dogs, a trend he found increasingly dangerous.[18]

Judy assured readers that the German shepherd had been "secured by artificial breeding," and there was not a drop of wolf blood to be found in the breed.[19]

On another page he posted a photograph of the head of a wolf, asking readers to compare the photograph with that of a German shepherd.[20] In comparing shepherds to "wild dogs," Judy stated that "perhaps the German shepherd dog … mirrors most closely the dog of nature," before man created the breed that the public had come to know, all of them "carefully planned and grooved."[21]

Judy wrote that similar to the German shepherd dog, "nature follows a somewhat distinct type of conformation." He stated that the body of the wild dog is long-backed, with ears set high and erect with rounded tips. Similar to a German shepherd, the eyes of the wild species are light brown tinged with yellow, its head long with a skull of medium width with a rib spread nearly as wide as that of a Saint Bernard; its long and bushy tail was held downward in a way that contoured to its hindquarters.[22]

Judy was not one to avoid controversy when it involved defending the reputation of a breed he believed provided value to man. The February 1925 issue of *Dog World* was packed with advertisements purchased by kennels that specialized in the breeding of the German shepherd dog. Despite Bert Finch's pleas for shorter more Americanized names, these shepherds displayed names such as Nores Von Der Kriminalpolizzi (Father of Strongheart),[23] Junker von Soolbad,[24] Litel Vom Wasserland[25] and Blinka von Graustein.[26]

The question of "shepherd quality" also came into focus. In a column headed, "His Master's Voice," the publisher welcomed letters on any subject pertaining to the dog industry, with the caution that *Dog World* was not responsible for any controversy a letter might present.[27]

Under the heading "Importing Biscuit Crushers," a dog enthusiast named R. C. McCallum, Jr., from Baldwin, L. I., New York wrote about the practice of inferior shepherds imported from Europe. "I would hate to tell the American fancy what most second-raters can be bot [bought] for in Germany," he began. The writer went on to recommend an embargo on shepherds imported from Germany that he claimed carried diseases.[28]

McCallum further stated that the best of the breed could not be found in Germany. Instead, he was quick to praise the English dog judges and breeders who valued "soundness" in a dog, which reflected overall health, something the writer believed to be the most important quality in all animals. A sound and well-bred German shepherd was one that possessed "light eyes, gray tails, cow hocks."[29]

McCallum complained that all that was required of the poorly bred imported dogs was "a gait to win and a long body with plenty of angulation."[30]

He acknowledged that while he was like most breeders, "after the mighty dollar," and liked to win on the dog show circuit, the importation of inferior German shepherd dogs needed to stop or there would be no "real winning thru-out the country." He advised those seeking to purchase a German shepherd not to patronize hobby breeders and to invest "real" money when doing so. On a final note he suggested that American dog owners stop importing "biscuit crushers" from Germany.[31]

An item titled "A Complaint," by B. Braakman of Chicago, who was identified as an early booster for a shepherd club in the Chicago area, discussed other problems experienced by shepherd breed enthusiasts. A disgruntled Braakman wrote that there were enough shepherd breeders in the Chicago area to present the largest and finest club if only the present leadership improved.[32]

Braakman claimed that the group had suffered from unfair management by leaders who made decisions without consulting membership and that this had undermined the success of the breed in the Midwest and elsewhere.[33]

The unsavory topic of something termed dog faking was also addressed in the issue. Judy discussed the topic of truthfulness in advertising when it came to dog breeding and admitted that even the experts at *Dog World* could be deceived by fraudulent breeders.

He shared that it had come to his attention that a dog that had been advertised for stud purposes in his magazine was actually no longer living when its picture was claimed to have been taken. Furthermore, he had learned that the name of the dog presented under the picture of this imposter belonged to another dog that was also no longer alive and that the picture was being "offered under the pedigree of another dog."[34]

A dramatic Judy ended this summation by noting that after all this had been disclosed to him, he fainted.[35]

Judy also had opinions on the pricing of purebred dogs. In a piece titled "The Minimum Price," he stated that the mongrel puppy and one that was pedigreed differed in what they cost to raise. He noted that while Mother Nature usually nursed the mongrel puppy, the raising of a pedigreed puppy typically entailed a greater expenditure from its care-takers.[36]

Judy relayed that the expenses incurred in all steps of responsible dog breeding were part of running a good breeding business. Items such as stud fee, price of the dam, and the feeding of the puppies combined with the time and effort required to produce a litter of healthy puppies and called for a fair price in their sale.[37]

It was suggested that a pedigreed puppy of any breed should sell for no lower than $20, which in the year 2011 would translate to approximately $300. Judy stated that "A rightful combination of sportsmanship and good business is proper and desirable in the dog fancy."[38]

In the column titled "Brik Bats and Bokays," under the heading "Beg Your Pardon," Judy used his wit to apologize for a typo in the December 24 issue that lead readers to believe a stud fee for a Schulzlust shepherd named Cesar von Hohentor was just an incredible $15 when the correct fee was $50.[39]

Judy's humor was in evidence when he wrote that the breeder, Mrs. Hattie M. Schultz, "had a special policeman to ward off the owners of bitches" who had descended upon her home in Chicago hoping to get in on this bargain. He added that he was grateful that this woman was kind enough not to bomb *Dog World* headquarters at 1922 Lake Street in retaliation for the editor's mistake.[40]

Another reader addressed the topic of the poor attitude of dog judges at dog show events. He wrote to Judy and suggested that "if judges would mingle with the exhibitors and in a friendly way," and engage the exhibitors in "good fellowship," instead of walking around being crabby and holding grudges, the conditions at dog shows would be more enjoyable. The writer concluded that exhibitors deserved the right to know why their dogs were "placed down."[41]

But it was suggested by other writers that perhaps these judges had good cause not to engage with disappointed handlers and owners, since they often proved to be a difficult and contentious lot. Edwin L. Pickhardt offered his personal views on good sportsmanship in his column "Collie Talk." He wrote that "we cannot all win, but we can play the game," and suggested that the dog show world adopt the attitude of the University of Illinois's football team, whose motto was, "To win without boasting; to lose without alibis." The writer reminded *Dog World* readers that the best sportsmen were those who were best prepared, be it for a dog show, a tennis match or even a football game.[42]

Judy appreciated well-written works on dogs and was happy to promote the works of his fellow authors. Under the heading of "Dog Book Column," several works of this genre were reviewed. One titled *First Aid to Animals* and published by Harper and Brothers in New York City was described as a useful volume written in a style that could be understood by anyone. Judy recommended this book to farmers, kennel owners and all those "who have an interest in animal life ... at least those who believe that the beasts of the field should be treated with kindness."[43]

Both *The 1924 Annual of the Dog World (London)* and its American counterpart received glowing reviews. It was noted that both editions were written and edited by women journalists, and Judy singled out the writing of the English version by Miss Phyllis Robson as clear, forceful and original. He further noted, "To the eye and feel of the printer, the 1924 annual is a thing of joy."[44]

No issue of *Dog World* would be complete without Judy's personal expression of the admiration and love he possessed for all dogs. In the February 1925 issue he extolled the value of all dogs writing, "I see something wonderful and beautiful in every breed—all different. But all in (or out) of order, meaning that in plain English, I am an honest-to-goodness dog lover." He proclaimed that he had just been born that way. To those who questioned him on this matter he noted with finality, "it is, has been, and always will be, and why not? So let it be!"[45]

The August 1947 issue of *Dog World* was now priced at 35¢. Its cover presented readers with the image of four dignified champion German shepherd dogs posing obediently. In post–World War II America the once feared and loathed German shepherd dog was experiencing new respect and popularity as a breed.

Under the heading of "Cover Calvacade," it was stated that these shepherds were owned by a breeder named Lloyd C. Brackett of Long-Worth K's of Allegan, Michigan. In presenting these credits, Judy announced that all the remaining magazine covers for 1948 had been accounted for and had proceeded to list which dog breeds had been selected to grace covers for issues extending well into 1951.[46]

By this time Judy was no stranger to being a regular guest on radio talk shows. In the August 1947 issue he informed readers that he had been interviewed while in Kansas for a dog event.

In the interview conducted by a member of the KFOR radio station staff, Judy was quizzed about the size of the current dog population in the United States and the cost to feed them all. It was asked of him if he could offer any words of advice to new dog owners, his personal opinion of those dog owners who allowed their dogs to run free in the streets, and his purpose for founding *National Dog Week* 25 years earlier.[47]

But these questions that seemed simplistic at first glance actually were designed to delve issues of a more sensitive nature. It was also inquired of Judy if the United States Army would continue to include war dogs "in its peacetime schedule," and if he believed "mongrels or plain mutts are smarter than canine bluebloods." Judy was also asked to give his personal take on the old saying, "The more I see of men, the more I like my dog."[48]

Another question centered on favoritism and popularity of specific breeds, and Judy was asked about which dogs were currently enjoying popularity and if he had a personal favorite.[49]

The topic of breed popularity literally dogged Judy wherever he went. By1947, although it appeared that German shepherd dogs fared better in perceived reputation, another breed was now the focus of public fear.[50]

In an article about bull terriers, Judy responded to an editorial that had appeared in the *Chicago Tribune* a month earlier with the spirit of a dog lover fighting against anti-dog propaganda. The editorial in question was titled "Murder-Dogs." It recounted the horrific account of a boy's death from an attack by two American bull terriers and the police officer who was seriously hurt while unsuccessfully attempting to save the life of the 11-year-old named Stanley Balaban of Bronx, New York.[51]

The dogs were owned by a man named Svend O. Sandgren, who told police that someone had come through an open window of his houseboat and let the dogs out. The owner also claimed that some of his dogs had been awarded ribbons at two dog shows.[52]

Although the writer of the editorial openly admitted to being ignorant as to what an American bull terrier was, he wrote, "It is our considered opinion that the breed ought to be exterminated by law." He further stated that bull terriers were specifically bred for fighting, killing other dogs as well as humans, and suggested that heavy fines be imposed on those who possessed a member of this breed or any one "engaged in breeding or selling these killers."[53]

The writer of the editorial acknowledged that some members of the breed were no doubt of good temperament, however he bluntly suggested that due to the increasing number of these horrible incidents, "they ought to be exterminated."[54]

Judy responded by acknowledging that while this incident was the third of its kind to have occurred in the nation within two years, "all three [were] unfairly connected in the public's mind with the bull terrier." He advised readers and members of the lay press to differentiate between the four distinct dog breeds that were frequently confused by the public. These according to Judy were the boston terrier, the bulldog, the bull terrier and the Staffordshire terrier.[55]

Judy gave this topic a lot of ink and noted that in their coverage of the killing of the Balaban boy the *New York Post* had referred to the dogs involved as "American bullterriers," while the *New York Times* described them as "white bull terriers."[56]

Judy placed the misunderstanding and ignorance about these breeds on those who trained dogs to fight. He urged that true dog lovers and members of the dog fancy must "cast into outer darkness, completely disown, all those dog owners ... who fight their dogs in pits or in formal encounters." Dogs for the purpose of fighting were identified as members of the Staffordshire terrier breed.[57]

Judy did not spare his readers the gory details of crunched and splintering bone and the blood that flowed freely from the jugular veins of those unfortunate dogs involved in organized dog fights. Of those who were involved in this activity, Judy wrote that these "sportsmen (?), dog lovers (?), and red-blooded he-men (?) did not deserve to be classified as humans."[58]

Identifying these fighting dogs as Staffordshire terriers, it was evident that Will Judy believed the much-beleaguered "Staf" had been unfairly treated by the public and faced prejudice within some parts of the dog industry. He relayed that he had spent over ten years compiling the breed standard for the Staffordshire terrier and had campaigned for full official recognition of the breed in 1926.[59]

Judy blamed those he mockingly referred to as "red-blooded Americans" for harming the development and progress of the Staffordshire. Their success in the dog fighting ring made them unwelcome in the dog show ring. He further condemned a dog magazine, established in 1912 and headquartered in Kalamazoo, Michigan, for their promotion and glorification of this blood sport.[60]

Judy concurred that the temperament of the Staffordshire could be "molded more easily than that of a human infant." To those who chose to breed these dogs, he advised that they do so only with dogs known to possess a dependable disposition, be able to provide the proper training and proper environment for their needs, and to only sell those puppies that had received plenty of human touch and socialization.[61]

Only responsible breeding and the public denunciation of those who continued to use Staffordshire and American bull terriers for the purpose of fighting would keep the Boston terriers and bulldogs, and their owners, outside of this "black circle."[62]

Judy railed against those who called for the wholesale murder of an entire breed because of the transgressions of a few. In his opinion this was as logical and intelligent as believing that "all negroes be massacred because a certain percentage of them commit crimes." He also likened this to proposing that all automobiles be destroyed by fire because 48,000 people lost their lives in car accidents each year.[63]

Judy wrote that some newspaper editors should be "hanged on the gallows" for their discriminatory publications. However, he made note that he was not going so far to call for the closing of the *Chicago Tribune* due to the business of certain scalawags.[64]

The heavy-hearted editor acknowledged the dreadfulness of the tragedy in the Bronx, but also reminded readers that the young boy had climbed an eight-foot fence to gain access to the property of the Castle Hill Bathing Park and was legally trespassing at the time of the incident.[65]

He further reminded them that although five dogs were present at the scene it was determined that only two had actually been involved in the attack. After they were destroyed by gunfire the remaining dogs had been found to be docile and were carefully placed in the wagon of the ASPCA without incident.[66]

Judy urged people to consider that "dogs, like humans, are subject to mob rule," and were capable of horrible acts as much as any human mob. Breed was not a factor in these attacks, and Judy placed the blame on irresponsible humans who allowed their dogs to run freely, creating dangerous situations.[67]

This particular issue was again highlighted in the August 1947 issue of *Dog World* in an article that offered an account of a Florida woman who had been killed by a gang of "staffs" two years prior.[68]

Judy relayed that he was compelled to report on the matter because the owner of the dogs, identified as a Mr. Munn, had been recently arrested and sentenced to a prison term of five years for his role in the woman's death.[69]

Judy urged dog owners to write to Florida's governor to request a pardon for Munn and quoted the convicted man's warning that "with cattle on the open range, every rancher in Florida faces the penitentiary."[70] Munn proposed that if he was found guilty, logic dictated that if a horse jumped a fence, and harmed or killed someone, its owner would also be held responsible by law.[71]

The role of dogs in the military continued to be of interest to Judy. Under the heading of "War Dog Training," Judy relayed details of his conversation with Captain Major Godsol, a colleague who had served two years as the Commanding Officer of the K9 Corps Detachment in Fort Robinson, Nebraska.[72]

Of the role of military dogs in World War II, Judy inquired what were "some of the basic policies which might have been changed?" Captain Godsol informed Judy that there had been too many camps for military war dog training and that too many dogs had been recruited.[73]

Godsol also added that these dogs should have been trained "for tactical or battle use at the beginning [of the war] … instead of training all dogs during the first year of operations solely for sentry duty."[74]

In closing, Judy reported that "a complete authenticated history" of American military canine forces had yet to be written and noted that this task had been placed in the hands of Captain Godsol. Judy also acknowledged that in addition to the captain's account, the Dogs for Defense planned to publish a history of its own activities.[75]

Judy truly understood the benefit of dogs in the military sector on and off the battlefield. In the August 1947 issue there appeared a brief item titled "Hospital Show," in which it was reported that a dog show had been held at the Veterans Administration Center in Waco, Texas, on May 17.[76]

It was written that the audience had immensely enjoyed talks on the subject of dogs, a presentation of champions and a demonstration of a guide dog at work. He ended the item with a suggestion that other dog clubs might replicate these types of activities in their own communities.[77]

On a lighter note, the ongoing issue of sportsmanship in the dog show circle was good naturedly revisited. The article used humor to describe an event that had taken place a few years prior in the southern region of the nation that had been held with the intent to cheer the sore losers of a dog show.[78]

On this occasion, the human halves of the dog showing teams gathered at the "wailing wall" over cocktails and consoled each other over the unfairness and criticisms of the dog show judges. Judy referred to this gathering as a meeting of the "Beaters Club," stating that this congregation was one that "never elects officers, never has any dues and knows no by-laws."[79]

Judy invited a man by the name of James T. Culp, of Slugger Hill Boxer Kennels in Dallas, to share with his writers why the Beaters Club had been established. Cult imparted that after many years of listening to the bickering and griping of participants at the dog shows he had attended in the south, he had decided to start a club with the intent to "promote good will and sportsmanship" among his colleagues. Culp wrote that in his home state of Texas these Beaters Club meetings had replaced contention and "cemented good will and friendship" between many a handler and exhibitor. He hoped that other states would follow their example.[80]

Judy certainly did. He shared a detailed account of a similar event he had attended after an important dog show event in Long Beach, California. Judy recalled being chauffeured off Ventura Boulevard and driven into the hills, to a gathering hosted by the Professional Handlers Association of the Pacific Coast and the so-called Beaters Club.[81]

On this festive occasion losers and winners of the dog show circuit mingled as they were entertained. The guests danced to the strains of an orchestra while enjoying "good food, [and] all sorts of beverages," in an atmosphere of goodwill with all bad feelings having been left at the entrance.[82]

In typical fashion Judy stated that in sharing these stories he had proven to readers that these meetings of the Beaters Club were more than just an excuse to "bend an elbow." He restated that these alliances were promoted to bring out what he believed to be the best in a good dog fancier; the ability to, "take a licking," in the show ring while remaining a good sportsman and competitor.[83]

Judy also took the opportunity to promote another society he held in high esteem. Under the heading "Not Many Are Eligible to Join This Group," the publisher wrote that it was a great distinction to belong to the Oldtimers of the Kennel World referring to a nonprofit organization he had founded years earlier.[84]

"The Old Guard passes on but never dies," Judy wrote. In its establishment, Judy addressed the fact that the typical career of breeders and exhibitors in the world of dog showing lasted approximately two years. The Oldtimers group served to perpetuate "the traditions and sportsmanship of the dog fancy," promoting goodwill among its members.[85]

Membership in this club was open to men and women who had been actively involved in some aspect of the dog show industry or any commercial field that centered on dogs. Those in the dog publishing industry or employed in the animal caregiving industry were also eligible to join. The novitiate was required to have been active in their work for at least 20 years.[86]

Of those who served for such a period Judy waxed poetic. "Like the sturdy oak which survived the storm," these dedicated dog enthusiasts upheld the longstanding traditions of the dog fancy.[87]

As in many of his books, Judy frequently imbued the pages of his magazine with spirituality. In this particular issue he reprinted a Russian prayer titled "Prayer For Animals" that began with the words, "Hear our humble prayer, O God, for our friends the animals, especially for animals who are suffering; for all that are overworked and underfed and cruelly treated; for all wistful creatures in captivity that beat against their bars; for any that are hunted or lost or deserted or frightened or hungry; for all that are in pain or dying; for all that must be put to death."[88]

This prayer was situated next to an item that conveyed the positive response of so many readers to the printing of Rudyard Kipling's poem, "The Power of the Dog." That poem had appeared in its entirety in the June issue of *Dog World* that year. Judy pleased his readers and reprinted a snippet of the poem.

> Buy a pup and your money will buy
> Love in flinching that cannot lie,
> Perfect passion and worship fed
> By a kick in the ribs or a pat on the head.[89]

September was just weeks away and Judy took the opportunity to remind dog lovers that *National Dog Week* would soon be celebrated, as it had been for the past 19 years. It was announced that "YOURS For Keeps" would be the theme for the event.[90]

The poster and seals for this observance featured a little girl holding a black and white puppy in her arms in celebration of the event's twentieth anniversary.[91]

Under a headline that announced "No Money Could Be Better Spent," it was declared that the Century Club of the National Dog Week Association had contributed $1,300 toward the "research fund in behalf of dogs."[92]

It was further explained that each year, a person or persons who had contributed the most to the advancement of dog health and medicine had been awarded $2,000 for their efforts. Judy personally thanked Mrs. Leicester Harrison of New York City for her contribution of $100. He stated that in offering her donation, this breeder and member of the Poodle Club of America had urged others to follow suit.[93]

Judy did so too. He wrote that it was not too much to ask, as these contributions brought about improvements in dog health care that would "not only benefit the dogs of the donor," but all dogs for many years to follow.

He was hopeful that medical science would soon offer "a perfect vaccine against rabies," a foolproof prophylactic against distemper, and a cure for infectious jaundice and encephalitis, as well as for follicular mange.[94]

Newbold Ely "of foxhound fame" identified as a prolific publisher of the magazine *Judge,* commented on the National Dog Week report on the prior year's observance. Ely wrote that he embraced the second objective for National Dog Week that urged for the elimination of stray dogs from city streets and further suggested that their elimination be encouraged in rural regions as well. Ely noted that the Pennsylvania Game Commission had issue with stray dogs that ran "game out of season," and killed rabbits and other wildlife.[95]

Although Judy remained active as the publisher of *Dog World*, in August of 1947 he fielded rumors that the magazine was for sale. He refuted all speculation and reported that "a group of New York persons recently made a written offer for the purchase of *Dog World* for the sum of $350,000." He confirmed that this offer had been declined and that there were no imminent changes in the ownership of the magazine.[96]

The August 1953 cover of *Dog World* magazine featured a black and white photograph of a sweet-faced little boy from Los Alamos, New Mexico. He posed happily beside a Belgian sheepdog. The image was set off by a crisp white border that floated on a bright red background.

Judy had remained at the publishing reigns of *Dog World* for three decades; his enthusiasm for this task had not waned and business was booming. A small item on page four of this issue led with the statement, "To sell, you must tell." It further advised, "SELL, SELL, SELL—month after month." Advertisers were informed that with each monthly issue of the magazine, "ALL CLASSES OF BUYERS" could be reached across America, Canada and 74 foreign countries. It was also stated that a typical issue of *Dog World* contained approximately 40,000 paid advertisements per issue.[97]

This was evident from the moment the reader opened to the first pages of the magazine to find countless advertisements purchased by a multitude of competitors in the vast dog market: a myriad of dog foods, shampoos, tick remedies, worm capsules, flea powders, vaccines, and skin treatments.

Each advertiser extolled the unique value of their products through clever ad copy and whimsical drawings and cartoons, with the back pages of the issue presenting ten pages of sales listings from kennels for almost every dog breed imaginable.

Countless industry-related items offered commentaries on the status of a variety of dog breeds written by guest contributors in the fancy, as well as several reports on news of obedience trials held throughout the nation and numerous advertisements by kennels promising champion bloodlines.

A mention of National Dog Week's Twenty-fifth Observance was also prominent. A black and white rendition of that year's National Dog Week Poster Seal featured the image a young girl posing with a boxer. It was announced that National Dog Week would be observed the week of September 20–26 with a theme of "Always Faithful."[98]

In answering his own question, "What is National Dog Week all about?" Judy explained that his mission was to educate humans that dogs were dependent upon them for their care and welfare, especially in urban areas.[99]

He stated that National Dog Week also highlighted the importance of respecting the rights of those who owned dogs as well as those who did not, the importance of keeping dogs off the streets, sharing improved methods of dog obedience training, the promotion of proper canine nutrition and educating the public about the current quality of rabies vaccines.[100]

But despite Judy's best efforts it appeared that the earnest and still idealistic publisher was frustrated at the lack of impact those efforts had made on the nation's view of canines.

Judy was disheartened by the way many of the nation's dog owners still regarded their dogs. He addressed the fact that even after 25 years of National Dog Week observances, millions of dog owners still regarded dogs as "just dogs—something that takes care of itself."[101]

He expressed disappointment that many dogs still slept outdoors in all kinds of weather, had to find their own food supply, barked all day and roamed about without purpose. Judy looked to use this important milestone to restate and define the mission of National Dog Week. He proclaimed, "We do not want more dogs so much as we want better dog owners."[102]

He urged his readers to write immediately to the National Dog Welfare Guild located in midtown Manhattan to request information on how to actively participate in the observance during the last week of September.[103]

A small item about Blanche Saunders also appeared in this issue. Saunders was a pioneering dog obedience trainer and author who would become an important feature in Will Judy's National Dog Week observances. It was noted that Saunders had celebrated her fifth "Spectacular Dog Act" at Yankee Stadium in June. Jack Thomsen of Ken-L-Ration had served as the event's announcer and then–New York City Mayor Impellitteri presented trophies.[104]

In Saunder's production, dogs representing the Poodle Obedience Training Club of Greater New York, Metropolitan Boxer Training Club, Keeshond Club and the Port Chester Obedience Training Club performed "intricate feats of jumping." It was an event that Judy credited for promoting interest in all things dog.[105]

In an item tilted "Feature," Judy, the consummate promoter, took the opportunity to inform readers that he also wrote a syndicated feature for newspapers called *Dog Talks,* which reached an audience of approximately 3 million weekly.[106]

Judy boasted that *Dog Talks* created "new interest in dogs and better care and a desire for more knowledge of dogs." He encouraged readers to contact their local newspaper editors to request that his column be made available to their readership and provided a detailed list of where it was currently offered.[107]

In the August 1953 issue of *Dog World* Judy also reported that 1,752 canines were currently engaged in the world's military forces. He wrote that while the European forces utilized 1,400 dogs in this capacity, the United States only claimed 137 dogs of war.[108]

In the U.S. it was reported that all German shepherd dogs that met the height requirement of 22 to 28 inches, weighed between 60 and 90 pounds and were between the age of one and a half to two years old were enlisted in active military service.[109]

Another subject that continued to concern Judy was the absence of responsible practices in the sale of dogs. An article titled "The Sale of Dogs Must Be Lifted to a Higher Plane of Merchandising" began with Judy's admonishment that "the whole field of merchandising in dogs needs to be brot to a modern and more logical basis."[110]

Judy addressed the fact that over 90 percent of all dog sales at that time occurred from afar. He offered sympathy for the dismayed and disgusted dog owners who had received sick puppies after paying fair market prices for a pedigree dog. He stated that no one should ever buy a puppy unless it had received shots for rabies and distemper and been provided guidelines for how and when these inoculations would be administered.[111]

Judy urged dog breeders to guarantee the safe and sound delivery of puppies and replace those pups that died within ten days of delivery. He further advised those breeders who advertised their dogs in the classified section of *Dog World* not to ship a puppy that displayed symptoms of illness within two days of the shipping date or when the outside temperature rose above 102 degrees. There was also a mention regarding problems experienced when shipping dogs through the use of airlines, which was to be addressed in a future issue of the magazine.[112]

Judy was no stranger to the controversy surrounding the antivivisection movement in America. Under the heading "American Humane Ass'n Not an Anti-Vivesection Organization," he addressed this subject. Judy took issue with the American Humane Association's Director of Field Services, Larry Andrews. Andrews had accused Judy of writing with "a chip on his shoulder," with his frequent attacks on the humane movement on the pages of *Dog World*.[113]

Andrews described these contentious items as "an insidious attempt to divide humanitarians on the issue of animal seizure legislation." Andrews claimed that Judy's writing supported the agenda of the National Society for Medical Research, which sanctioned the seizure of animals from shelters for the purpose of laboratory experimentation.[114]

Judy was accused of being a dog lover as long as those dogs qualified to be registered with the American Kennel Club. Andrews made the claim that Judy did not like mixed breeds and that he referred to them as "mongrels" and "strays."[115]

Andrews also cynically stated that Judy had devoted a "couple of valuable inches" in his maze of magazine columns to deride national humane societies for their attempts to assist mixed-breed dogs that Judy and his colleagues deemed of lesser quality than purebreds.[116]

In a chilling indictment, Andrews accused Judy of promoting the drowning of those said mongrels and strays in cold water, while allowing a single pup to live only as a measure to prevent the "mother's breast from caking."[117]

In his response, Judy accused Andrews of resorting to "the usual sophistry of misquoting, misinterpreting," and generally distorting the truth.[118]

Andrews countered that Judy had not had any contact with the American Humane Association in the past 18 months. He referred to that single meeting as the occasion when Judy gave a speech that "fulminated against" the society's policies regarding the placement of homeless animals.[119]

Judy acknowledged that he had given a talk at the Cleveland Convention in October of 1951, where the content of his speech "blew such cold draft ... that the brutal truth gave them a chill and they never have forgiven us."[120]

Andrew's conviction that the readers and staff of *Dog World* cared only for the purebred dog remained steadfast. He inquired of Judy and his colleagues that inhabited an elite group of dog enthusiasts how they would feel if asked to sacrifice their own beloved dogs and puppies for medical research or had their kennels raided for procurement of laboratory animals. He also suggested that those dog breeders who put down dogs that were deemed not suitable for sale might consider offering *them* up for the purpose of medical research.[121]

On these issues, a reader from San Francisco defended Judy. In an impassioned letter to *Dog World*, the devoted reader wrote about her displeasure concerning the vicious assaults made against Judy that had appeared in the February and March issues of the *National Humane Review*. It was stated that these accusations would not go unchallenged by the Dog Defenders League of California.[122]

The writer also suggested that an officer of the ASPCA named Mr. Coleman, of New York City, had been more than happy to be considered for a humane award granted by the "evil" publisher of *Dog World* himself. It was also proposed that those who raged against Judy should redirect their anger toward a man named Anton Ross, who was identified as a supporter of "Dr. Carlson's pound-dog procurement legislation."[123]

Judy referred to these impassioned exchanges as ongoing episodes of a "friendly battle between World War I Captain (infantry) Will Judy and Seaman Second-class World War I, Larry Andrews." He referred to his magazine as "Space Ship Dog World," and those siding with Andrews as "Jet Rocket Humanitarian," and asked his readership who they thought would win this battle.[124]

Judy urged readers to stay tuned for reports on this continuing battle and promised that proceeds from all sales of *Dog World* would go "for the better care, treatment and understanding of dogs, both purebred and mongrel." It was additionally stated that the magazine and its staff did not practice favoritism toward the purebred dog.[125]

Expressing no animosity, Judy encouraged *Dog World* readers to subscribe to *The Humane Review,* noting that readers would get their money's worth with their expenditure of $1.50.[126]

Judy promised that a story about his visit to the new state-of-the-art animal shelter in Long Beach, California, would be published in an upcoming issue of *Dog World.* He described the facility in glowing terms as being one of the best planned, most efficient shelter facilities in the nation.[127]

Despite this show of support for America's shelter systems, some dog breeders viewed "pounds" as a source of competition. A woman from New York wrote to *Dog World* complaining about a current television advertisement that was promoting the "adoption" of shelter dogs. The reader was dismayed to see "a lovely sable and white collie," offered by the shelter for the price of $15. During the commercial it was announced that the typical adoption fee for shelter animals was $5, however, the cost of this collie was higher due to the fact that this dog "had papers."[128]

The woman identified herself as a breeder of purebred dogs and claimed these offerings hurt her dog breeding business as her customers balked at the prices she requested for the puppies her purebred dogs produced. "Why should they when they can go the animal shelter and pick their choice of 65 or 70 dogs for as low as $5?" This clearly did not benefit her because they could acquire someone's surrendered purebred dog at a third of her prices.[129]

7

The Enduring
Influence of *Dog World*

A black and white photo of Pekingese champion Wei Tiko of Peke-boro and Rob Kai peered out from the cover of the September 1958 issue of *Dog World* magazine underneath a subheading that read, "Some Folks Who Shouldn't Own Dogs."[1] It was also noted that this was the "NAT'L DOG WEEK ISSUE." It would be the next to the last issue to be published by William Lewis Judy.

Inside the cover pages, crammed with the requisite advertisements for dog food and dog care products, mingled with the standard newsy items that provided updates on dogs and the law, and the registration of dogs and articles about dog sales, it was business as usual, until page 14, where readers were met with a dramatic headline: "FLASH! FIRE DESTROYS *DOG WORLD* HOME!"[2]

The startling item was composed by editorial assistant Dave Kuhlman and relayed that in the early morning of July 30 a terrible fire had been set by arsonists, who had broken into the front portion of the four-story Judy Building on South Michigan Avenue.[3]

Kuhlman wrote that the thieves had entered the building through a fire escape and then gained access to Judy's office. It was surmised that the intruders were searching for cash, and after they cracked the publisher's safe and discovered nothing of value, they had set fire to the building.[4]

It was noted that this building had served as the home base for the Judy Publishing Company and *Dog World* magazine for over 27 years and also as the headquarters for the recently formed Judy-Berner Publishing Company for three years.[5]

The brick walls still stood, but they were "weakened and out-ofplumb." The building's roof was missing, as well as a large plate glass window, and the interior had suffered major water and smoke damage.[6]

Judy stated that the Chicago newspapers had been negligent in their reporting of the incident in placing damages at approximately $12,000. Of the total loss, Judy wrote, "Actually, ten times that couldn't cover all losses." He further stated that no dollar amount could replace the magnitude of this loss that included hundreds of articles and items of sentimental value.[7]

It was reported that in an instant over 35 years of Judy's personal collections and the *Dog World* library had been destroyed. Among items claimed by the fire were invaluable company files "of news, ad, book and magazine fotos and cuts" for use in future books and issues of *Dog World* magazine, and back issues of the periodical.[8]

The third floor of the building that housed the classified advertising and circulation departments also suffered severe damage, with the losses of business ledgers, Judy's personal library of rare dog books, display ads and audits and mailing supplies and equipment. Items housed in the rear portion of that floor also suffered smoke and water damage, seriously harming the all-important subscription files, Judy's collection of rare dog paintings and etchings, personal stationery and correspondence as well as priceless gifts of statuettes and plaques and mementos.[9]

Gone too were many of Judy's treasured personal items acquired from the days before "his entry into dogdom." These included his collection of books from his school and college years, certificates, rare books that were not entirely about dogs, a copy of the Bible, Judy said, was the first to be printed west of the Allegheny Mountains, and his personal souvenirs from his service during World War I and ensuing service in the National Guard.[10]

The intrepid spirit of Judy infused the tone of the article, and in typical fashion he implored his readers to excuse the tardy delivery of the October issue of *Dog World*.[11]

It was acknowledged that although the Judy-Berner headquarters had been "jolted" by this devastating event, it was just a matter of time before business was running at or close to its regular publishing schedule. It was noted that this great setback would be overcome with hard work to "earn our BIS in the publishing end of the dog field."[12]

In another article Judy expressed his disappointment at his inability to engage a young generation of dog enthusiasts to be more active in the world of dogs. He wrote that he had gone to great lengths and expense to establish a Junior Kennel Club of America and had even provided bylaws for local chapters, paid for the printing of membership cards and issued charters.[13]

Despite his best efforts over the period of two years, he expressed that he was discouraged that only 31 local chapters were active across the nation and that this endeavor had produced a deficit of approximately $7,000.[14]

Judy was also discouraged by his inability to motivate adult dog enthusiasts to handle the responsibility of supervising these fledgling chapters. He cited the lack of interest on the part of kennel clubs in general when it came to establishing junior divisions. He suggested that "many kennel clubs should get off their fannies and really do something for man's best friend."[15]

This issue of *Dog World* introduced an informative new section that focused on the topic of dog laws. On these pages Judy's formal law training was showcased. He called the September 1958 *Dog World* "The dog owner's rights issue," and he advised readers to retain the issue as a permanent resource on the topic.[16]

Judy was aware that every day somewhere in the United States a multitude of dog owners faced important legal matters that affected them in a very personal manner. The lawyer turned dog advocate explained that the National Dog Week Association had made it their business to educate and update the public regarding the legal issues and the rights of their dogs in all regions of the nation. It was also noted that the editor of *Dog World* was a member of the bar of the state of Illinois.[17]

Legal matters discussed in this issue included rabies inoculation requirements, the killing of stray dogs, property taxes on dogs and insurance policies to protect the dog owner. It was also noted that the laws affecting dog ownership would be discussed on a state-by-state basis.[18]

Judy reminded readers that unless an attack was imminent, it was unlawful to kill stray dogs, including those that had wandered onto a home owner's property. Judy also shared that because dogs were considered personal property, much like furniture, dog owners were responsible for any damages incurred by them.[19]

It was also noted that in some instances an owner could not be found responsible for the afflictions of their dogs. Judy wrote about a case in which the owner of a rabid dog was not held accountable for damages inflicted by the sickened dog.[20]

The subject of rabies inoculation remained a controversial subject.

Judy wrote that despite its unpopularity among many dog enthusiasts, the compulsory inoculation for rabies would inevitably be enacted by all cities in the entire nation.[21]

Judy agreed with many of those active in the dog industry that this mandate was not fair, since many of the dogs that spread rabies were strays owned by humans who took no responsibility for them or were unable to control them. He noted that this requirement that all dogs be inoculated for rabies might "impress upon the public the necessity of better dog control."[22]

Judy wrote that there had never been a case heard in a higher court that challenged compulsory rabies vaccinations as unconstitutional. In 1958 the state of Illinois required dogs to be inoculated unless they were retained in an enclosed environment at all times, with the exception of kennels. But under this law it was revealed that municipalities of a certain size were able to enact ordinances that required compulsory inoculation of all dogs, kenneled or not.[23]

In an item headed "Veterinary Notes," Judy discussed the current state of veterinary practice in the United States and questioned recent findings reported by the *Modern Veterinary Practice*. It had been stated by that publication that approximately 50 percent of the 900 June graduates of veterinary colleges in the nation and Canada that year were headed to small animal practices. The article Judy referenced further noted that during the course of the next 25 years, the need for small practice veterinarians would double.[24]

Judy did not agree with this conclusion and countered by writing that in the specialty of small animal practice, namely dog-centric practices, there was a saturation point. He pointed out that the nation already had approximately 1,800 dog hospitals and doubted that the American dog population would increase in such a manner that more of these practices would be required.[25]

Judy commented that there had been "a lot of bosh publicized" surrounding the growth of America's cat and dog populations and noted that nearly 425 veterinarians were lost each year through death, or a myriad of other causes.[26]

It displeased Judy that despite the fact that great strides had been made in the implementation of police dogs around the world, some still did not fully understand their value. In this September 1958 issue, it was noted that in London, England, police dogs had actually proven to be too efficient.

Judy wrote that it was "not good news" that the city had officially discontinued its use of police dogs in efforts to disband street crowds and to quell mob activity.[27] Prior to the use of police dogs, horses had been employed for protective and policing duties. Due to abuses and damages suffered by the crushing force of approximately 400 police horses, it was determined that police dogs were a better choice for crowd control and law enforcement.[28]

Judy revealed that the *Chicago Daily Tribune* had reported that two police dogs had been successfully employed to quell mobs in England during incidents that involved political protests and major disputes on Downing Street and in the city of Manchester. But he pointed out that unlike horses, dogs responded to aggression with their own protective instincts, which presented different challenges.[29]

This was evident in the case where a police dog had bitten a group of teenage boys as a result of having been kicked repeatedly. While a healthy respect for the police dog force had been instated in public forums, Judy was upset that "some yappers, complained that these police dogs were too vicious."[30]

He reminded readers that trained police dogs had been used to make the parks of many cities safer after dark, had thwarted the efforts of many purse snatchers and had decreased the number of police forces required to patrol and guard warehouses and docks in many areas of the nation.[31]

The ever-present topic of the fairness of judging in the show ring was also covered. Under the heading "Judges Have a 'Hard' Life," Judy discussed the status of the 2,400 licensed dog judges in the nation, noting that the American Kennel Club had discontinued the use of the word "licensed" for legal reasons.[32]

It was duly noted by the publisher that over 40,000 people purchased *Dog World* magazine to obtain a better understanding of "the passing dog scene each month." To help with that effort Judy declared that he welcomed the opinions of breeders and judges, but admitted that many times he was in "violent disagreement" with many of those that were "exprest."[33]

So many breeders and dog owners had complained about the unfairness of dog show judging that Judy expressed his personal desire to publish a series that presented what judges thought of the exhibitors.[34]

Under the heading of "The Dog's Own Week," the thirtieth occasion of National Dog Week received full coverage. Judy wrote that it was "easy and pleasing" for him to write about this subject. That year's observance took place during the week of September 21 with Judy set to act as the "honorary president of the National Dog Welfare Guild," the organization that sponsored the event. Judy reminded his readers that he was the acknowledged founder of this annual honorary week established to pay tribute to America's dogs.[35]

Judy noted that there were a myriad of weeks dedicated to all kinds of things and it was important for dog lovers to remember that the cumulative influence of three decades of National Dog Week observances were not to be trivialized. He derived great satisfaction that countless American dogs were receiving better care, "and a more sympathetic consideration on the part of their owners," due to the observance.[36]

Judy reminded people that this special week called for "a concentration of emphasis in order to get action," and encouraged schools, clubs and all organizations, as well as the press, to work together during these seven specified days to improve the manner in which dogs were cared for and controlled, and to reduce the population of stray and nuisance dogs.[37]

"'You' are the Volunteer," readers were reminded. Judy made it clear that the nation's dog owners bore the responsibility of keeping the spirit of the observance alive. He implored all dog lovers to volunteer as their local National Dog Week Chairman or to help by putting up posters supplied by the National Dog Week Association. "Do not expect 'George' [Berner] to do the work—your dog expects YOU to come forward to volunteer."[38]

It was promised by the editors of *Dog World* that this week just for dogs would receive plenty of publicity and be covered by newspapers, radio and television. A number of events were also planned to mark its special 30-year observance that featured organized obedience training demonstrations to be held at schools, window displays in stores, informal dog shows and special community meetings.[39] It was also proclaimed that these organized activities were meant to be embraced by all dog owners, including those with mixed-breed dogs.[40]

Judy listed the objectives of that year's observance, which included the finding of good homes for all dogs, the elimination of stray dogs as much as possible, the teaching of kindness toward dogs, placing an emphasis on the usefulness of dogs, the achievement and enforcement of fair and just dog laws and respecting the rights of those who did not particularly care for dogs.[41]

Under a column "House Chat," Judy's personal and business plans for September were discussed. It was reported that he would spend the Labor Day holiday in his hometown mountain village in Pennsylvania, where he would host his annual dinner for the village's seniors age 75 years and older. He good-naturedly attributed the longevity of the locals to the "mountain ozone."[42]

Judy also wrote about his upcoming duties as the "country-wide chairman" of National Dog Week. It was noted that on the twentieth of September he would spend his birthday at the band shell of Grant Park in Chicago to participate in the opening ceremonies for the observance with a Mrs. James Compton, who would serve as the co-chair for National Dog Week in Chicago. Two days later Judy was scheduled to speak at the dedication of the newly opened Purina Dog Food Research Kennels in St. Louis, Missouri.[43]

Closing ceremonies for that year's National Dog Week would prove to be especially meaningful to Judy. It was reported that on September 27, a Saturday, Judy was scheduled to arrive in Warrensburg, Missouri, to serve as the principal speaker at the historic dedication of the monument to Old Drum, the hound immortalized in Graham Vest's "Tribute to a Dog."[44]

Another item titled "Folks Who Shouldn't Own Dogs" weighed in on the subject of the population of irresponsible dog owners in America as it pertained to the observance of National Dog Week. After 30 years of observances Judy had gained a new perspective on his perception of the modern American dog owner.[45]

Judy noted that while a previous slogan of an early observance of National Dog Week, "A dog in every home," had been intended to help dogs, he and his colleagues had quickly realized the slogan had been a mistake.[46]

Judy admitted that most of the "problem dogs," those that roamed city streets unattended, were involved in street fights and caused damage to livestock, belonged to people who did not care, and had no regard for the responsibilities of dog ownership or the desire to become enlightened on the subject.[47]

The frustrated publisher further chastised the many dog owners who did pay annual license fees for their dogs and mistakenly believed that their dogs should be allowed to run about freely without supervision. Of this Judy wrote, "About the only thing a dog license fee gives the owner is the right to be arrested for not taking out a license for owning the dog."[48]

Judy also took to task those families who acquired dogs because it was fashionable, owners who allowed their dogs to roam free without having them inoculated with the rabies vaccine, and "lazy dog owners" who did not brush, groom, bathe or exercise their dogs.

Also included on Judy's list of irresponsible dog owners were those who allowed their dogs to leap on others or trespass on the property of neighbors, and those who publicly pretended to be dog-lovers only to neglect and treat them unkindly in private or failed to obtain timely and adequate veterinarian care for a sick dog.[49]

Despite these negative issues surrounding dog ownership, it was clear that more American homes were determined to acquire one. It was reported in this issue of *Dog World* that *Look Magazine* had completed a survey of pet owners in the nation and concluded that dogs were the most popular pet. *Look* disclosed that 49.9 million Americans shared their residences with one or more dogs. It was also revealed that 25.4 million cats were kept as pets in the United States. This was of special note, as it set to rest the issue of cat popularity versus that of the dog in America.

Judy commented that an earlier news release had reported that cats were the first choice of American pet owners, something Judy had naturally questioned and humorously attributed to the reporting of "a black cat at mid-night."[50]

A black and white drawing of champion Threethorne Honeybee, a bulldog owned by Mr. and Mrs. Raymond L. Dickens of Oklahoma City, graced the cover of the December 1965 issue. This serious-faced rendition of a dog with soulful eyes floated under the subheading that boasted "Five Decades of Dog Breeding: *50th Anniversary Issue.*" *Dog World* had reached a publishing milestone.

Cover art credit was bestowed on Barry A. Michaels of Ferndale, Michigan, a renowned pet portrait artist who specialized in "life-like" pastel renditions of man's best friend.[51]

Dog World was now priced at 50¢ and the cover of this landmark issue promised coverage of an eclectic list of relevant topics that included, but was not limited to: a retrospective of the history of the American Kennel Club, a review of the important advancements in Veterinary Medicine, a look at a "Half Century of Breed Changes," and an article titled "New Puppy After Christmas."

George Berner now served as the magazine's president-publisher, however, Judy's presence was strong. In the issue's first pages the name of Will Judy appeared in an article that attributed the success of *Dog World* to his foresight and direction that spanned five decades. Judy was credited for his astute decision to purchase the magazine 42 years earlier when it was "little more than a pamphlet with a total of 400 subscribers."[52]

The article told of how Will Judy was considered one of the world's "outstanding dog authorities," credited for building the magazine into the world's largest publication devoted to man's best friend.[53]

In this golden anniversary issue it was evident that *Dog World* was not only dog-friendly, but also supported women in the workplace and the contribution made by its female staff. In a display of black and white photos of the 25 executives showcased in the magazine's masthead, 18 were female. That included the magazine's executive vice president, Carmela Szybinski, and Olga Dakan, who was listed as the magazine's vice president of advertising.[54]

Of the latter it was noted that after working hours Mrs. Dakan was known as Mrs. Tony Pocius, an unusual practice for female executives in 1965. Mrs. Dakan was credited for having served at the magazine for almost 25 years and was responsible for all aspects of advertising. Furthermore, it was noted that her success was achieved by the help of another woman named Gladys Bauer, who was in charge of classified ads.[55] This was a very important and prestigious responsibility, considering the huge advertising revenue of *Dog World.*

The accomplishments of the hardworking staff were praised by Berner, who wrote, "We salute each of them." He promised that the magazine would continue to offer quality customer service, top of the line expertise and knowledgeable contributors and writers. As Judy had done for years, Berner also continued to welcome any and all suggestions and criticisms from his devoted readership.[56]

In a heartfelt tribute to the endurance of *Dog World,* Associate Editor Harry Miller presented a page-length article that gave testimony to the magazine's ongoing role in the welfare of America's dogs, and those in foreign lands. Miller humbly noted how earlier readers, leafing through the pages of the magazine's premier issues, would have most likely found its content quite unremarkable and probably would have condemned it as having "a poor future."[57]

On the occasion of proving itself a leader in the publishing field, *Dog World* was not shy about the major role it had played in boosting the popularity of dogs in America and beyond. Miller reminded readers that 50 years later, those doubters had been proven very wrong. The proud associate editor explained how *Dog World* had not only come to mirror the world of dog fanciers, but was now considered by those in the dog industry a "fantastic, fabulous phenomenon of the twentieth century."[58]

This celebratory issue served as an eye-opening barometer of the popularity of dogs in the United States. It was noted that by 1965 the current canine population in America had exceeded 26 million. Although there were no official statistics available for the earliest portion of the twentieth century available data for the period of the late 1920s revealed that there were approximately seven to eight million dogs residing in the nation by that time, reflecting a significant increase in 35 years.[59]

America now boasted the largest dog population in the world, "the biggest one on a per capita basis." Miller noted that by 1965 two out of five American families owned a dog and that the nation's canine population was growing more quickly than that of its humans.[60]

Demographics revealed that most of the nation's dogs lived on farms, but this was changing as the number of farms in the United States was declining. Miller noted, however, that although farms were in decline, the number of hunters who relied on their hunting and field dogs more than made up for that loss. Of important note, it was disclosed that approximately 19 million suburban families were rapidly acquiring dogs as family pets, with 20 percent of them acquiring more than one.[61]

Miller noted that nearly 50 percent of suburban families and 25 percent of those who lived in cities were now among the ranks of American dog owners. Of the latter, it was indicated that many urban dwellers relied on their dogs to prevent burglaries and many others who were single, elderly or living alone valued them as companions.[62]

The boom in the number of dogs and the increasing concern about their care and health needs had created a lucrative market for products and services that catered to those who owned dogs. Miller reported that by the middle of the decade the dog industry employed tens of thousands of people who were active in an industry that generated over one billion dollars in revenue.[63]

Products such as dog foods, houses, carriers, beds, blankets, collars, leashes, dishes, tags, toys, soaps, shampoos, and accessories were in demand, as were the services of veterinarians, groomers, trainers and even those providing dog burial services. But perhaps most importantly for the staff of *Dog World,* those who published relevant material were in demand.

Facilities as diverse as those that hosted dog racing operations, institutions that trained guide dogs for the blind and the rapid development of hundreds of shelter facilities across America created a multitude of job and career opportunities.

Industries that catered to those in the dog show and breeding world were also experiencing a boom. According to Miller, this included 55,000 private kennels with facilities specifically designed for the breeding and selling of one million puppies a year.[64]

Those who handled and showed AKC-registered dogs, as well as those employed in writing about these activities, were also cited as benefitting from the increased popularity of dogs in the nation. In a matter highly relevant to readers of *Dog World,* Miller noted that by 1965, 40 percent of American-owned dogs were purebreds. This accounted for the dramatic rise in the number of dogs registered by the American Kennel Club.[65]

Miller informed readers that this commemorative issue summarized the progress of the American Kennel Club's quest to educate the American public about dogs and their care, the presentation of newly recognized breeds and the evolution of dog shows in America and abroad.

A special focus was also placed on the burgeoning dog food industry and the area of veterinary medicine. Miller noted that major developments and improvements had been accomplished during the last five decades in those sectors and had greatly contributed to the better overall health and longevity of American dogs.

In 1965 alone, over three billion pounds of dog food produced in the nation accounted for a national expenditure of over $500 million. To illustrate the staggering impact of this figure, the associate editor pointed out that it was equivalent to what Americans spent on packaged detergents, and more than coffee, cereals, toilet soaps and baby foods, noting that those items were purchased by *every* home in the United States.[66]

It was reported that a man by the name of Robert F. Hunsicker, president of the Allen Products Company, identified as a division of Ligget and Myers Tobacco Company, forecasted that in that year the sale of pet foods in America would exceed the billion dollar mark. It was duly noted that 80 percent of that expenditure would be spent on the nation's dogs.[67]

Miller observed that over the course of several decades the dog food industry, unlike most other sectors, had implemented an unprecedented amount of new research and development initiatives to enhance the nutritional value of commercial dog foods. Prepared dog foods were now routinely supplemented with vitamins, minerals and amino acids to sustain a longer and more healthful life for dogs.[68]

By 1965 America had over 20,000 practicing veterinarians, which was almost three times the amount in active practice a half century earlier. Of these veterinarians, over half earned an estimated gross combined income of $380 million. It was also noted that more than half of the total income of the nation's veterinarians was derived through the care of dogs.[69]

According to the article, with these advancements in veterinary medicine thousands of dogs had survived serious ailments, and their average lifespan had been prolonged beyond the average age of eight years.[70]

Under the heading "50 Years of Veterinary Medicine," full-scale coverage of the state of veterinary medicine was presented by the president of the American Veterinary Medical Association, Don H. Spangler, D.V.M.

This extensive and detailed article was hailed as "an historical sketch" of the evolution of the veterinary practice in America over the course of 50 years. Spangler noted that he was honored to have been asked to write on this topic on the occasion of *Dog World*'s golden anniversary. The contributor noted that it was the American Veterinary Medical Association's way of saying, "Congratulations to a great magazine."[71]

Spangler wrote that with the increase of companion animals in the households of the nation, the focus of pet care now centered on the mutual responsibility and teamwork between pet owners and their veterinarians. It was noted that *Dog World* magazine, through its publishing services, was largely responsible for defining this new relationship model.[72]

According to Dr. Spangler, the period from the mid–1920s to 1965 marked a time in which "the relationship between pet owner and veterinarian matured." He rejoiced in the fact that the veterinary practice had come through a dark period and had entered a new age of prosperity and enlightenment.[73]

In pre–World War I America, those who practiced veterinarian medicine were highly valued for their role in equine health. In 1900 the care of horses accounted for approximately 80 percent of the practices of 8,000 veterinarians nationwide. In sharp contrast, by 1920 equine care comprised only 10 percent of the practice of the 14,000 veterinarians in the nation.[74]

Spangler wrote that the onset and growth of the automobile industry was the demise of the horse's role in the nation's mode of transportation. With the automobile's development the number of professionals who cared for horses slowly declined and the field of veterinary medicine suffered.[75]

This once-prestigious and profitable field now found it difficult to attract capable men and women to its ranks. The number of students enrolled in veterinary medicals schools steadily declined with each passing year, and subsequently the number of veterinary training facilities decreased. It was noted by Spangler that from 1924 to the following year only ten schools in the entire nation specialized in veterinary medicine, with their total enrollment numbering only 504.[76]

But the status of the field of veterinary medicine gradually improved over time with the continued shift from equine-centric care to the study and care of a wider variety of animals. Under the leadership of the American Veterinary Medical Association, improvements made in standards for admission to these institutions bolstered the core curriculum of these new programs.

In 1926 there were 13 colleges and universities that offered course studies in veterinary medicine in the United States and Canada. By 1928, the year Will Judy introduced the first observance of National Dog Week, enrollment in these institutions experienced an upward trend.[77]

This new approach to training placed a greater emphasis on scientific study. The veterinarian was no longer viewed as just the caretaker of cows, horses or farm animals. A growing number of domesticated household pets, animals housed in large city zoos and smaller petting zoos now required the services of medically competent veterinarians. By 1965, Dr. Spangler observed, "the health of any living being has in some fashion become the responsibility of the veterinarian."[78]

Spangler saw a bright future for those in the profession on several levels. He wrote that these trained professionals would serve as guardians of the welfare and health of the nation's livestock and sources of food and fiber. He also foresaw an increased role of pets as providers of "support for emotional stability for many."[79]

Spangler noted that during the American Veterinary Medical Association convention of 1922, only one full day of talks and lectures was dedicated to the emerging field of small animal specialties. However, from 1955 to 1965 the number of veterinarians specializing in small animal care had almost doubled. By the middle of the 1960s, nearly one-third of the 4,000 animal hospitals in the United States offered specialized practices not solely for the care of cats and dogs, but also including animals such as monkeys, caged birds, raccoons and a legion of other species.[80]

According to Spangler's article, a total of 18 veterinary colleges were active in the United States and two in Canada in 1965. Enrollment in these programs averaged over 4,262, of which 257 were female. But it was an arduous course of study, with only about 1,000 students graduating from these programs each year.[81]

This modern curriculum for veterinarian training consisted of a minimum two year course of pre-veterinarian study at the college level that required 5,000 class hours. Clinical study in anatomy, physiology, pathology, surgery, public health and preventive medicine were listed among a myriad of required subjects.

Spangler declared that "today's veterinarian is virtually a medically trained professional." He stated that these doctors were highly capable of administering in the animal health sector as well as those areas that concerned public health in general.[82]

Although many veterinarians sought careers in the care of small animals, others found lucrative and rewarding careers specializing in the care of livestock. In all regions of the United States diseases like bovine tuberculosis, scabies found in sheep and cattle, bacterial dysentery, hog cholera, cattle tick and anthrax that had once devastated farm communities were now greatly reduced or eradicated due to advances in veterinary training.[83]

Under the subheading "Versatile Veterinarians," Spangler lauded this new connection between the advancement of animal care and the health of humans, calling it "the hallmark of the modern veterinarian." The improved health of the American livestock supply was a case in point, but Spangler also wrote that the area of laboratory animal medicine presented another. He proposed that laboratory animal medicine was one of the "most significant links between veterinary and human medicine."[84]

In a section titled "One Medicine," Spangler claimed that between

40 and 50 million animals were used in medical research, laboratory instruction and drug testing, with 250 practicing veterinarians employed as laboratory animal specialists. Others found employment among the ranks of research and development in large pharmaceutical firms.[85]

Spangler wrote that the work of these veterinarians had dramatically improved the health of humans in matters concerning radiology, air quality, cardiac health, and food and milk inspections, as well as matters concerning sanitation and the study of allergies and infectious diseases. He asserted that modern veterinarians were now regarded as active partners in "the total effort to combat the physical, mental, and economic ills of modern society."[86]

Under the heading "Medical Milestones," Spangler cited the works of several renowned men of veterinarian medicine whose research ultimately improved or saved the lives of millions of humans.

Included among them was Dr. Maurice Hall of the United States Department of Agriculture. Hall developed the drug tetrachorethylene for the treatment of human hookworm disease. Australian veterinarian Franz Benesch's research on cattle and horses ultimately perfected the epidural method of anesthesia for humans. While working in Canada on the causes of sweet clover poisoning in cattle, Dr. Frank Schofield helped to develop the anticoagulant drug Dicumaro. Major Walter Reed's fight against malaria was accelerated by the observation made by yet another veterinarian, Dr. Fred Kilborne, who proved that insects transmitted disease between animals and man.[87]

These vast and dramatic medical breakthroughs discussed by Spangler clearly illustrated the inseparable link between the healthcare of animals and humans. But Spangler wrote that the most powerful innovation in modern medicine was found in the area of rabies control.

In an item written by Dudley Baker titled "Progress in Infectious Diseases," a detailed confirmation of Spangler's claim was offered. Baker expanded on Spangler's piece on the history of veterinarian medicine. In marked contrast to Spangler's straightforward writing style, Baker's article opened with a fiery and dramatic start and read like a thriller.

In his first sentences Baker presented a scene inspired by the first 60 lines of Homer's *Iliad*, where the god Apollo's bows downed mules and dogs "as swift as a flash of silver" before striking down men. Baker likened these deadly arrows to an anthrax epidemic, and since anthrax was the only disease proven to be fatal to both man and animal he asserted that anthrax was the cause of these swift deaths.[88]

The article explained that the study and eventual cure of anthrax presented one of the "best examples of how progress in knowledge through thousands of years led eventually to understanding" that resulted in life-saving measures for both humans and animals. Baker noted that rod-shaped anthrax bacilli multiplied and formed spores that were transmitted aerobically. These anthrax bacilli were capable of surviving in extreme weather conditions for many years and were readily spread by way of dust particles, flooding and by way of human and animal foot traffic.[89]

Dogs were sickened by the disease when they consumed the carcasses of infected animals or were fed infected batches of bone meal. Cases of anthrax in humans were traced to infected cheese supplies and contact with the fur, hides, wool or hair of animals that carried the anthrax spores. Baker wrote that he found it incredible that anthrax, which was a disease that had caused so many deaths in ancient Greece, had been eradicated only 80 years prior to the writing of his article.[90]

He wrote that leaders and scientists of ancient civilizations, from the "Mohemmadans" to those of major European cities in the Middle Ages, were aware that disease was transmitted from animal to man and took whatever precautions were available to curb the spread of infectious disease.[91]

Bubonic plague was transmitted by the fleas carried by rats. "The Black Death," as it is called, had eradicated half the population of England in the fourteenth century. Bovine, avian and human forms of tuberculosis also took their toll on human and animal populations worldwide. Of these illnesses, bovine flu was found most often in cats and humans, but not dogs. Similar to anthrax, the avian bacilli remained active in soil for prolonged periods, sickening domestic and wild fowl.[92]

It was noted that the study of immunology also had its origins in the study of animals. Scientists noted that individuals who recovered from diseases did not subsequently become reinfected. Baker imparted that in the ancient civilizations of China, Arabia and Turkey, people were deliberately exposed to disease as a form of prevention and control. He also cited the work of Edward Jenner, who discovered a cure for smallpox after it was disclosed to him by dairy farmers and milkmaids that they were immune to the disease after being exposed to cowpox.[93]

Baker wrote that even at the time of Abraham Lincoln's presidency in the early part of the 1860s, scientists still did not comprehend the role of microbes in bacteriology and how they were invisibly transported through air.[94] Lincoln had contracted smallpox, which manifests in grotesque pocks that cover the face and body. Of his illness Lincoln famously quipped, "Now I wish all of the job-seekers would come to see me. At last I have something I could give them."[95]

While all of these discoveries were remarkable in their own right, Baker observed that nowhere was the connection between the study of human and animal disease more relevant than in the area of rabies control. The medical breakthroughs of Louis Pasteur are numerous and far-reaching.

Baker informed the readers of *Dog World* that Pasteur had rescued the silk industry through his extensive research into the cause of death of silk worms, but it was noted that the scientist was best recalled as the man who developed the first vaccine for rabies.[96]

In his research, Pasteur "attenuated the virulence" of the live virus found in infected dogs and injected the resultant samples in the spines of laboratory rabbits. Injections were given at intervals, with doses that were increasingly more potent as tolerance to the virus was developed.[97]

Baker likened Pasteur's successful efforts in the field of rabies research as "miracles of modern science." But he reminded readers that rabies remained "enzootic" in the United States and that all warm-blooded species, including man, were susceptible to the disease.[98]

This article on infectious diseases was relevant to the readers of *Dog World* because, Baker asserted, the health and welfare of humans hinged on the research related to dogs in particular. Baker noted that rabies was seldom "found in dogs in those localities where dogs are kept protected by periodic vaccination." In terms of medical advancement, Baker observed that dogs suspected of being infected by the rabies virus were currently administered tests that had not been available at the time of Pasteur's original vaccine.[99]

Baker wrote that similar to Pasteur, Robert Koch of Germany had advanced the study of bacteria through his study of anthrax and tuberculosis. Through the use of photography Koch devised a way to capture clear images of bacilli, and in doing so he and his colleagues developed a method of staining bacteria with chemicals to make them more visible and easier to classify.[100]

It was noted that over 200 years had passed since the construction of the first microscope by Dutch scientist Van Leeuwenhoek. With many improvement over the years, the microscope had gone from being an instrument of amusement to an invaluable tool in bacterial research.[101]

Baker informed readers that by 1965 these dramatic improvements in the way bacteria and viruses were classified made it possible for nearly 300 diseases to be "isolated, studied, and classified" in groups that ranged from adenoviruses to pox viruses to what Baker designated as the most useful category, "miscellaneous."[102]

Classification was a key factor in major advancements in preventive measures and control of diseases. It was now understood that there was an endless variety of bacteria with specific "preferences, and shapes." Some bacteria existed at extreme temperatures and survived in boiling water; however, it was discovered that most pathogenic bacteria survived and reproduced at 98.6 Fahrenheit in man and approximately 100 to 103 Fahrenheit in dogs.[103]

Baker noted that advancements in electric power and refrigeration had additionally aided in the advancement of vaccine research and development. Through the process of refrigeration purified viruses could be kept frozen in air-tight vials. Electricity allowed fertile eggs to be incubated and electric ovens and dishwashers allowed for necessary sterilization of equipment and containers. Baker wrote that even in 1965 some foreign nations were not able to produce effective vaccines due to the lack of a dependable source of electricity in those regions.[104]

That last observation reminded readers of *Dog World* that in 1965 America was literally leading the pack in the area of dog and human healthcare initiatives. Baker suggested that the veterinarian's work was not just confined to this planet, boldly proclaiming that "the responsibility of the veterinarian reaches the frontier of man's activity in space." As America's space exploration program expanded, veterinarians participated in the care and training of animals used in space flights and the subsequent interpretation of the data collected.

With the publishing of *Dog World's* fiftieth anniversary issue it was clear that a myriad of mind-boggling developments had occurred in the dog industry since the magazine's inauspicious debut in 1916. The world of dogs and mankind had been through some dramatic changes, but the influence of its pioneering publisher remained.

By 1965 the Oldtimers of the Kennel Club established by Judy in the late 1920s had proved to be a very good investment. On the occasion of its golden anniversary, *Dog World* listed the names and years of service for the entire membership of the club. It was stated that their "continued patronage made the golden anniversary possible." These devoted long-term advertisers and loyal supporters of Judy had helped to build and sustain this venerable magazine and now were acknowledged as "good friends."[105]

Like Judy, George Berner continued to support those who authored books on dogs, even those not published by him. Under the heading of "Books About Dogs," contributor Herm David reported that over the course of the past 50 years "writers, researcher and artists" had been highly productive in their contributions to the dog industry.[106]

David took on the daunting challenge to compose a list of those titles he believed represented the most influential books of pioneering initiatives in the study of dogs, those that portrayed dogs through art exceedingly well and those that he felt encouraged readers "to explore outside of their own breeds," something he stated led to the better understanding of all dogs.[107]

In celebrating the remarkable legacy of the magazine it was only fitting that Will Judy himself presented a few words on his role in the history and success of *Dog World* magazine. Tucked away on page 37 his picture appeared next to the heading that read, "After Fifty Years."[108] Of his role in the success of the magazine Judy wrote, "To say that *Dog World* is 'Will Judy's Puppy' seems rather farfetched," and questioned the logic of comparing a magazine that had celebrated several decades of success to a puppy. "But time passes—or rather we pass ... time remains," he observed.[109]

Judy recalled how *Dog World* had been "whelped" by Fred Fromeneck with its first issue produced in the basement of 1333 South California Avenue in Chicago in January 1916. Judy wrote about the day he answered a classified ad to inquire about the sale of a "sporting magazine." After some negotiation a deal was finalized and the first issue of *Dog World* was published under Judy's ownership in January of 1923.[110]

Judy confided to readers that in the publication's early days the entire circulation of the magazine could be carried in two mail sacks that were delivered to the post office on Madison Street by a man named Cleve Bardine. Judy pointed out that Mr. Bardine had remained a loyal *Dog World* employee, who in 1965 served as a district circulation agent.[111]

It gratified Judy to see how his dog publishing empire had prevailed as a leader in the fields of "news, service and scientific guidance" in the dog industry. He wrote that despite increased competition, *Dog World* still "ranked first throughout the world in the field of canine journalism." He based his figures on those provided by the Audit Bureau of Circulation.[112]

Relating how the growth of the American Kennel Club was recorded in history, canine press coverage contributor Arthur Jones shared that he had joined the AKC staff in 1924 when it was "almost impossible to sell sports editors" on the topic of dog-related activities. At the time most media outlets did not want to report on events that affected only 50 to 60 breeds of dogs. Jones wrote that prior to 1924 only a few daily newspapers even "bothered to cover dog shows."[113] Most reporters scoffed at the notion that dog showing was a sport, and prior to that time the only newspaper in the New York vicinity that reported on dog shows was the *New York Herald-Tribune*.[114]

Jones wrote that eventually reporters such as Frank Dole of the *New York Herald Tribune* and Roland Kilbon led the way in serious dog show reportage. It was noted that Kilbon had reported on dog news for the New York *Evening Sun* under the pseudonym of Arthur Roland.[115]

Of his personal involvement in dog reporting, Jones relayed how he had convinced the sports editor of the *New York Times* to allow him to write a column on dogs for the Sunday edition of that venerable newspaper. His column was so successful that the *Times* eventually hired a reporter from the *Boston Transcript* by the name of Harry Isley to provide regular news coverage about the New York City dog scene.[116]

Jones wrote that over time he had helped to convince sports editors from across the nation to welcome "usable items about dogs" in their news outlets, which in turn introduced readers to the name of the American Kennel Club and their purposes, since many were not familiar with the organization.[117] During the period leading up to World War II, the American Kennel Club was so regularly covered by the press that it was no longer necessary for the organization to actively seek publicity. Shortly after the attack on Pearl Harbor and up to the end of World War II, the task of providing newspaper editors with "dog copy" was delegated to Roland Kilbon on behalf of Dogs for Defense.[118]

In 1965 *Dog World* (magazine) remained protective of those dog breeds that suffered from misconceptions of the general public. In a piece titled "Neighborhood Rejection," contributor Betty A. Radzevich defended the reputation of large breed dogs such as the German shepherd. Radzevich appealed to those who owned large breed dogs to always be considerate of their neighbors. In particular she advised them not to leave their dogs tethered and unattended for long periods of time, to discourage excessive barking and howling.[119]

Honesty and diplomacy were recommended when dealing with the problematic dog of a neighbor. Readers were reminded to never allow their dogs to relieve themselves on neighborhood lawns, to give their dogs regular exercise and to provide for proper obedience training. Of the latter it was advised that dogs should not receive "serious" training until six to eight months of age and only then in what was termed a "fun manner," writing that "a dog is only a product of the owner's training."[120]

For dogs in group training classes he reminded owners to have all dogs inoculated and groomed before class and to have their dogs relieve themselves before each session. Participants were to be punctual, considerate of trainers and classmates and to be "tolerant and kind" to their own dogs.[121]

Like it had on the cover of the February 1925 issue of *Dog World*, the words of Graham Vest's "Tribute to a Dog" still resonated on the pages of this golden anniversary issue.[122]

In a contribution by Harry Miller headed "Must Memorize Vest's Tribute," the associate editor wrote about a situation that involved two youths from Henryette, Oklahoma. These boys had sprinkled flammable liquid on a dog and set the animal on fire. A woman who had witnessed the crime filed a complaint and the pair was fined $20 and charged with cruelty to animals by a municipal judge.[123]

Miller wrote that an attorney by the name of Harry Pitchford learned of the incident and called for further punitive measures.[124] Pitchford observed that if the charge had been filed in the county court system the boys could have received a maximum sentence of five years in prison. Pitchford ordered the boys to memorize Graham Vest's "Tribute to a Dog," and to report to him in 30 days. Of this unusual request the lawyer stated, "This could be a good way to show them what a dog can mean."[125]

It was a testament to the impact of Judy's publishing legacy that Vest's words had endured and influenced a generation of dog lovers though their inclusion on the cover and pages of a magazine that had educated and enlightened a generation of dedicated American dog enthusiasts for decades. In the seventy-fifth anniversary issue of *Dog World* magazine published in 1991, an article titled "Two Memories" presented the recollections of Maxwell Riddle and William W. Denlinger.

Denlinger recalled how he came to know of Will Judy as a young boy when Denlinger's father, Milo, commenced a personal correspondence with Judy that included the exchange of dog stories and jokes. William Denlinger relayed that his father had submitted a poem for publication in *Dog World*. The poem was titled "Heaven Can Wait," in which the word "hell" appeared three times. Judy wrote to the senior Denlinger and told him that although he had never published that word in his magazine, he was willing to make an exception in this case because he thought that "this poem hit the target so well."[126]

Denlinger eventually became a member of Judy's Old Timers of the Kennel World thanks to Judy's kindness and sense of humor. Denlinger's father was a "gold pin" member of the organization and the young Denlinger had attended the Old Timers annual dinner for years. At the age of about 30, Denlinger recalled trying to join the Old Timers, but came up short in the required years needed to become a member. On his application form Denlinger informed the committee that he hadn't been born, but was whelped. Judy wrote back to him and acknowledged that the young applicant had been indeed "raised in a kennel," and approved his membership.[127]

It was relayed by Riddle that Judy did more than write and report on the relationship between humans and canines. He recalled that during his military service in Europe, Judy was so impressed with how the Germans and the French forces employed military dogs that he purchased a Doberman pinscher upon his return to the United States. He named the dog Major, the first in a line of dogs owned by Judy that would share that name.[128]

Riddle wrote that at one time Judy's collection of dog-related books was larger than the American Kennel Club's but had been lost in the fire that had destroyed Judy's publishing offices in 1958.[129] Riddle also recalled a story of how Judy had studied Spanish to prepare for a dog judging assignment in Brazil, only to learn afterward that Portuguese was spoken in that country.[130]

Riddle described Judy as a "restless genius" and credited him for bringing "American dogdom to a cohesive whole" and infusing the dog industry with a spirit that had not been present before his emergence in the publishing field.[131]

Back issues of magazines can be excellent historical sources. Through the classified ads, columns and trade advertisements, back issues of *Dog World* chart the careers and accomplishments of "famous dogs" along historical timelines and track the emergence of particular dogs, the fluctuation in the popularity of dog breeds, and the contributions of noted authors who expanded the public's knowledge of dogs.[132]

Although Judy's publications have been criticized by readers and those in the publishing field for an overreliance on the generic and "boiler plate" presentation of material, his ability to educate a vast audience on how to love and care for dogs had a profound effect on the American dog owner. His writings have endured and are as meaningful now as they were when written decades ago.[133]

8

When Every Dog
Had Its Week: Seven Days to
Honor the American Dog

National Dog Week ... has had the basic goal not so much
of more dogs, but of better dog owners and better care for
the dogs we already have.
　　　　—Will Judy, founder of National Dog Week[1]

Will Judy referred to National Dog Week as a movement. A movement is defined as a series of organized activities working toward an
objective. With the use of that word it is clear that its founder intended
for this tribute to the dogs of America to be observed enduringly and
enthusiastically throughout the United States during the last full week
of each September.

In the pages of *Don't Call a Man a Dog,* Judy stated, "We do not
plead for more dogs, but for better dog owners and better care for the
dogs we already have."[2] That mission statement would serve as the foundation of all the National Dog Weeks to come.

To those who might have dismissed the need for a full seven
days devoted to dogs, Judy reminded them in minister-like fashion
that "no one ever sinned greatly by being too kind, too helpful, too
humane."[3]

With his National Dog Week initiative, Judy reached out to engage
the members of what he called "the cult of dog ownership ... founded
upon a warm heart" and for those who still thought he had gone too far,
he added, "An error of the heart is never altogether that."[4]

Educating the public about National Dog Week at the time of its
initial observance was challenging. Imploring the nation to spend time

and money on the care and maintenance of dogs during uncertain economic conditions proved daunting, even for such a master of marketing as Will Judy.

Six months before the advent of National Dog Week, the *Chicago Daily Tribune* published an item that showcased Will Judy's concern for the dogs of his city. The brief item titled "Dog is Man's Friend, Give Him a Pound" described a speech that Judy had delivered to the Committee on Animal Protection of the Women's City Club. In it, Judy urged that "every Chicagoan should back the committee" that had been trying get a modern facility built to shelter the city's stray animals.[5]

During its official launch in September 1928, Clara Bow graced the cover of *Film Weekly*,[6] Louise Brooks starred in the film *Beggars of Life*,[7] and a wire-haired fox terrier named Talavera Margaret was named top dog at the Westminster Dog Show in New York City.[8]

In the nation's capital, President Calvin Coolidge was serving the last of his term and although there is no record of it, Coolidge was likely to have been a great fan of National Dog Week.

President Coolidge and his wife, first lady Grace Coolidge, were noted animal lovers, especially when it came to dogs. Coolidge once remarked, "Any man who does not like dogs and want them about does not deserve to be in the White House."[9]

It has been suggested that in his childhood, the shy Coolidge found comfort and companionship in the quiet presence of animals, something that appears to have stayed with him as an adult. The Coolidge White House was home to several canines throughout his administration, including Peter Pan, Paul Pry (the half sibling of Warren Harding's famous Airedale, Laddy Boy), Tiny Tim, Calamity Jane, Blackberry, Ruby Ruff, Palo, King, Kole, Bessie, and two white German shepherd dogs named Rob Roy and Prudence Prim, the last two being personal favorites of the first couple.[10]

Within a year Herbert Hoover occupied the presidential office and the White House remained a dog-friendly place. First dogs that "served" during his administration included a collie by the name of Glen, Yukon the malamute, Patrick the Irish wolfhound, Eaglehurst Gillette, Weejie the elkhound, fox terriers Big Ben and Sonnie, and perhaps the best known, German shepherds Pat and King Tut.[11]

It has been suggested that photos of Hoover posing with King Tut made him appear more friendly and approachable and may have helped him win the presidential election. The big nervous shepherd came to be known as "the dog that worried himself to death," due to his vigilant patrol of the White House lawn as he served his master and family in the period following the 1929 stock market crash.[12]

With its first official observance, Will Judy's enthusiasm for National Dog Week even managed to cross the Atlantic Ocean, as documented by a headline of the *Ottawa Citizen* in September 1928 that proclaimed, "Every Dog in England Had His Day This Week in National Campaign." According to this news item, London celebrated the very first occasion of the week's observance with "8,500,000 dogs wagging their tails in glee" during its closing ceremonies. It was further reported that "sermons on dogs were preached in many churches. Flag days, dances and other forms of entertainment were organized to raise money for veterinary institutes."[13]

Two years later, a story in *Time Magazine* reported that a "stylish dog doctor" named Arthur W. Smith had established a hospital for dogs suffering nervous conditions in West Orange, New Jersey. Details included how each canine patient would have a private rook and be fed a diet of scientifically prepared foods. In the event of their death, they would have the privilege of burial in a cemetery located on the grounds of the infirmary with graves covered with fresh flowers.[14]

But with the crash of the stock market in October 1929 and the economic devastation that followed, not everyone exhibited this devotion to dogs, and National Dog Week was a victim of poor timing. With the nation's jobless rate at approximately 25 percent, how could Americans lavish their dog population with seven days of attention when so many people were just struggling to get by each day?

Despite his best efforts, the future of Will Judy's National Dog Week initiative appeared doomed from the start. The effects of the economic downturn influenced the unfortunate canine citizens of the nation. In January 1932, a *New York Times* article clearly defined the situation, declaring, "Depression Felt by Homeless Pets; Women's League for Animals Reports Big Gain in Work as Result of Hard Times."[15]

A search of national newspaper archives reveals an absence of media coverage of the observance of National Dog Week during the Depression. Despite the examples set by the residents of 1600 Pennsylvania Avenue, not everyone was as enamored of dogs as the nation's leaders or thought of them as friendly companions.

A *Time* magazine article of February 1931,[16] for example, tells of how agents for the ASPCA of New York secretly investigated a woman as she stealthily sprinkled a mysterious powdery substance outside the homes in an upscale Park Avenue neighborhood.

The agents had been alerted by local residents who had reported that a dozen area canines had suffered agonizing deaths within a short period of time. Upon inspection, authorities discovered that the dogs had perished from arsenic poisoning.

When first confronted, the suspect, a Mrs. Helen Corel, the housekeeper of a local realtor, claimed to be trying to poison rats, but soon confessed of her desire to rid the neighborhood of dogs. She explained that while dogs were fine in the great outdoors where they had plenty of room to roam, she resented how they were increasingly infringing on the quality of life in her neighborhood. According to this woman, roving dogs dirtied the basement windows, destroyed plants and shrubs, and annoyed everyone with their incessant barking and howling. As to the demise of those 12 local dogs, she placed the real blame on the owners who failed to restrain them. For her crime, she was fined $5.

Two decades later, Will Judy (who no doubt would have also placed the real blame on those negligent dog owners) in his new post as head of the Dog Defenders League, would have slapped Mrs. Corel with a fine 20 times that amount, a whopping $100![17]

"National Dog Week Almost Got by Unnoticed," bemoaned a headline in the *Free Lance-Star* of Fredericksburg, Virginia, on September 20, 1934.[18] The article began with the statement, "Here it is Thursday of National Dog Week and not a thing done about it." The news item told of how local dog lover George Berner, colleague and business associate of Will Judy, had personally reminded the city desk about the week, but nothing had been done to promote it locally. Upset at the prospect of the week slipping by unobserved, he took it upon himself to distribute "25 posters and 1,000 small stickers" promoting that year's slogan, "A Dog in Every Home."[19]

By 1935 the nation was making a slow recovery and Will Judy, operating his publishing company from Chicago, was decidedly out of the power circle of national dog fanciers and writers who called New York City home. In a move to close the 750-mile gap that separated him from this hub of dog activity, Judy joined forces with fellow writer Maxwell Riddle to establish the Dog Writer's Association in New York, later to be renamed the Dog Writer's Association of America.[20] In doing so Judy and his colleagues were able to honor those writer-members whose work best exemplified the importance of dog welfare in the nation.

For the first time in the history of American journalism, writing and reporting about dogs and the activities surrounding them was distinguished by its own category. This association with only 30 members at its inception now has a membership of over 500.

With the spirit of a natural teacher, Captain Judy mentored and influenced a generation of premier dog writers, including Maxwell Riddle. Riddle wrote a monthly column for *Dog World* magazine for 50 years, authoring nine dog-related books of his own. Today, the Maxwell Medallion is among the highest honors to be presented each year to a member of the DWAA.[21]

The establishment of the DWAA enabled Judy to promote and nurture his cherished dream of seeing National Dog Week observed more widely, and consequently celebrated on a much larger scale. The time had come for dog lovers across the nation to receive comprehensive news coverage of National Dog Week.

In August of 1938, *Chicago Tribune* reporter Bob Becker wrote about National Dog Week in his column "Mostly about Dogs."[22] In the article titled "National Dog Week Has Seven Aims," Becker noted that "National Dog Week was a movement sponsored without thought of monetary gain and made possible solely through the help of dog fanciers."

Becker imparted that the seven objectives of National Dog Week included the elimination of stray dogs; a good home for each of them; rabies education; promotion of responsible dog ownership; educating young people and adults to be kind and considerate of dogs and animals in general; emphasizing dogs for protection, companionship and servitude; the implementation of fair laws for dogs and their owners; and being respectful to those who did not own dogs or particularly care for them.

The following month, Becker published an article with the headline, "Chicago Joins U.S. in Paying Tribute to Dog."[23] He wrote of how throughout the entire designated week of the dog, thousands of Americans, along with their dogs, would find many ways to celebrate National Dog Week.

This item gave an account that Governors of New York, Pennsylvania, Washington, Oregon, Utah, Nevada, Maryland, Massachusetts and Texas had given their official endorsement of paying tribute to "America's dog population."

Becker told of meetings, dog shows and parades that would be held to call "attention to the service that dogs render to man." He reported that the observance's founder, Captain Will Judy, would be a guest speaker among several leading dog experts in a meeting to be held at the Anti-Cruelty Society Building located at 157 Grand Avenue in that city.

Becker astutely observed that the canine industry had become one of the most important businesses in the United States, and it was reported that American dog lovers had spent approximately $125 million the previous year on their canines, with almost half of that spent on their feeding alone.

National Dog Week had now gained the attention of celebrities. "Actress and Dog Friends: Alice Brady Will Direct National Dog Week Here"[24] announced a headline of the *Los Angeles Times* on September 14, 1936. Alice Brady, former star of the silent screen who had made a successful transition to talkies, succumbed to cancer three years later.

An affiliation with a Hollywood star had over the years proved to be a helpful means to promote this week devoted to dogs. In 1938, the *New York Times* announced on September 22, "Paddy Is Star Model at Dog Fashion Show."[25] The article related how Paddy Reilly, the dog mascot of the Humane Society and National Dog Week, "found himself in some dazzling canine company yesterday afternoon."

The story told of how Paddy, dressed in evening clothes, had visited the president of the Dog Welfare Association. Honoring that year's slogan, "Justice for Dogs," he had been the recipient of an award wired directly from screen star Bette Davis, the current president of the Tail-wagger's Club, for saving "about forty lives, mostly human, but including dogs and even a canary."

Young people of the nation were viewed as the future generation of Dog Week supporters and encouraged to make National Dog Week part of their lives. In a story appearing in the *New York Times* two weeks after the Paddy item, readers were informed that ten-year-old Frances Puccio's essay about her dog had won top honors from the Humane Society in a contest held in recognition of National Dog Week.[26]

The essay, accompanied by a beaming photo of the girl, told the story of how on a beautiful summer day Frances was walking through Central Park. She observed a beautiful young police dog that had been severely injured by a car. Not being able to locate its owner, the caring girl had sought medical attention for the dog and was ultimately allowed to keep him. Within three weeks of his adoption the pup had succumbed to its injuries and died.

In her touching essay Frances wrote of how, even in their short period of time together, she and the dog had bonded and how she had admired its loyalty to her. The essay ended with Frances's quote, "This expression has always been used, and I will again use it—man's best friend is his dog."

That year a short story titled "Lassie Come Home" appeared in the *Saturday Evening Post*. Written by author Eric Knight, the story about a rough-coated collie evolved into a novel length work in 1940.[27] Three years later, Metro-Goldwyn-Mayer adapted the book for a popular movie of the same title. The success of both further fueled the dog craze sweeping the nation.

Just as Will Judy had hoped, the nation seemed to be taking his lead and going to the dogs in a big way. Through celebrity connections, mascots, and contests and favorable cultural influences, Judy and his like-minded colleagues appeared to be finding a measure of success for their National Dog Week movement.

By 1940, with Franklin Delano Roosevelt in the White House, the arrival of his beloved Scottish terrier, Fala, proved to be auspicious. With Fala's arrival on the national scene, Americans watched as an honored canine was welcomed without reservation into the most famous of homes and the heart of its revered master.

Fala, a Scottish terrier originally named "Big Boy," was a gift to the president from his cousin Margaret "Daisy" Suckley. When the little black dog came to live at the White House, he was renamed Murray the Outlaw of Falalhill, after a Scottish ancestor of Roosevelt's. FDR and Fala became close companions, traveling the world together.[28]

In 1944 Fala accompanied his master to the Aleutian Islands. Rumors circulated that the terrier had been accidentally left on one of the islands. In the presidential election campaign that soon followed, opponents of FDR accused him of spending exorbitant amounts of taxpayer money to recover the little dog. Roosevelt addressed his accusers in a speech he delivered at a dinner given by the International Brotherhood of Teamsters, Chauffeurs, Warehousemen and Helpers of America.

In his famed Fala Address, Roosevelt deflected blame for the stock market crash and the depression, but most importantly defended the reputation of his dog. "These Republican leaders have not been content with attacks on me, or my wife, or on my sons. No, not content with that, they now include my little dog, Fala."

Roosevelt went on to explain how Fala resented the falsehoods circulating about his master and that Fala's "Scottish soul was furious," claiming his dog hadn't been the same since the incident.[29]

This sentiment was echoed by Will Judy who stated a few years later in *Don't Call a Man a Dog*, "Speak ill of a man, ridicule his work, and endeavors, even remark evilly of his wife—he is miffed; but berate his dog and there is battle!"[30]

The well-trained Fala performed tricks and even smiled for famous visitors to the White House. The first dog even slept in the same room as his master, which was a scenario that captivated the nation. In 1945, Fala attended the president's funeral, and he lived out the remainder of his days with Mrs. Roosevelt.[31]

The Fala years at the White House delighted the public and made it difficult for any future president of the United States to reside without a canine. But it appears that even during the dog-loving Roosevelt years, not every dog enjoyed such good living conditions as Fala. The occasion of National Dog Week also served to remind Americans of this and the hard fact that not every dog had a home.

In a *New York Times* article posted on September 24 of 1940, around the same year that Fala inhabited the White House, the headline declared, "It's National Dog Week and Pound Mutts Seek Homes."[32]

At this time, the well-orchestrated New York City dog week festivities kept the glamour and sportiness in its observance, which had now become a much-anticipated and celebrated event. A report in the *New York Times* that September announced, "Champions Parade in Dog Exhibition; Obedience, Retrieving Also Figure in City's Tribute to Thoroughbreds."[33]

In that year's observances, onlookers at Rockefeller plaza watched for two hours as retrievers delivered ducks from land and water to the hands of their trainers. For the citified denizens of Manhattan this may have been the only opportunity to watch dogs doing the work for which they had been born and bred.

In Manhattan some dogs knew how to make friends in high places. "Mrs. Jiggs to Aid Dog Week," proclaimed the headlines of another *New York Times* article in September 1940. It was relayed here that Mrs. Jiggs, a toy bull mascot of the Humane Society of New York, would be stationed on Broadway in front of the Saks Thirty-fourth Street department store during National Dog Week. The dog would be encouraging donations on behalf of the Humane Society in connection with the observance of

National Dog Week. The brief news item ended with the *National Dog Week* slogan, "Every Dog Needs a Good Home."[34]

Americans were becoming increasingly aware of the sacrifices dogs had been making all along for the country's war efforts. Dogs with names like Stubby and Rin Tin Tin and his descendants became poster dogs for the canines of war, and accounts of their military contributions brought greater depth to the observances of National Dog Week.

Unlike the militarily trained dogs of European forces during World War I, the dogs of the United States Armed Forces were something of unintentional warriors. Dogs like the famous Stubby, a brindle pit bull mix, had an unofficial part of the United States Army.

In 1917 Stubby was adopted by then–Private John Robert Conroy when the dog wandered onto the Yale University campus where soldiers trained and prepared for their deployment. Stubby endeared himself to all he met and was eventually smuggled overseas where the tough little dog served in the 26th Yankee Division in France for well over a year.[35]

Stubby took part in 17 battles, enduring injuries and assaults in the trenches. But the intrepid dog prevailed, learning to alert his unit to duck for cover from incoming artillery, finding wounded soldiers, warning his humans of lethal gas attack and cheering up his wounded comrades in military hospitals. Stubby even mastered his own manner of saluting, passing a paw across his brow when prompted.[36]

By war's end, the highly decorated Stubby was promoted to the rank of Sergeant and brought back to the states by his owner, where he met the dog-loving Presidents Wilson, Coolidge, and Harding. Eventually he became the mascot for the Hoyas of Georgetown University.[37]

In *Don't Call a Man a Dog*, Will Judy wrote about Harding's love for his own dog, an Airedale terrier named Laddie Boy. In 1921, Judy recalled watching the happy-go-lucky dog as he romped about on the White House lawn.

Judy poignantly recounted how Laddie watched from the sidelines as the president and first lady embarked on their long cross-country automobile journey known as the "Voyage of Understanding."[38] Harding would never return to the White House; he succumbed to congestive heart failure in August of 1923 while visiting the West Coast.

Like Fala would years later, Laddie Boy kept a hopeful and vigilant watch for his master's return and intently inspected every automobile that came into view. Judy recalled how the devoted and once happy dog died consumed with grief, never fully recovering from his loss.

The beloved Rin Tin Tin of cinema fame also made his presence known in America during war time. At only five days old, the legendary German shepherd puppy was discovered among a litter of puppies living in a bombed out war dog kennel in Lorraine, France, in September 1918.[39] A man by the name of Corporal Lee Duncan rescued two pups from the litter, naming them after a pair of popular French puppets known as Rin Tin Tin and Nannette.

Duncan was impressed with the way the Germans had trained their shepherds for their armed forces and aspired to achieve similar results with these pups. He took the two dogs back home to Los Angeles with him, but Nannette succumbed to distemper.[40]

Rin Tin Tin proved to be an intelligent and athletic dog. By 1922 the shepherd was drawing admiration with his feats of agility at local dog exhibitions, where his activities caught the eye of a man named Charles Jones. Jones had been experimenting with a new type of camera that recorded moving pictures and through his camera's lens recorded the talents of this special dog for the world to see.[41]

As talented an actor as he was, even Rin Tin Tin was not spared the rejection experienced by the human members of the film industry. It was only through the tireless persistence of his owner that the shepherd dog found fame as a movie star.

Used on a movie set as an impromptu substitute for an incorrigible wolf, the dog quickly became a hit. His recurring roles in subsequent productions captured the nation's heart and rescued the faltering Warner Brothers Studio from bankruptcy. The original Rin Tin Tin appeared in 26 motion pictures before his death in 1932.[42]

But Duncan had come to understand the true potential of the breed and did not rest on the laurels of Rin Tin Tin's film accomplishments. During the Second World War, with the help of Rin Tin Tin the Third, he convinced the United States Army to establish a military training facility for dogs in Camp Hahn in California. Ultimately over 5,000 dogs and their handlers were trained for military combat under this program.[43]

Will Judy recalled meeting the famous "Rinty," as he was called, when Corporal Duncan brought his dog for an interview for a popular radio show Judy produced for WGN in Chicago. On the occasion of this Sunday afternoon broadcast in the 1930s, Judy recalled how he needed the police to escort him through the throngs that had gathered to meet the German shepherd dog.

During the interview Duncan put the dog through a series of maneuvers. Judy told of how the powerful Rinty knocked Judy and his microphone to the floor with a "mighty leap," and of how he and the dog only "made friends" when the dog was so commanded by his master![44]

The headline of the *Milwaukee Journal* of September 22, 1941, announced, "Defense Will Be Stressed During Nation's Dog Week,"[45] with talks to be given on the subject at 32 local schools. Will Judy's effort to honor our canines of war was catching on as that same year the *Berkley Daily Gazette* of Illinois announced that 200 cities across the nation would hold celebrations for National Dog Week.[46]

In Pennsylvania, the *Reading Eagle* on September 13, 1943, pronounced "5 Dogs Accepted for Armed Forces: Kennel Club Officials Resume Tests Here."[47] These dogs included Bud, a shepherd mix; collies Rover and Spunk; Wow, a Belgian shepherd; and Major, a German shepherd. The article noted that Boots, a German shepherd, and an Airedale named Trixi had been deferred.

Three months later, the *Pittsburgh Gazette* announced "Small Dogs Sought for War Services," noting that "for the first time since Pearl Harbor small dogs are wanted by the K-9 Corps to help win the war."[48] The story went on to note that the Dogs for Defense, Incorporated, the official procurement agency for war dogs, had announced that the War Department was requesting a large number of cocker spaniels, basset hounds in addition to bloodhounds and springer spaniels. That week, a similar call went out in the *Palm Beach Post,* reminding dog owners that dogs needed to be at least one year old and no more than five to be eligible for military deployment.

In a promotional effort during the National Dog Week campaign of 1943, the *Pittsburg Post Gazette* featured a uniformed man posing with a photogenic bull dog. The article announced that children age five through thirteen were encouraged to enter a letter-writing contest by writing to First Class Happy Gismo, Mascot of the local Marine Corps Recruiting Office, telling him how they would treat a dog during the week dedicated to dogs and beyond.[49]

Those civilians who had offered up their cherished canines for the military were not forgotten. "War Dogs Are Treated Kindly," offered a soothing headline in the *Spokane Daily Chronicle* on February 10, 1944. The article was intended to ease the minds of anxious dog owners. Individuals who had pledged their canines to the war effort were assured that their beloved dogs were being carefully tested for physical defects, given two weeks to acclimate to their handlers and new surroundings, and were receiving short training periods while being kept in insulated houses and fed once daily.[50]

By the arrival of National Dog Week 1945, the war had ended, but the contributions of the dogs of war were not forgotten. "Dog to Have His Day Here Marks National Week,"[51] declared the *Milwaukee Journal* in September 1945. That year's observance paid tribute to the members of the K-9 Corps throughout the world with the slogan, "In War, in Peace, Man's Best Friend," with Robert L. Ripley of *Believe It or Not* notoriety serving as the chairman of the observance.

Patriotic war veteran Will Judy was among those who truly understood the ultimate sacrifices dogs had made for the nation. Finally, after a decade of hard work, his notion to help the dogs of the nation brought to light his quest to honor the dogs of war, in addition to ensuring that every dog had a good home and a responsible, caring owner.

From urban centers like New York City and Los Angeles, to small town America, dogs were ready to take center stage. They put on a grand show while posing with celebrities of the entertainment world and luminaries of the elite dog circle, making the last week in September a dog-lover's paradise with no expense spared.

In September 1948, the *Palm Beach Post* declared that the Greater Miami Dog Club, Inc., would pay for the citywide celebrations held for local dogs during that week. Dale Carnegie, Gabriel Heater, and Gene Tunney would serve in the advisory capacity for National Dog Week.[52]

"21st Observance of Dog Week Set," the *New York Times* reported on August 29, 1948, declaring its organizer's express goal was to make that year's twenty-first consecutive observance of National Dog Week the most successful ever.[53]

The ensuing article informed readers that heavyweight boxing champion Gene Tunney, at age 51, would act as the event's chairman during the week of September nineteenth. James Joseph "Gene" Tunney held the title of world heavyweight boxing champion from 1926 to 1928 and had defeated Jack Dempsey two times in 1926, and again in 1927, before retiring undefeated one year later.

The special objectives of this particular celebration urged that every dog be trained in "obedience, guard or other useful work," and that all canines should receive proper care and feeding under "post-war conditions." A third objective concerned itself with the elimination of stray dogs, urging dog owners to control their pets with the use of leashes.

One month later, the heading "A Canine Cavalcade in Plaza of Rockefeller Center"[54] floated above two large photos of National Dog Week being celebrated in all its glory in New York City.

The accompanying article described how over 3,000 observers watched as Tunney, general chairman of the event, and comedian Joe E. Brown, chairman of the New York committee, presided over the activities.

The famous prize fighter and the huge crowd became absorbed in the elaborate pageantry of this event. Members of the North American Sheep Dog Society held a demonstration of border collies herding sheep around the Rockefeller Center Plaza while a parade of 26 different dog breeds was led by Boy Scout Troop 718 of Manhattan. During the procession dog owners and handlers displayed flags of several nations, with an Alaskan malamute named Chisholm's Viking representing Alaska, and a Chesapeake Bay retriever by the name of Laddie's Rowdy wagging his tail and an American flag.

Adding to the spectacle was the appearance of Blanche Sanders, the first lady of poodle obedience. Sanders was a rare breed herself as she was a female dog trainer in what was considered at the time to be primarily a man's profession. Sanders and her entourage of trained poodles became a prominent fixture in future dog week observances.

Throughout the 1940s dog lovers everywhere embraced the concept of National Dog Week wholeheartedly, with its numerous observances recorded at a greater rate in the pages of local newspapers. A *Pittsburgh Post Gazette* headline of 1944 announced, "National Dog Week Brings New Jewelry for Pet Protection Medallion."[55] The *Milwaukee Sentinel* of September 1945 told of how 50 homeless dogs housed by the Humane Society waited to celebrate the week.[56] In 1948, the *Hartford Courant* reported that "Youth Groups Observe National Dog Week."[57] An item in the *Evening Independent* of St. Petersburg, Florida, in 1949 reminded readers that National Dog Week would be celebrated in that city.[58] That year, the *Telegraph* of Nashua, New Hampshire, noted the Salvation Army's involvement in the event.[59]

But not everyone appreciated Will Judy's veneration of dogs as demonstrated in a column titled "Our Town," appearing in the *Toledo Blade* on September 20, 1948, the occasion of Will Judy's fifty-seventh birthday.[60]

The commentary, written by Arthur Peterson, provided a biting review of Will Judy that mocked his dedication to and love of dogs. "Captain Judy edits *Dog World* magazine and has earned himself a couple of yards and hootnanny chevrons for piling up a monumental hunk of fruity prose in honor of the four-footed friends that aint cats!" wrote Peterson.[61]

In this scathing piece Peterson also ridiculed Gene Tunney and his role as chairman of National Dog Week, wondering why an athlete like Tunney wasn't out pursuing women and drink instead of hanging out with dogs of the four-legged variety. Peterson wrote that Tunney's people had been urging him to write something about Dog Week and referred to the pile of clippings of Judy's writing samples as "the fruitiest of material and bilge."[62]

Peterson ended his column wondering if it was possible that the nation had become so dog-obsessed because people "got the dogs for things that we ought to be giving each other and getting from each other?"[63]

Despite its critics and detractors, National Dog Week had come a long way from its humble beginnings. These impressive and tightly orchestrated performances and press coverage helped to usher in a new era of dog training and obedience awareness in America.

In the post–World War II era, Will Judy's challenge remained to remind American dog owners that National Dog Week had been established to provide a voice for those who could not speak for themselves and that the phrase man's best friend also required man to be the dog's best friend.

At the opening ceremonies of the 1952 National Dog Week observance held in midtown Manhattan, photographers stood at the ready as Ace, a four-year-old German shepherd, prepared to jump through a paper-covered hoop flanked by a flurry of American flags. Ace had been chosen among 50 other dogs for this honor.[64]

As Ace hurdled toward his target emblazoned with the words *NATIONAL DOG WEEK*, an enthralled audience watched and waited with great anticipation. The big dog skidded to several stops, which were followed by two more attempts to pass *under* the giant hoop. Ace successfully accomplished this feat on the eighth try. The amused and relieved spectators reacted with laughter and applause.[65]

German shepherds, like the hoop-jumping Ace, stole the spotlight; the American public was fascinated with the highly trainable German shepherd breed was gaining favor due to the popularity of dogs like Rin Tin Tin of motion picture fame.

After Ace jumped *through* his hoop, a four-year-old shepherd named Topper entertained the crowd by retrieving a brown chicken egg and running approximately 50 feet with it before placing the unbroken egg in his owner's hand. His mistress, a Mrs. Theodore Strickland of Greenwich, Connecticut, proceeded to crack the egg in a glass bowl, then offered it as a tasty reward for Topper.[66]

Not to be outdone, five-year-old German shepherd Toots, of Manchester, Connecticut, wowed onlookers as he soared through a *flaming* hoop and then performed as a draft animal, pulling a delighted four-and-a-half-year-old girl in a one-dog shay.[67]

Smaller dog breeds also stole the hearts of that year's National Dog Week celebration. White-haired ankle-high Maltese terriers put on vaudeville-style acts as they jumped over foot-high barriers to retrieve objects almost as large as their bodies.[68]

The following year, another headline in the *New York Times* relayed information about another National Dog Week event held at Rockefeller Center, where 60 well-behaved dogs of a variety of breeds put on a show for an audience that numbered in the thousands.[69] It was announced that breeds of dogs as diverse and exotic as Russian wolfhounds, Lhasa Apsos, and Keeshonden, "all house pets trained by their owner/handlers," demonstrated for the audience the "pleasure of owning or raising an obedient animal."[70]

In the splashy National Dog Week observance of 1952, Ace and Topper shared the spotlight with actress Faye Emerson and actor Johnny Johnston, who co-starred with Shirley Booth in the film *A Tree Grows in Brooklyn,* serving as chairperson and master of ceremonies respectively.[71]

Faye Emerson was a glitzy and popular personality in the early days of television and added a touch of glamour and allure to National Dog Week. Ms. Emerson had once been married to Elliot Roosevelt, the son of Franklin Delano Roosevelt, owner of the fabulous Fala. It is also reported that the television industry's illustrious "Emmy" award was named for her.[72]

Twelve years had elapsed since reporter Bob Becker of the *Chicago Tribune* had posted the seven objectives of National Dog Week. But in the polite orderliness of post–World War II American society, an eighth item noted by Becker was now emphasized. In keeping with the teachings of Will Judy, Becker had proposed that the responsibility of proper dog obedience training be placed on educated dog owners, so as not to infringe on the rights of non-dog owners.

To help carry out this objective, Blanche Saunders and her entourage of obedient and entertaining poodles became a mainstay of National Dog Week observances during the 1950s and 1960s.

Saunders was the daughter of a Baptist minister and a graduate of the Massachusetts Agriculture College. A woman ahead of her times, Saunders began training dogs in 1934, quickly forming a partnership with Mrs. Whitehouse Walker, who had prescribed the modern formula for obedience training in the nation.

Helene Whitehouse Walker was a breeder of standard poodles, a breed that was often regarded as the "sissies" of the dog world. But Walker thought differently and approached dog clubs and breeders about the possibility of holding competitive obedience trials at dog shows similar to those that were being held in England.[73]

By 1933, through her persuasiveness and persistence, Whitehouse Walker had organized the first obedience trial in the United States. Held in Mount Kisco, New York, the event featured eight canine competitors. In 1936, the year dog obedience training was officially recognized by the American Kennel Club,[74] Saunders and Walker embarked on a 10,000 mile transcontinental trek in a 21-foot trailer, showcasing their training abilities, with a mission to spread the word about the benefits of obedient canines. Wherever a dog show was being held, the pair would appear on the scene and put on an exhibition. Through their efforts, the mantra "train your dog" became ingrained in the minds of the American dog owner.[75]

The late 1950s brought Saunders to places as distant as Alaska, instructing dog owners on how to handle and train their pets. On her way back east, via Seattle, she was welcomed by 15 training clubs that had enrolled in advance for her conference. Some traveled as far as 1,500 miles just to meet her and to participate in her training program.[76]

Saunders was the training director with the American Society for the Prevention of Cruelty to Animals in New York City for 16 years. During that time, she oversaw the training of 17,000 dog-human partners. Successful graduates of her course were now knowledgeable dog owners and good canine citizens carrying out the objectives of National Dog Week.[77]

Wherever Saunders and her dogs went, an appreciative crowd was entertained and enlightened. Her pregame demonstrations performed at Yankee Stadium in New York enthralled cheering baseball fans and dog lovers alike. Under the headline "An Astute Dog Judge," a *New York Times* article printed in July of 1961 chronicled the life of the intrepid Ms. Saunders and her enterprising spirit. Through her numerous appearances at National Dog Week events held at Rockefeller Plaza, the news item declared that "she showed out-of-towners what a well-behaved New York pup could do after some obedience training."[78]

Like her colleague Will Judy, Saunders was an accomplished author, writing about her favorite topics: dogs and the importance of intelligent canine ownership. Saunders authored seven books; her first, *Training You to Train Your Dog* (1946), sold more than 100,000 copies.[79]

Despite Judy's best efforts, by the early 1950s it seemed that the dogs of America still suffered from neglect and homelessness. The plight of the homeless dog was spotlighted by Mayor Earl J. Glades of Salt Lake City while observing the National Dog Week of 1952. He commented in the *Deseret News,* "The Humane treatment of dogs and other animals is a responsibility held by all members of civilized society."[80] In that same article, City Pound Superintendent Henry Eskelsen called attention to the large amount of stray dogs that were taken into the pound on a daily basis. At that time, "pound" was the acceptable term for animal shelter, however, in this case, the descriptive term also emphasized the weightiness of the matter.

By the early 1960s, National Dog Week observances took on a lighter tone with their positive slogans, such as "Deserve to Be Your Dog's Best Friend," with the focus on proper dog obedience training remaining a constant.

By 1961, at the personal request of Captain Judy, the sponsorship of National Dog Week was transferred to the Pet Food Institute, who took up the baton in the effort to breed good manners in the nation's canines. The pet food industry wasted no time launching a campaign that offered dog training tips for the nation's dog owners during that September's celebration. In the promotional style of Will Judy, the Pet Food Institute invited readers to contact its headquarters in Chicago for a free training booklet.[81]

In a lighthearted item in the *Palm Beach Post,* a reporter lamented how difficult it was to keep up with the demands of gifts, treats, and attention bestowed on his dog for seven whole days. The following year another reporter for the *Milwaukee Sentinel,* in response to his editor's request for National Dog Week coverage, posted the headline, "Hounded Reporter Wants People Week."[82]

By 1967, five years before the passing of Will Judy, a question posted by a reader to the *Reading Eagle* inquired "what the purpose of National Dog Week was." This question demonstrated that the popularity of National Dog Week had declined, despite great effort on the part of its founder. The editorial response to this reader's inquiry focused on the importance of paying tribute to the thousands of dog breeders who spent large amounts of time, money, and energy to provide the public with breed education and a supply of healthy pups. It went on to say that the mission of National Dog Week was also to appreciate those who cared for and fed homeless animals and shelter pets.[83]

The benefits of intelligent dog breeding continued to be emphasized, as noted in an item in the *Lakeland Ledger* of September 18, 1972. The article reminded dog owners to be knowledgeable about their dog's heredity and instincts when choosing a breed, to ensure the owner's lifestyle and breed were a good fit. This article concluded, "The better the physical and psychological match of pooch to person, the more blessings to count."[84]

In 1973, just shy of Will Judy's death, Italian-American actress Carmelita Pope served as National Dog Week chairperson. The *Lodi News Sentinel* on September 15 told of Ms. Pope's 40,000 mile trek through the nation to promote the cause of pet welfare. "Everywhere I go I see the pleasure that dogs so unselfishly give people," she commented in the true spirit of the observance. The article went on to reinforce the ongoing goals of National Dog Week.[85]

Four years later, a headline in the September 18 *Ocala Star-Banner* summed up the situation when it asked, "Whatever happened to National Dog Week? We're in it—but it's called Pet Responsibility Week," an event that addressed similar themes, but dealt with broader issues.[86]

By November 1970, the American Dog Owners Association (ADOA) was established in Detroit, Michigan, by a man by the name of Duncan Wright and 85 individuals who wanted to stop dog fighting in their area. The ADOA, the first national organization of dog owners and fanciers working together to protect the rights of dogs and their owners, has participated in the promotion of National Dog Week over the past several years.[87]

In the spirit of Will Judy's mission for improving the welfare of canines in America, the ADOA preserved the special relationship between dogs and mankind by protecting and defending the rights of responsible dog ownership.[88]

In the year 2000, an online item on the pet education website sponsored by Doctors Foster and Smith cited Bob Duffy, at the time the executive director of the ADOA, now disbanded, announcing that the theme of that year's event would be "Friends for Life: Companions Forever."[89]

Despite the efforts of dedicated followers and dog week enthusiasts, with the passing of its founder, National Dog Week had disappeared for the most part, as if unleashed, wandering the back roads of America in search of a new master.

But another legend in the dog industry had been exerting his own influence on the state of the dog in the states of the nation, and like Will Judy had, was changing the way modern-day America regarded dogs. That man was Captain Arthur J. Haggerty, regarded by many as the "grandfather of modern dog obedience in America," and just the master needed to lead the week of the dog into a new generation.

9

Captain Arthur J. Haggerty Shares Will Judy's Mission of National Dog Week with a New Generation

An article titled, "Captain Will Judy: An American Original," appeared in the October 2003 issue of *Dog World* magazine. It was followed by the subtitle, "A dedication to dogs and a flair for business established Judy, the founder of *National Dog Week*, as an icon in the sport." The piece was written by a Captain Haggerty, who described Judy as "unique, different, he marched to a different drummer."[1] This extraordinary tribute was written by the late Captain Arthur J. Haggerty, who is often referred to as the "grandfather of modern dog obedience training in America."[2]

It was noted at the time that Haggerty was the youngest member of the Oldtimers of the Kennel World group founded by Judy and an occasional contributor to *Dog World*.[3] Many members of the dog obedience industry cite Haggerty as one of the most influential individuals to have shaped the field.[4]

Although Judy and Haggerty shared a common affection and enthusiasm for all things canine, they were products of very different times, backgrounds and demeanors. Judy wrote in the manner of a spiritual advisor and employed an old-fashioned, gentle approach with his following. In sharp contrast, Haggerty was bold and flamboyant and utilized the modern technologies of television, film and the advent of the internet to get his ideas across.

National Dog Week had been observed just three times by the time Arthur Haggerty was born on December 3, 1931.[5] That year the "Star

Captain Arthur Haggerty elicits a positive response from an obedient client, c. 1980s (courtesy of Babette Haggerty).

Spangled Banner" became the national anthem, the construction of the Empire State building was completed and, fittingly, a wire fox terrier named Ch Pendley Calling of Blarney, a dog breed with an Irish heritage, reigned as the American Kennel Club's Best in Show.[6]

Born to Arthur P. and Helen Jean Haggerty in Manhattan, Arthur and his younger brother Gerard were raised in the Bronx section of New York, in an Irish-American dog-loving family.[7] Haggerty, whose father and grandfather were breeders of Irish setters and Boston terriers, once quipped that he had cut his teeth on a feed pan.[8] In his youth Haggerty preferred dog shows to ball games and by the age of ten he was training dogs; at age fifteen he was showing terriers and boxers.[9]

In the years of his youth, an organized, professional field of dog obedience training had yet to be established in America and the young dog enthusiast set his sights on becoming a professional dog handler.[10]

Those who knew the youthful Haggerty recalled that he displayed the ferocity of a Doberman pincer and the tenacity of a Jack Russell terrier. During his enrollment at Saint Nicholas of Tollentine High School in the Bronx, when faced with a challenge Haggerty "would fight to the death."[11]

Haggerty also served in the United States armed forces, commencing a ten-year military tour that began with the Korean Conflict in 1950. During his service in the United States Army he was awarded a Bronze Star, received for his efforts during the Battle of Pork Chop Hill; he was subsequently awarded three Purple Hearts.[12]

It was during his military career that Haggerty first worked as a professional dog handler, when he served as an Army Ranger and Commanding Officer for the 25th and 26th Scout Dog Platoons.[13]

After completing his active military service, Haggerty joined forces with a colleague named Dick Maller to form the Tri-State School for Dogs, located at several locations in New York. His timing was fortuitous because the crime rate in the region was rising and the need for trained guard dogs was growing.[14]

Not long after opening Tri-State, Haggerty met Betty Ann Lamott at a function for dog enthusiasts. They married and soon afterward he and Maller disbanded their business partnership, allowing Haggerty to create and shape a unique and pioneering center for dogs and their training. He restructured and renamed his enterprise the Captain Haggerty's School for Dogs, which became the largest dog training facility in the nation.[15] With locations in Brooklyn, Queens, Manhattan, the Bronx and upstate New York, Haggerty trained and provided dogs for guard work.[16] Big name department stores like Gimbel's, Macy's, Korvette's, Alexander's, Bonwit Teller, Ohrbach's, and B. Altman, among others, relied on guard dogs professionally trained by Haggerty.[17]

In the early 1960s professional dog training facilities in the nation were essentially nonexistent. Haggerty became a mentor for others in his profession in a manner similar to Will Judy. His services as a "trainer of trainers" were in demand and he went on to pioneer a new field that launched the careers of a new generation of dog professionals.

By the middle of the decade, Captain Haggerty's facility employed seven full-time workers with over 200 satisfied customers. Haggerty's unique stance was based on his belief that not all dogs were created equally. He employed training techniques that focused on specific breed characteristics that shaped the innate instincts of each particular dog.

In a *New York Times* article of 1965, Haggerty discussed his training philosophy by declaring that breeds in particular were not stupid, but some were quick to learn and easier to work with than others. Similar to Blanche Saunders, Haggerty considered standard poodles to make excellent students and also included both miniature and toy poodles in that category.[18]

Haggerty was a master of promotion and marketing and retained his title of captain throughout his career, since he believed it suited his image. He knew it was a moniker people would remember and one that distinguished him as someone who took command of any situation, especially when it involved dogs.

And he could easily take command without the utterance of a single word, for everything about the captain commanded attention and obedience. At a towering six-foot-three, the imposing figure of Haggerty with his large bald head was unforgettable. He was direct and outspoken and was often referred to as the "General Patton" of dog trainers."[19]

In his methods Haggerty was clear and unambiguous and never shy when it came to offering his opinion. He believed the secret of great dog trainers was to let a dog know who was boss. "The dogs don't have to wonder about me, they know exactly what I want."[20]

This point was illustrated by Haggerty's vivid account of an interaction with a client. "Okay, take the dog [that] barks and barks relentlessly. The desperate renter will have to get rid of the dog if the problem isn't fixed," he stated. He proceeded to offer his solution to the problem. "Here's what I do. I wait with the owner in the [building] hallway. Sure enough, the dog starts barking and I explode into the house and scare the living shit out of the dog."[21]

For Haggerty the problem had been resolved in a proper and successful manner. The dog remained alive and in its home and his client had gotten their money's worth. He concluded in his direct manner, "After one session with me—if the owner follows up—the dog lives. Period."[22]

When it came to dog obedience training, Haggerty was "old school." He remarked, "We have a nation filled with sissy dogs."[23] He denounced those dog trainers who espoused the total use of positive reinforcement techniques because he found they did not get the "job" done and referred to their approach as "namby pamby."[24] But even those who attracted this harsh criticism respected him. When he passed in 2006, his daughter Babette, a renowned dog trainer in her own right, recalled how many of them responded with immediate and heartfelt condolences upon hearing of the sad news.[25]

Whether he was training a military or police dog to detect mines, explosives, or drugs, or to search for bodies buried under avalanches, guard stores, sell products, or act out a scene in a movie, Haggerty was admired and respected because his methods worked.

Like Judy had been, Haggerty was also a clever self promoter and marketing mastermind and knew how to run a profitable business while doing what he loved. He never forgot "that it was all about the dogs," and not so much the humans who took credit for training them.[26]

"Too much is being made of technique and equipment," Haggerty complained. It was a source of frustration for him that modern dog trainers who received media attention were quick to take credit for achieving results with their claims of "I was the first to use food," or "I was the first to do this or the first to that." For Haggerty, the most important goal in the dog training field was "helping the client, and helping the dog. End of story."[27]

During his service on the board of The Guild of Animal Theatrical Agents, Haggerty trained countless dogs for Hollywood movies, Broadway shows, and television productions and series. Dogs trained by Haggerty appeared in over 150 film and television productions. Haggerty dogs were even seen on popular soap operas, such as *As the World Turns, All My Children* and *Another World*.

His clientele was diverse, and with his commanding appearance and entertaining style it was just a matter of time before his talents were sought by those in the entertainment industry. Haggerty became the "go to" trainer for the dogs of the rich and famous and the canines that increasingly appeared in television shows, commercials and movies. Celebrities and entertainers such as James Woods, Hugh Hefner, Diane Keaton, Racquel Welsh, Liza Minelli, and Hugh Hefner all sought Haggerty to help them handle and train their dogs.[28]

By the late 1980s Haggerty had carved an enviable niche market that provided dogs for television and print advertisements. In an article that appeared in the *New York Times* in March of 1987, Haggerty discussed the increasing demand for these camera-ready trained dogs. When television and movie producers or advertising agencies needed a qualified canine actor, it was the services of Haggerty they sought. Whether a dog was required to sit quietly and gaze contentedly out a window or perform a series of intricate movements and tricks, Haggerty had the dog for the job and a lucrative branch of his dog training enterprise emerged.

The fee for a dog provided for a commercial and its handler could run as high as $2,000. But it was a good investment; advertising executives understood that animals, especially dogs, won the hearts of consumers and helped to sell almost anything.[29]

Over the past several decades, the sight of a happy, fun-loving dog in a multitude of advertisements has caused consumers to think more positively about products, ranging from tires to coffee makers or insurance. The commercially captivating canines of Arthur Haggerty appeared in more than 450 televised advertisements and contributed to many of those advertising success stories.[30]

Captain Haggerty became the darling of television talk shows with his numerous guest spots. He appeared twice on *The Johnny Carson Show,* three times with Joe Franklin, made eight appearance on *Mike Douglas Midday Live,* and was seen on the sets of the Merv Griffin and David Frost shows. He also made two guest appearances on *Saturday Night Live.*[31]

Most will likely remember him for his 26 appearances on the *Late Night with David Letterman Show.* Haggerty's visits on that set featured him performing stunts with his dogs that always guaranteed a laugh and are said to be the inspiration for the popular "Stupid Pet Tricks" segment that became a staple of *Late Night.*[32]

Given his charismatic demeanor it was inevitable that Haggerty himself would at some point emerge from behind the camera to become part of the on-screen action. He made his first film appearance in 1973 while supplying dogs for the movie *Shamus,* starring Burt Reynolds. Buzz Kulik was the director of the film and spotted Haggerty's imposing figure on location. Kulik thought the dog trainer would make a perfect on-screen "goon" and cast Haggerty in a role that called for him to chase Reynolds through Central Park. For his effort Haggerty endured a smack with a log delivered by Reynolds himself. Despite the roughness endured during his small role, Haggerty thoroughly enjoyed the experience and subsequently appeared in over a dozen film productions.[33]

Haggerty appeared in additional film and television roles that included small parts in such movies as *Married to the Mob, The Last*

Embrace, The Eyes of Laura Mars, The Great Gatsby, Home Movies and *Honeymoon in Vegas.* He also appeared in the television pilots for *Just for Fun with Bill Boggs, Murder Ink,* and *Nero Wolfe.*[34] He appeared in over 65 commercials and his likeness served as the inspiration for the original "Mr. Clean," before the famous icon was animated.[35]

Haggerty also worked and appeared in live theatre productions. He trained Sandy, the beloved dog of the Broadway production of *Annie,* and took to the stage as well appearing in the productions of *On the Rocks, The Sellout,* and *The Prophet.*[36]

Similar to Judy, Haggerty also enjoyed success as an author specializing in the dog book market. He is credited for writing over 1,000 articles on dogs and many of his books were the recipients of awards presented by the venerable Dog Writers Association of America (DWAA).

Among his many publishing accomplishments Haggerty is credited for writing the dog training section for the Encyclopedia Britannica. Books he authored include *Dog Tricks,* written with trainer Carol Lea Benjamin, *The American Breeds, How to Get Your Pet Into Show Business, How to Teach Your Dog to Talk, Service Dogs: Their Training and Employment,* and one of a more contemplative approach, *The Zen Method of Dog Training,* a book he worked on for several years but never completed.[37]

Despite all his accomplishments in the theatrical and literary world, it was the more serious work he performed with dogs that really made a difference in the lives of humans and showcased the amazing capabilities of our canines. From his work as the civilian consultant to the United States Army's Dog Breeding Program at the Aberdeen Proving Grounds in Maryland for the Super Dog Program, in which he trained scout dogs to patrol for and detect explosives, to his work on the *Aggression Newsletter,* Haggerty never forgot to inform his readers about the value of dogs to humans.[38]

During the activities surrounding the 133rd Annual Westminster Kennel Club Dog Show in 2009, Babette Haggerty presented writer/producer Harris Done with the Captain Arthur J. Haggerty Award from the Alliance of Purebred Dog Writers. This award was bestowed on Done for his documentary *War Dogs of the Pacific.* The film documented the bond between a platoon of young marines and the dogs that were trained to serve them during World War II.[39]

The moving stories of "ordinary" dog owners who donated their beloved pets to the war effort were also presented. Many of these people never saw their dogs again and several soldiers who became deeply attached to these dogs had to relinquish them to their original owners by the end of the war. The soldiers in the documentary shared their first-person accounts and powerful memories of these events.

War Dogs of the South Pacific exemplified the causes and concerns surrounding service and military dogs in a manner that Will Judy had hoped to accomplish with the continued observances of National Dog Week over the years. Haggerty believed it was important for dog lovers of America to become reacquainted with Judy's legacy and began a personal crusade to honor his mentor and to revive America's interest in what was referred to as the National Dog Week movement.

Will Judy, in his role as publisher of *Dog World*, toiled in his Chicago office late into the evening clacking away on an old-fashioned manual typewriter and ringing up colleagues on a pedestal phone. He had much to say about the welfare of canines, but may have been disheartened by those who have termed his era as "the Silent Generation," due to its lack of high-tech communication outlets.

Despite being a member of that generation, there was nothing silent about Judy as he utilized whatever methods were available to him at the time as a means to reach the public. Those busy pages of *Dog World* were infused with the distinct personality of its creator, and Judy's editorials concerning the welfare of dogs were always passionate and written from the heart.[40] With a myriad of classified ads and testimonials, an issue of *Dog World* was the equivalent of a modern day website and provided information for both the average American dog owner, enthusiast and those who made their living working with dogs.

Years later when Haggerty opened his pioneering Tri-State School for Dogs, the medium of television had been only available to most Americans for approximately 20 years. He utilized this relatively new media outlet to promote himself, his training philosophies, and some camera-ready canines.

In 2003 Haggerty paid the ultimate tribute to Judy and his cherished National Dog Week movement on the pages of *Dog World* and in 2005 launched a website dedicated to the observance of National Dog Week. The site was a veritable dog week central that aimed to engage a new generation of supporters for its observance.

Haggerty's website presented a documentation of how National Dog Week had evolved over the decades, complete with photos of past celebrations, tips to help carry out Judy's mission during these special seven days and a sample "Proclamation" to be used by ordinary citizens to get their city, town, and state officials to officially recognize National Dog Week for their communities. In crediting those who played a major role in many organized National Dog Week observances, Haggerty gave special mention to Harry Miller and Evelyn Monte of the Gaines Dog Research Center and dog trainer Blanche Saunders.[41]

At the heart of the now inactive site was Haggerty's poignant reminder to Americans that "dogs have always been at our sides to comfort and help us," urging his supporters to "return all those favors bestowed on us by the dog."[42]

Haggerty shared that people of all ages and from all walks of life could contribute to and participate in National Dog Week. He suggested numerous ways in which they could participate that ranged from simple steps to grand gestures. He called for citizens to become dog week ambassadors and encouraged independent action. "You can do it on your own," he declared. "There is no need for you as an individual or club to clear everything through the NDW Committee." In exchange for their efforts, individuals and groups were to receive official recognition on the National Dog Week website.[43]

Haggerty reached out to dog lovers and urged them to become grassroot volunteers in an effort to generate publicity through the use of press releases and the media. He shared tips gleaned through his own experience in the film and television industry and advised those who spoke for National Dog Week and its mission to "focus on what you want to discuss." He recommended that those who were new to public speaking should rehearse their presentations using sound bites of three or four words to get ideas and points across. He coached his messengers on how to deflect the inevitable difficult questions of naysayers and negative interviewers and suggested they request the services of a "wise guy" to pose a few tricky practice questions.[44]

He encouraged promoters of National Dog Week to organize demonstrations in conjunction with local dog clubs, dog obedience schools, and other relevant institutions. When approaching schools about arranging events he suggested introducing the topic of dog safety and to involve local police and fire departments and their trained canines.[45]

Despite his industry experience and popularity, Haggerty faced challenges in his efforts to promote the National Dog Week movement. The turbulent economic conditions that existed in 2005 were similar to

National Dog Week
Sept. 19-25
2011
Help Bring it Back!

2011 National Dog Week poster, "Help Bring It Back," created by Oregon-based artist Donald E. Brown.

those that had plagued Judy's launch of its initial observance. Haggerty was an astute businessman and navigated these obstacles. He advised those involved in National Dog Week efforts to carry out activities "on the cheap," and to approach media personalities known to be dog-friendly and willing to be generous with their help during tough economic times.[46]

Haggerty suggested that simple press releases be accompanied with a photo to keep things "visually interesting." When dog week advocates were ready to stage their first media presentations, they used venues such as restaurants that were dog-friendly, animal shelters, pet supply chains, and shopping malls. With a bag full of simple dog treats and a handful of publicity material everyone could be on the National Dog Week press team.

Haggerty stated that it was the dogs themselves that were ultimately the best promoters of National Dog Week. He encouraged dog lovers and enthusiasts to promote their favorite dogs through local breed and rescue groups, kennel clubs, and through their own personal businesses. If you happened to know an American Kennel Club "show dog," or a local dog hero, he suggested that they be invited to make a personal appearance at an event.[47]

Directing a dog-loving nation through his website, Haggerty served as a cheerleader, coach and caring contributor to this cause closest to his heart. Those reading his heartfelt pleas on behalf of Will Judy's National Dog Week movement couldn't help but to come away with a desire to be part of the cause.

As a special tribute to his hero, Captain William Lewis Judy, Haggerty shared an excerpt from Judy's "Why the World Likes Dogs" that Judy had printed in *Don't Call a Man a Dog*. The essay poignantly reflected the feelings both held for man's best friend and began with the line, "The most unselfish living thing in the world is your dog.... The most patient thing in the world is your dog." The remainder of the poem extolled dogs as the most grateful, friendly, forgiving and overall most perfect living thing on the planet.[48]

Haggerty also presented a section titled the "National Dog Week Proclamation," where he encouraged participants to have the week "proclaimed" by community leaders of large cities, small towns, and governors of states. He urged a grassroots approach and requested anyone with political connections to approach their local officials. Everyone's contributions were equally important. He stated that a lack of connections shouldn't hold a person back from seeking the help of those in office.[49]

Arthur Haggerty was a motivator and a leader who offered a mission accompanied by a plan of action. He provided a sample proclamation to be adapted regionally across the nation; he urged everyone "to use your imagination," and he made it clear that all were free to script their own by stating, "We welcome additions."[50]

Photograph of a patriotic National Dog Week celebrant taken by photographer Joseph Frasciello, recognized as the official image for National Dog Week 2012 (courtesy J. Frazz studios).

National Dog Week Proclamation

Whereas, this is the 82nd Anniversary of National Dog Week, and whereas, the dog has valiantly served humans for 17,000 years, and whereas, the dog has served us in war and peace, and whereas, the dog has distinguished itself by delivering the life-saving serum in [insert town or city], and whereas, dogs such as Chips and the Marines Devil Dogs have fought for the United States during World War I, and World War II, whereas, other dogs followed in this pattern during Korea, Vietnam, Afghanistan and Iraq, and whereas, dogs worked around the clock after 9/11 to find buried people and continued on under the most adverse conditions to find bodies to offer the families closure, and whereas, dogs have helped children with deep-seated psychological problems in many programs to help them adjust, and whereas, the visually handicapped have been guided by dogs in the country for over 80 years, Be it resolved that September ___ through September ___will be proclaimed National Dog Week in the year ____.

Therefore, I, _____, Mayor of the City of _____, affix my signature to this proclamation for all the dogs on this date _____.[51]

With Haggerty's passing in 2006, the dogs of America lost another best friend. One can only imagine what might have been had he lived long enough to see his vision for National Dog Week realized. Now it would be up to the professed dog lovers of the nation to carry on the tradition of National Dog Week and its mission.

Just as much of our national history is recorded in the written word, so too is the history of the American dog. Among those rows upon rows of dog books at your local book store you probably will not find one published by Will Judy. However, the spirit of his work and what he hoped to accomplish is often contained in the pages of these books written by authors who may never have heard of Will Judy and his influence on the modern American dog and their owners.

Humans help dogs and dogs help humans; end of story, as Arthur Haggerty might have declared. But the story of Will Judy and his legacies of *Dog World* magazine and National Dog Week are in actuality the beginning of a great story—a tale that has no ending for those who wish to keep the pages turning.

Chapter Notes

Preface

1. "Pets by the Numbers," The Humane Society of the United States, 27 September 2013, accessed December 2013, http://www.humanesociety.org/issues/pet_overpopulation/facts/pet_ownership_st atistics.html.
2. Captain Arthur Haggerty, "Captain Will Judy: An American Original," *Dog World*, October 2003, 64.
3. Ibid.
4. Will Judy, *Don't Call a Man a Dog* (Chicago: Judy Publishing Co., 1949), 68.
5. Ibid., 7.
6. Captain Arthur Haggerty, "National Dog Week: History of National Dog Week," defunct website.
7. Ibid.
8. Steve Dale, "A Salute to Captain Arthur Haggerty," *Hartford Courant* via Tribune Media Services, 5 July 2006.
9. Captain Arthur Haggerty, "National Dog Week: History of National Dog Week," defunct website.
10. Will Judy, *Don't Call a Man a Dog*, 114.
11. Ibid., 7.
12. Ibid., 102.
13. Will Judy, "Who Is to Be Blamed for Low Sales Prices in the Dog Field!" *Dog World*, September 1958, 6.
14. Will Judy, *Don't Call a Man a Dog*, 20.
15. Will Judy, "Barks: The Livest Page of Dog News in America," *Dog World*, February 1925.
16. Will Judy, *Don't Call a Man a Dog*, 27.
17. "Pet Overpopulation," The Humane Society of the United States, accessed December 2013, http://www.humanesociety.org/issues/pet_overpopulation.
18. Will Judy, *Don't Call a Man a Dog*, 13.
19. Ibid., 8.
20. Ibid., 28.

Chapter 1

1. Will Judy, *Don't Call a Man a Dog*, 27.
2. "English-Word Information," accessed December 2013, http://wordinfo.info/unit/3465/page:2.
3. Will Judy, *Don't Call a Man a Dog*, 17.
4. Ibid.
5. Ibid., 22.
6. Ibid.
7. Ibid.
8. Ibid.
9. Ibid., 23.
10. Ibid., 16.
11. Ibid.
12. "Regarding Henry: A 'Bergh's-Eye' View of 148 Years at the ASPCA," American Society for the Provention of Cruelty to Animals, accessed December 2013, http://www.aspca.org/about-us/about-the-aspca/history-aspca.
13. "How American Humane Association Began," American Humane Association, accessed December 2013, http://www.americanhumane.org/about-us/who-we-are/history.
14. Will Judy, *Men and Things: Fifty Essays About Human Nature, the Ways of Men, and Their Private and Public Conduct* (Chicago: Judy Publishing Co., 1927), 61–62.

15. "The Foremother to American Animal Advocacy: Caroline Earle White," American Anti-Vivisection Society, accessed December 2013, http://www.aavs.org/site/c.bkLTKfOSLhK6E/b.6452381/k.1E3C/The_Foremother_to_American_Animal_Advocacy.htm.

16. "Vernon and Irene Castle," Wikipedia, accessed December 2013, http://en.wikipedia.org/wiki/Vernon_and_Irene_Castle.

17. "Our History," Orphans of the Storm, http://www.orphansofthestorm.org/About/OurHistory.html.

18. "Stands by Helpless as 90 Dogs Burn," *Pittsburgh Post-Gazette*, 2 February 1930.

19. "Champion of All Dogs," *Spokesman-Review*, 31 July 1936.

20. Will Judy, *Don't Call a Man a Dog*, 26.

21. Ibid., 27.

22. Alan Jalowitz, "Judy, William Lewis," 5 November 2009, http://pabook.libraries.psu.edu/palitmap/bios/Judy_Will.html.

23. *Somerset Daily American* 24 May 1938.

24. "Garrett, Pennsylvania," Wikipedia, accessed December 2013, http://wikipedia.org/wiki/Garrett,_Pennsylvania.

25. Will Judy, *Don't Call a Man a Dog*, 75.

26. "The Story Behind Dog World Magazine" *Boxer Reviews*,October 1956 (Press Release).

27. "Basic Beliefs Within the Church of the Brethren," Brethren Rivival Fellowship, 18 November 2009, http://www.brfwitness.org/?p=88.

28. Maxwell Riddle, "Two Memories of Will Judy and a Look at *Dog World*'s Roots," *Dog World*, January 1991, 34.

29. Alan Jalowitz, "Judy, William Lewis," 5 November 2009, http://pabook.libraries.psu.edu/palitmap/bios/Judy_Will.html.

30. "Native Son to Talk," *Somerset Daily American*, 24 May 1938.

31. Ibid.

32. Ibid.

33. "The Story Behind Dog World Magazine" *Boxer Reviews*,October 1956 (Press Release).

34. "Native Son to Talk," *Somerset Daily American*, 24 May 1938.

35. Alan Jalowitz, "Judy, William Lewis," 5 November 2009, http://pabook.libraries.psu.edu/palitmap/bios/Judy_Will.html.

36. Will Judy, *A Soldier's Diary: A Day to Day Record in the World War* (Chicago: Judy Publishing Co., 1930), 9.

37. Ibid.

38. Ibid.

39. Ibid.

40. Ibid.

41. "The Story Behind *Dog World* Magazine," *Boxer Review*, October 1956, 1.

42. Ibid.

43. Ibid.

44. "Dog World Rate Card," *Dog World*, February 1925, 3.

45. "The Story Behind *Dog World* Magazine," *Boxer Review*, October 1956, 2.

46. Captain Arthur Haggerty, "Captain Will Judy: An American Original," *Dog World*, October 2003, 65.

47. Mary Ellen Tarman, "Old *Dog Worlds*: A Bountiful Yield for the Canine Collector," *Canine Collectibles Quarterly*, Winter 1993.

48. Ibid., 4.

49. Promotional material (possibly from a book cover) hand-dated 1945 (Juniata College).

50. "The Story Behind *Dog World* Magazine," *Boxer Review*, October 1956, 1.

51. Ibid.

52. Ibid.

53. Ibid.

54. Ibid.

55. "The Story Behind *Dog World* Magazine," *Boxer Review*, October 1956, 2.

56. Ibid.

57. *Capt. Judy Retires from Dog World After 36 Years*, promotional material (Juniata College Alumni File, 1958).

58. Ibid.

59. *The Big 6*, promotional material (Juniata College Alumni File).

60. Ibid.

61. Ibid.

62. *Capt. Judy Retires from Dog World After 36 Years*, promotional material (Juniata College Alumni File, 1958).

63. Will Judy, "The Female," 3rd edition (Chicago: Judy Publishing Co., 1963).

64. John Wall, Dir. Media Relations, Juniata College, e-mail message to author regarding the Will Judy Lectureship Fund (1958), 19 November 2009.

65. Ibid.
66. *The Big 6*, promotional material (Juniata College Alumni File).
67. Captain Arthur Haggerty, "Captain Will Judy: An American Original," *Dog World*, October 2003, 65.
68. Ibid.
69. Will Judy, *Don't Call a Man a Dog*, 28.
70. Ibid., 26.
71. Alan Jalowitz, "Judy, William Lewis," 5 November 2009, http://pabook.libraries. psu.edu/palitmap/bios/Judy_Will.html.
72. Ibid.

Chapter 2

1. Will Judy, *Don't Call a Man a Dog*, 7.
2. Ibid.
3. Ibid.
4. Ibid.
5. Ibid.
6. Nancy Pearl, "These Books Have Gone to the Dogs," 6 November 2006, accessed January 2014, http://www.npr.org/templates/story/story.php?storyId=6431059.
7. Ibid.
8. Beautiful Joe Heritage Society, http://beautifuljoe.org.
9. "Beautiful Joe," Wikipedia, http://en.wikipedia.org/wiki/Beautiful_Joe.
10. Ibid.
11. Will Judy, *Don't Call a Man a Dog*, 2.
12. Ibid.
13. Ibid., front dust jacket.
14. Ibid., 5.
15. Ibid.
16. Ibid.
17. Ibid.
18. Ibid., 7.
19. Ibid., 8.
20. Ibid., 83.
21. Ibid.
22. Ibid., 84.
23. Ibid.
24. Ibid., 86.
25. Ibid., 13.
26. Ibid.
27. Ibid.
28. Ibid., 14.
29. Ibid.
30. Ibid., 15.
31. Ibid.

32. Ibid.
33. Ibid., 16.
34. Ibid.
35. Ibid.
36. Ibid., 17.
37. Ibid.
38. Ibid.
39. Ibid., 24.
40. Ibid.
41. Ibid., 25.
42. Ibid.
43. Ibid.
44. Ibid., 26.
45. Ibid., 28.
46. Ibid.
47. Ibid.
48. Ibid.
49. Ibid., 29.
50. Ibid., 30.
51. Ibid., 32.
52. Ibid., 46.
53. Ibid., 31.
54. Ibid., 48.
55. Ibid., 52.
56. Ibid., 36.
57. Ibid., 37.
58. Ibid., 38.
59. Ibid.
60. Ibid., 40.
61. Ibid.
62. Ibid.
63. Ibid.
64. Ibid., 43.
65. Ibid., 45.
66. Ibid.
67. Ibid., 46.
68. Ibid., 47.
69. Ibid.
70. Ibid., 49.
71. Ibid., 48.
72. Ibid.
73. Ibid., 49.
74. Ibid.
75. Ibid., 50.
76. Ibid., 52.
77. Ibid.
78. Ibid.
79. Ibid.
80. Ibid.
81. Ibid.
82. Ibid., 57.
83. Ibid., 53.
84. Ibid.
85. Ibid.
86. Ibid.
87. Ibid., 55.
88. Ibid., 54.

89. Ibid., 57.
90. Ibid., 58.
91. Ibid., 59.
92. Ibid., 60.
93. Ibid.
94. Ibid., 62.
95. Ibid.
96. Ibid.
97. Ibid., 64.
98. Ibid.
99. Ibid.
100. Ibid., 66.
101. Ibid., 67.
102. Ibid., 68.
103. Ibid.
104. Ibid.
105. Ibid., 70.
106. Ibid., 69.
107. Ibid., 70.
108. Ibid.
109. Ibid., 79.
110. Ibid.
111. Ibid., 73.
112. Ibid., 76.
113. Ibid.
114. Ibid., 77.
115. Ibid., 78.
116. Ibid.
117. Ibid., 79.
118. Ibid.
119. Ibid.
120. Ibid., 80.
121. Ibid., 81.
122. Ibid., 82.
123. Ibid.
124. Ibid., 88.
125. Ibid., 90.
126. Ibid., 99.
127. Ibid., 100.
128. Ibid.
129. Ibid., 97.
130. Ibid., 112.
131. Ibid.
132. Ibid., 113.
133. Ibid.
134. Ibid.
135. Ibid.
136. Ibid., 112.
137. Ibid.
138. Ibid., 114.
139. Ibid.
140. Ibid.
141. Ibid., 115.
142. Ibid.
143. Ibid., 124.
144. Ibid.
145. Ibid.
146. Ibid., 120.
147. Ibid.
148. Ibid.
149. Ibid., 121.
150. Ibid.
151. Ibid.
152. Ibid., 93.
153. Ibid.
154. Ibid., 102.
155. Ibid.
156. Ibid.
157. "Ben Hur Lampman," Oregon Poetic Voices, accessed January 2014, http://oregonpoeticvoices.org/poet/2.
158. Judy, *Don't Call a Man a Dog*, 140.
159. Ibid.
160. Ibid.
161. Ibid., 141.
162. Ibid., 127.
163. Ibid.
164. Ibid., 136.
165. Ibid.
166. Ibid.
167. Ibid., 138.
168. Ibid.
169. Ibid.
170. Ibid.
171. Ibid.
172. Ibid.
173. Ibid., 146.
174. Ibid.
175. Ibid.
176. Ibid., 136.
177. Ibid.
178. Ibid., 148.
179. Ibid., 148.
180. Ibid., 149.
181. Ibid.
182. Ibid., 150.
183. Ibid., 151.
184. Ibid.
185. Ibid., 152.
186. Ibid., 153.
187. Ibid.

Chapter 3

1. Will Judy, *Training the Dog* (Chicago: Judy Publishing Co., 1941), x.
2. Will Judy, *Training the Dog* (Chicago: Judy Publishing Co., 1953).
3. Ibid., 176.
4. Ibid., 4.
5. Ibid., 5.
6. Ibid.

7. Ibid.
8. Ibid.
9. Ibid.
10. Ibid.
11. Ibid.
12. Ibid.
13. Ibid., 6.
14. Ibid.
15. Ibid.
16. Ibid.
17. Will Judy, *Training the Dog* (Chicago: Judy Publishing Co., 1932), 9.
18. Ibid., 52.
19. Ibid., 54.
20. Ibid. 52.
21. Ibid.
22. Ibid.
23. Ibid., 56.
24. Ibid.
25. Ibid.
26. Ibid.
27. Ibid., 57.
28. Ibid., 76.
29. Ibid.
30. Ibid.
31. Ibid.
32. Ibid.
33. Ibid., 53.
34. Ibid., 78.
35. Ibid., 52.
36. Ibid.
37. Will Judy, *Training the Dog* (Chicago: Judy Publishing Co., 1941), 80.
38. Ibid., 46.
39. Will Judy, *Training the Dog* (Chicago: Judy Publishing Co., 1932), 42.
40. Will Judy, *Training the Dog* (Chicago: Judy Publishing Co., 1941), 42.
41. Will Judy, *Training the Dog* (Chicago: Judy Publishing Co., 1932).
42. Ibid., 42.
43. Will Judy, *Training the Dog* (Chicago: Judy Publishing Co., 1941), 16.
44. Ibid.
45. Ibid.
46. Ibid., 17.
47. Ibid., 18.
48. Ibid., 20.
49. Ibid., 15.
50. Ibid., 16.
51. Ibid.
52. Ibid.
53. Ibid., 22.
54. Ibid.
55. Ibid.
56. Ibid., 148.
57. Ibid.
58. Ibid., 149.
59. Ibid.
60. Ibid.
61. Ibid., 150.
62. Ibid., 151.
63. Ibid.
64. Ibid.
65. Ibid., 16.
66. Ibid., 84.
67. Ibid.
68. Ibid., 85.
69. Ibid., 84.
70. Ibid., 85.
71. Ibid., 86.
72. Ibid.
73. Will Judy, *Training the Dog* (Chicago: Judy Publishing Co., 1932), 36.
74. Ibid.
75. Ibid.
76. Ibid., 35.
77. Ibid.
78. Ibid.
79. Ibid., 36.
80. Ibid., 37.
81. Ibid.
82. Ibid., 103.
83. Ibid.
84. Ibid.
85. Ibid.
86. Ibid.
87. Ibid., 104.
88. Ibid.
89. Ibid.
90. Ibid., 105.
91. Ibid., 104.
92. Ibid.
93. Ibid.
94. Ibid., 105.
95. Ibid.
96. Ibid., 106.
97. Ibid.
98. Ibid.
99. Ibid., 107.
100. Ibid.
101. Ibid.
102. Ibid., 108.
103. Ibid.
104. Ibid., 107.
105. Iibd.
106. Ibid., 110.
107. Ibid.
108. Ibid.
109. Ibid.
110. Ibid., 108.
111. Ibid.
112. Ibid.
113. Ibid.

114. Ibid., 109.
115. Ibid.
116. Ibid.
117. Ibid.
118. Ibid.
119. Ibid.
120. Ibid.
121. Ibid., 110.
122. Ibid.
123. Ibid.
124. Will Judy, *Training the Dog* (Chicago: Judy Publishing Co., 1941), 145.
125. Will Judy, *Training the Dog* (Chicago: Judy Publishing Co., 1932), 120.
126. Will Judy, *Training the Dog* (Chicago: Judy Publishing Co., 1941), 97.
127. Ibid.
128. Ibid.
129. Ibid.
130. Ibid., 98.
131. Ibid.
132. Ibid., 142.
133. Ibid.
134. Ibid.
135. Ibid.
136. Ibid.
137. Ibid.
138. Ibid., 143.
139. Will Judy, *Training the Dog* (Chicago: Judy Publishing Co., 1953), 151.
140. Ibid., 150.
141. Iibd., 152.
142. Ibid.
143. Ibid.
144. Will Judy, *Training the Dog* (Chicago: Judy Publishing Co., 1941), 150.
145. Will Judy, *Training the Dog* (Chicago: Judy Publishing Co., 1953), 150.
146. Will Judy, *Training the Dog* (Chicago: Judy Publishing Co., 1941), 144.
147. Ibid.
148. Ibid.
149. Will Judy, *Training the Dog* (Chicago: Judy Publishing Co., 1953), 153.
150. Ibid.
151. Ibid., 154.
152. Ibid.
153. Ibid.
154. Ibid.
155. Ibid.
156. Ibid.
157. Ibid.
158. Ibid.
159. Ibid.
160. Ibid., 156.
161. Ibid.
162. Ibid.
163. Ibid.
164. Ibid.
165. Ibid.
166. Ibid.
167. Ibid.
168. Ibid., 157.
169. Ibid.
170. Ibid., 156.
171. Ibid.
172. Ibid., 173.
173. Ibid., 174.
174. Ibid.
175. Ibid.
176. Ibid.
177. Ibid.
178. Ibid.
179. Ibid., 175.
180. Ibid.
181. Ibid.
182. Ibid., 176.
183. Ibid., 175.
184. Ibid., 176.
185. Ibid.
186. Ibid.
187. Ibid., 10.

Chapter 4

1. Will Judy, *Handy Dog Booklets: Anatomy of the Dog* (Chicago: Judy Publishing Co., 1948), 2.
2. Ibid., 3.
3. Ibid., 15.
4. Ibid.
5. Will Judy, *Handy Dog Booklets: Handling the Mating of Dogs* (Chicago: Judy Publishing Co., 1950), 3.
6. Ibid.
7. Ibid., 4.
8. Ibid., 9.
9. Ibid., 3.
10. Will Judy, *Handy Dog Booklets: The Stud Dog's Care and Management* (Chicago: Judy Publishing Co., 1951), 3.
11. Ibid.
12. Ibid.
13. Ibid.
14. Ibid., 5.
15. Ibid.

16. Ibid., 6.

17. Will Judy, *Handy Dog Booklets: Feeding the Dog* (Chicago: Judy Publishing Co., 1950), 2.

18. Ibid.

19. Ibid.

20. Ibid.

21. Ibid., 10.

22. Ibid., 13.

23. Ibid., 8.

24. Ibid.

25. Ibid.

26. Ibid.

27. Ibid., 9.

28. Ibid., 10.

29. Ibid.

30. Ibid.

31. Ibid.

32. Ibid.

33. Ibid.

34. Ibid., 9.

35. Ibid., 10.

36. Ibid., 11.

37. Ibid., 15.

38. Ibid., 13.

39. Ibid., 11.

40. Ibid.

41. Ibid.

42. Ibid., 16.

43. Will Judy, *Handy Dog Booklets: Housebreaking the Dog* (Chicago: Judy Publishing Co., 1948), 3.

44. Ibid., 5.

45. Ibid., 14.

46. Ibid.

47. Ibid., 5.

48. Ibid., 16.

49. Ibid., 12.

50. Ibid., 6.

51. Ibid.

52. Will Judy, *Handy Dog Booklets: Puppies and Their Care* (Chicago: Judy Publishing Co., 1951), 2.

53. Ibid.

54. Ibid.

55. Ibid., 3.

56. Will Judy, *Handy Dog Booklets: Laws on Dogs* (Chicago: Judy Publishing Co., 1949), 2.

57. Ibid.

58. Ibid.

59. Ibid.

60. Ibid.

61. Ibid.

62. Ibid.

63. Ibid.

64. Ibid., 3.

65. Ibid., 4.

66. Ibid., 3.

67. Ibid.

68. Ibid.

69. Ibid.

70. Ibid.

71. Ibid.

72. Ibid., 4.

73. Ibid.

74. Ibid.

75. Ibid.

76. Ibid.

77. Ibid., 11.

78. Will Judy, *Handy Dog Booklets: How to Sell Dogs* (Chicago: Judy Publishing Co., 1951), 2.

79. Ibid.

80. Ibid.

81. Ibid.

82. Ibid., 3.

83. Ibid.

84. Ibid.

85. Ibid.

86. Ibid., 4.

87. Ibid., 8.

88. Ibid.

89. Ibid., 4.

90. Ibid.

91. Ibid., 6.

92. Ibid., 14.

93. Ibid.

94. Ibid.

95. Ibid.

96. Will Judy, *Handy Dog Booklets: How To Ship Dogs* (Chicago: Judy Publishing Co., 1951), 10.

97. Ibid.

98. Ibid., 11.

99. Will Judy, *Handy Dog Booklets: The Dog in the Show Ring* (Chicago: Judy Publishing Co., 1950), 3.

100. Will Judy, *Handy Dog Booklets: Dog Shows and Rules* (Chicago: Judy Publishing Co., 1951), 3.

101. Ibid.

102. Ibid.

103. Ibid., 4.

104. Ibid., 5.

105. Will Judy, *Handy Dog Booklets: The Dog in the Show Ring* (Chicago: Judy Publishing Co., 1950), 3.

106. Ibid.

107. Ibid.

108. Will Judy, *Handy Dog Booklets: Dog Shows and Rules* (Chicago: Judy Publishing Co., 1951), 8.

109. Ibid., 6.

110. Ibid., 9.
111. Ibid.
112. Ibid.
113. Ibid., 10.
114. Will Judy, *Handy Dog Booklets: The Dog in the Show Ring* (Chicago: Judy Publishing Co., 1950), 4.
115. Ibid.
116. Ibid.
117. Ibid., 6.
118. Ibid.
119. Ibid., 7.
120. Ibid., 8.
121. Ibid.
122. Ibid., 7.
123. Ibid.
124. Ibid., 8.
125. Ibid.
126. Ibid.
127. Ibid.
128. Ibid., 9.
129. Ibid.
130. Ibid., 10.
131. Ibid., 11.
132. Ibid., 12.
133. Ibid., 14.
134. Ibid., 11.
135. Ibid., 12.
136. Will Judy, *Handy Dog Booklets: Dog Shows and Rules* (Chicago: Judy Publishing Co., 1951), 16.
137. Ibid.
138. Ibid.
139. Ibid.
140. Ibid.
141. Will Judy, *Handy Dog Booklets: The Dog in the Show Ring* (Chicago: Judy Publishing Co., 1950), 16.

Chapter 5

1. Will Judy, *Men and Things* (Chicago: Judy Publishing Co., 1927).
2. Ibid., title page.
3. Ibid., inside cover.
4. Ibid.
5. Ibid., dedication page.
6. Dugald Chaffee, "Edmund B. Chaffee and the Labor Temple," *The Courier: Syracuse University Library Associates* Vol. XI, number 1, accessed January 2014, http://surface.syr.edu/libassoc/31.
7. Will Judy, *Men and Things* (Chicago: Judy Publishing Co., 1927), back dust jacket.

8. Ibid.
9. Ibid.
10. Ibid., introduction.
11. Ibid.
12. Ibid.
13. Ibid.
14. Ibid., 14.
15. Ibid., 61.
16. Ibid., 63.
17. Ibid., 89.
18. Ibid., 115.
19. Ibid., 117.
20. Ibid.
21. Ibid., 119.
22. Ibid., 121.
23. Ibid., 122.
24. Ibid., 123.
25. Ibid., 122.
26. Ibid., 123.
27. Ibid.
28. Will Judy, *A Soldier's Diary* (Chicago: Judy Publishing Co., 1930), 216.
29. Ibid.
30. Weimar Port, *Chicago the Pagan* (Chicago: Judy Publishing Co., 1953), title page.
31. Ibid.
32. Will Judy, *Sayings of Rammikar* (Chicago: Judy Publishing Co., 1962), title page.
33. Ibid., 6.
34. Ibid.
35. Ibid., 8.
36. Ibid.
37. Ibid.
38. Ibid.
39. Ibid., 9.
40. Ibid.
41. Ibid., publisher's note, 7.
42. Ibid., 54.
43. Ibid., 55.
44. Ibid., 159.
45. Ibid.
46. "Will Judy Lectureship Fund (1958)," Juniata College, http://www.juniata.edu/services/activities/speakers/sponsors/will_judy.html.
47. Ibid.

Chapter 6

1. Cover, *Dog World*, February 1925.
2. Will Judy, *Don't Call a Man a Dog* (Chicago: Judy Publishing Co., 1949), 136.

3. Cover, *Dog World*, February 1925.

4. F. D. Hart, "The Newfoundland—The Dog with a Soul," *Dog World*, February 1925, 5.

5. Ibid.

6. Ibid.

7. Ibid.

8. "Bert Finch's Ideas," *Dog World*, February 1925, 8.

9. Ibid.

10. Ibid.

11. Ibid.

12. Ibid.

13. "The Airedale Slump," *Dog World*, February 1925, 12.

14. Ibid.

15. Ibid.

16. "The Man-Eating Shepherd Dog," *Dog World*, February 1925, 10.

17. Ibid.

18. Ibid.

19. Ibid.

20. Image, *Dog World*, February 1925, 10.

21. Will Judy, *Don't Call a Man a Dog* (Chicago: Judy Publishing Co., 1949), 20.

22. Ibid.

23. *Dog World*, February 1925, inside cover.

24. Advertisement, *Dog World*, February 1925, 1.

25. Ibid.

26. Advertisement, *Dog World*, February 1925, 7.

27. "Importing Biscuit Crushers," *Dog World*, February 1925, 13.

28. Ibid.

29. Ibid.

30. Ibid.

31. Ibid.

32. "Shepherd Shouts—A Complaint," *Dog World*, February 1925, 32.

33. Ibid.

34. "Dog Faking," *Dog World*, February 1925, 12.

35. Ibid.

36. "The Minimum Price," *Dog World*, February 1925, 12.

37. Ibid.

38. Ibid.

39. "Beg Your Pardon," *Dog World*, February 1925, 13.

40. Ibid.

41. "A Complaint," *Dog World*, February 1925, 32.

42. "Attention Fanciers," *Dog World*, February 1925, 16.

43. "Dog Book Column," *Dog World*, February 1925, 8.

44. Ibid.

45. "A Splendid Opportunity," *Dog World*, February 1925, 8.

46. "Cover Calvacade," *Dog World*, August 1947, 12.

47. "Radio Interview on Dogs," *Dog World*, August 1947, 7.

48. Ibid.

49. Ibid.

50. "Bullterrier Has Its Biggest Fight Still Ahead," *Dog World*, February 1947, 8.

51. Ibid.

52. Ibid.

53. Ibid.

54. Ibid.

55. Ibid.

56. "Bullterrier Faces Need for Enlightenment," *Dog World*, August 1947, 120.

57. Ibid.

58. "Bullterrier Has Its Biggest Fight Still Ahead," *Dog World*, February 1947, 8.

59. Ibid.

60. Ibid.

61. Ibid.

62. Ibid.

63. Ibid.

64. Ibid.

65. "Bullterrier Faces Need for Enlightenment," *Dog World*, August 1947, 120.

66. Ibid.

67. Ibid.

68. Ibid.

69. Ibid.

70. Ibid.

71. Ibid.

72. "War Dog Training," *Dog World*, February 1947, 34.

73. Ibid.

74. Ibid.

75. Ibid.

76. Ibid.

77. Ibid.

78. "Beaters Beat the Drum and Bend the Elbow," *Dog World*, August 1947, 22.

79. Ibid.

80. Ibid.

81. Ibid.

82. Ibid.

83. Ibid.

84. "Not Many Are Eligible to Join This Group," *Dog World*, August 1947, 29.

85. Ibid.
86. Ibid.
87. Ibid.
88. "Prayer for Animals," *Dog World*, August 1947, 29.
89. "Famous Kipling Poem," *Dog World*, June 1947, 29.
90. "No Money Could Be Better Spent," *Dog World*, August 1947, 36.
91. Ibid.
92. Ibid.
93. Ibid.
94. Ibid.
95. Ibid.
96. "No Change in Ownership," *Dog World*, August 1947, 42.
97. Ad promotion copy, *Dog World*, August 1953, 4.
98. "It's for Your Dog and You," *Dog World*, August 1953, 18.
99. Ibid.
100. Ibid.
101. Ibid.
102. Ibid.
103. Ibid.
104. "Yankee Stadium Is Scene of Spectacular Dog Act," *Dog World*, August 1953, 26.
105. Ibid.
106. "Feature," *Dog World*, August 1953, 27.
107. Ibid.
108. "How Many Dogs in the Army," *Dog World*, August 1953, 26.
109. Ibid.
110. "The Sale of Dogs Must Be Lifted to a Higher Plane of Merchandising," *Dog World*, August 1953, 29.
111. Ibid.
112. Ibid.
113. "American Humane Ass'n Not an Anti-Vivisection Organization," *Dog World*, August 1953, 22.
114. Ibid.
115. Ibid.
116. Ibid.
117. Ibid.
118. Ibid.
119. Ibid.
120. Ibid.
121. Ibid.
122. Ibid.
123. Ibid.
124. Ibid.
125. Ibid.
126. Ibid.
127. Ibid.
128. "Complains Against Sales Competition from Animal Shelters," *Dog World*, August 1953, 22.
129. Ibid.

Chapter 7

1. Cover, *Dog World*, September 1958.
2. "Flash! Fire Destroys Dog World Home!" *Dog World*, September 1958.
3. Ibid.
4. Ibid.
5. Ibid.
6. Ibid.
7. Ibid.
8. Ibid.
9. Ibid.
10. Ibid.
11. Ibid.
12. Ibid.
13. "JKC No Longer," *Dog World*, September 1958.
14. Ibid.
15. Ibid.
16. "Dog Laws," *Dog World*, September 1958, 1.
17. Ibid.
18. Ibid.
19. Ibid.
20. Ibid.
21. Ibid.
22. Ibid.
23. Ibid.
24. "Veterinary Notes," *Dog World*, September 1958, 39.
25. Ibid.
26. Ibid.
27. "Dogs Prove Too Efficient," *Dog World*, September 1958, 23.
28. Ibid.
29. Ibid.
30. Ibid.
31. Ibid.
32. "Judges Have a 'Hard' Life," *Dog World*, September 1958, 29.
33. Ibid.
34. "The Dog's Own Week," *Dog World*, September 1958, 20.
35. Ibid.
36. Ibid.
37. Ibid.
38. "'You' Are the Volunteer," *Dog World*, September 1958, 40.
39. Ibid.
40. Ibid.

41. "The Dog's Own Week," *Dog World*, September 1958, 20.

42. "House Chat," *Dog World*, September 1958, 21.

43. Ibid.

44. Ibid.

45. "Folks Who Shouldn't Own Dogs," *Dog World*, September 1958, 25.

46. Ibid.

47. Ibid.

48. Ibid.

49. Ibid.

50. "Dog Owners Are a Good Lot," *Dog World*, September 1958.

51. "Pastel Portrait on This Issue," *Dog World*, December 1965, 115.

52. "Mast Head," *Dog World*, December 1965, 4.

53. Ibid.

54. Ibid.

55. "Mast Head," *Dog World*, December 1965, 5.

56. "Mast Head," *Dog World*, December 1965, 4.

57. Ibid.

58. "50 Fantastic Years," *Dog World*, December 1965, 13.

59. Ibid.

60. Ibid.

61. Ibid.

62. Ibid.

63. Ibid.

64. Ibid.

65. Ibid.

66. Ibid.

67. Ibid.

68. Ibid.

69. Ibid.

70. Ibid.

71. "50 Years of Veterinary Medicine," *Dog World*, December 1965, 15.

72. Ibid.

73. Ibid.

74. Ibid.

75. Ibid.

76. Ibid.

77. Ibid., 51.

78. Ibid.

79. Ibid., 86.

80. Ibid.

81. Ibid., 85.

82. Ibid.

83. Ibid.

84. Ibid.

85. Ibid.

86. Ibid.

87. Ibid.

88. "Progress in Infectious Diseases," *Dog World*, December 1965, 18.

89. Ibid.

90. Ibid.

91. Ibid.

92. Ibid.

93. Ibid., 31.

94. Ibid.

95. Ibid.

96. Ibid., 74.

97. Ibid.

98. Ibid.

99. Ibid.

100. Ibid., 75.

101. Ibid.

102. Ibid.

103. Ibid.

104. Ibid., 76.

105. "Our Special Thanks," *Dog World*, December 1965, 38.

106. "Books About Dogs," *Dog World*, December 1965, 30.

107. Ibid.

108. "After Fifty Years," *Dog World*, December 1965, 37.

109. Ibid.

110. Ibid.

111. Ibid.

112. Ibid.

113. Arthur Jones, "History of the A.K.C.," *Dog World*, December 1965, 9.

114. Ibid.

115. Ibid.

116. Ibid.

117. Ibid.

118. Ibid.

119. Betty A. Radzevich, "Neighborhood Rejection," *Dog World*, December 1965, 77.

120. Ibid.

121. Ibid.

122. "Harry Miller at Large: Must Memorize Vest's Tribute," *Dog World*, December 1965, 27.

123. Ibid.

124. Ibid.

125. Ibid.

126. William W. Denlinger and Maxwell Riddle, "Two Memories of Will Judy," *Dog World*, January 1991, 34.

127. Ibid., 36.

128. Ibid., 34.

129. Ibid., 35.

130. Ibid.

131. Ibid.

132. Mary Ellen Tarman, "Old *Dog Worlds*: A Bountiful Yield for the Canine

Collector," *Canine Collectibles Quarterly*, Winter 1993, 4.

133. Ibid., 5.

Chapter 8

1. Will Judy, *Don't Call a Man a Dog* (Chicago: Judy Publishing Co., 1949), 7.

2. Ibid., 8.

3. Ibid.

4. Ibid.

5. "Dog Is Man's Friend, Give Him a Pound," *Chicago Daily Tribune*, 21 March 1928.

6. "Magazine Covers Archive—September 1928," accessed November 2011, http://www.whosdatedwho.com/sections/magazines/archive/1928/September.

7. IMBd, accessed January 2014, http://www.imdb.com/title/tt0018684/?ref_=fn_al_tt_3.

8. "Who Won the 1928 Westminster Dog Show," accessed November 2011, http://whowonthe.com/westminster-dog-show/1928/winner.

9. "White House Pets," Presidential Pet Museum, accessed January 2014, http://presidentialpetmuseum.com/whitehousepets-2.

10. David Pietrusza, "Coolidge Pets," accessed December 2011, http://davidpietrusza.com/coolidge-pets.html.

11. "White House Pets," Presidential Pet Museum, accessed January 2014, http://presidentialpetmuseum.com/whitehousepets-2.

12. Ibid.

13. "Every Dog in England Had His Day This Week in National Campaign," *Ottawa Citizen*, September 1928.

14. "Animals: Modern Doggery," *Time*, 29 September 1930, http://www.time.com/time/magazine/article/0,9171,740423,00.html.

15. "Depression Felt by Homeless Pets; Women's League for Animals Reports Big Gain in Work as Result of Hard Times," *New York Times*, January 1932.

16. "Animals: Poisoner Caught," *Time*, 9 February 1931, http://content.time.com/time/magazine/article/0,9171,741046,00.html.

17. "'Mr. Dogdom' of America," Pollard Press Syndicate, undated press release.

18. "National Dog Week Almost Got by Unnoticed," *Free Lance-Star* (Virginia), 9 September 1934.

19. Ibid.

20. Captain Arthur Haggerty, "Captain Will Judy: An American Original," *Dog World*, October 2003, 64.

21. Pat Santi, "The Maxwell Medallion," Dog Writers Association of America, accessed January 2014, http://www.dwaa.org/dogwriters-maxwell_medallion.php.

22. Bob Becker, "Mostly About Dogs: National Dog Week Has Seven Aims," *Chicago Tribune*, 7 August 1938.

23. Bob Becker, "Chicago Joins U.S. in Paying Tribute to Dog," *Chicago Daily Tribune*, 19 September 1938.

24. "Actress and Dog Friends: Alice Brady Will Direct National Dog Week Here," *Los Angeles Times*, 14 September 1936.

25. "Paddy Is Star Model at Dog Fashion Show," *New York Times*, 22 September 1938.

26. "Girl's Essay on Dog Wins Silver Medal," *New York Times*, 5 October 1938.

27. "Lassie Come Home," Wikipedia, accessed January 2014, http://en.wikipedia.org/wiki/Lassie_Come_Home.

28. "White House Pets: Fala Biography," Presidential Pet Museum, accessed 29 December 2009, http://www.presidentialpetmuseum.com/Pets/fala.htm.

29. "Campaign Dinner Address of Franklin Delano Roosevelt," 23 September 1944, accessed January 2014, http://www.wyzant.com/resources/lessons/history/hpol/fdr/fala.

30. Will Judy, *Don't Call a Man a Dog*, 7.

31. Mark Derr, "Fala, the Presidential Dog: How a Special Little Dog Made America's House His Home," *The Bark*, accessed January 2014, http://thebark.com/content/fala-presidential-dog.

32. "It's National Dog Week and Pound Mutts Seek Homes," *New York Times*, 24 September 1940.

33. "Champions Parade in Dog Exhibition; Obedience, Retrieving Also Figure in City's Tribute to Thoroughbreds," *New York Times*, September 1940.

34. "Mrs. Jiggs to Aid Dog Week," *New York Times*, 23 September 1940.

35. "Stubby," The Price of Freedom: Americans at War, accessed January 2014, http://americanhistory.si.edu/militaryhistory/collection/object.asp?ID=15.

36. Ibid.

37. Ibid.
38. Will Judy, *Don't Call a Man a Dog*, 129.
39. "The Legendary Rin Tin Tin," Rin Tin Tin Pet Products, accessed January 2014, http://www.rintintin.com/the-hero.html.
40. Ibid.
41. Ibid.
42. Ibid.
43. "Rin Tin Tin," Wikipedia, http://en.wikipedia.org/wiki/Rin_Tin_Tin.
44. "Players Guild of Evanston to Present Series: Bishop Warne to Speak Tomorrow," *Chicago Daily Tribune*, 19 July 1931.
45. "Defense Will Be Stressed during Nation's Dog Week," *Milwaukee Journal*, 22 September 1941.
46. *Berkley Daily Gazette*, September 1941.
47. "5 Dogs Accepted for Armed Forces: Kennel Club Officials Resume Tests Here," *Reading Eagle*, 13 September 1945.
48. "Small Dogs Sought for War Services," *Pittsburgh Post-Gazette*, September 1943.
49. *Pittsburgh Post-Gazette*, September 1943.
50. "War Dogs Are Treated Kindly," *Spokane Daily Chronicle*, 10 February 1944.
51. "Dog to Have His Day Here Marks National Week," *Milwaukee Journal*, September 1945.
52. *Palm Beach Post*, September 1948.
53. "21st Observance of Dog Week Set," *New York Times*, 29 August 1948.
54. "A Canine Cavalcade in Plaza of Rockefeller Center" *New York Times*, 24 September 1948.
55. "National Dog Week Brings New Jewelry for Pet Protection Medallion," *Pittsburgh Post-Gazette*, September 1944.
56. *Milwaukee Sentinel*, September 1945.
57. Arthur Peterson, "Our Town," *Toledo Blade*, 20 September 1948.
58. Ibid.
59. Ibid.
60. Ibid.
61. Ibid.
62. Ibid.
63. Ibid.
64. "Full of Mischief, Dog Steals Show," *New York Times*, 28 September 1951.
65. Ibid.
66. Ibid.
67. Ibid.
68. Ibid.
69. "60 Polite Pets Star in Dog Week Show; Thousands See Various Breeds in Obedience Demonstration at Rockefeller Center," *New York Times*, 26 September 1952.
70. Ibid.
71. Ibid.
72. Ibid.
73. Mary R. Burch, "The Evolution of Modern-Day Dog Training," National Animal Interest Alliance, 8 January 2012, accessed January 2014, http://www.naiaonline.org/naia-library/articles/the-evolution-of-modern-day-dog-training.
74. Ibid.
75. Ibid.
76. Walter R. Fletcher, "An Astute Dog Judge," *New York Times*, 20 July 1961.
77. Ibid.
78. Ibid.
79. Ibid.
80. *Deseret News*, September 1952.
81. "This Is National Dog Week, a Fine Time to Teach Your Pet the Five Basic Commands," *Eugene Register Guard*, September 1961.
82. "Canine Week Exhausts Master," *Palm Beach Post*, September 1961.
83. "Hounded Reporter Wants People Week," *Milwaukee Sentinel*, September 1961.
84. *Lakeland Leger*, 18 September 1972.
85. *Lodi News Sentinel*, 15 September 1973.
86. "Whatever Happened to National Dog Week? We're in It—But It's Called Pet Responsibility Week," *Ocala Star-Banner*, 18 September 1977.
87. http://www.adoa.org/about-adoa.
88. Ibid.
89. "National Dog Week: September 24–30, 2000," Doctors Foster and Smith, accessed January 2014, http://www.peteducation.com/article.cfm?c=22+1275&aid=1283.

Chapter 9

1. Captain Arthur Haggerty, "Captain Will Judy: An American Original," *Dog World*, October 2003, 64.
2. "International Hall of Fame: Captain Arthur Haggery, Dog Trainer," International Association of Canine Professionals, accessed January 2014, http://

www.canineprofessionals.com/index.php ?option=com_content&view=article&id= 37:international-hall-of-fame&catid= 20:site-content&Itemid=118.

3. Haggerty, "Captain Will Judy: An American Original," *Dog World*, October 2003, 64.

4. Steve Dale, "A Salute to Captain Arthur Haggerty," *Hartford Courant* via Tribune Media Services, 5 July 2006.

5. "International Hall of Fame: Captain Arthur Haggery, Dog Trainer," International Association of Canine Professionals, accessed January 2014, http://www.canineprofessionals.com/index.php?option=com_content&view=article&id=37:international-hall-of-fame&catid=20:site-content&Itemid=118.

6. Ibid.

7. Steve Diller, "Dogs Lost a Champion But I Lost a Friend," Babette Haggerty's School for Dogs, accessed January 2014, http://www.haggertydog.com/bio.html.

8. Stephen Miller, "Captain Haggerty, 74, Dog Trainer, Dog Author, Dog Cineaste," *New York Sun*, 17 July 2006, http://www.nysun.com/obituaries/captain-haggerty-74-dog-trainer-dog-author-dog/36127.

9. Steve Diller, "Dogs Lost a Champion But I Lost a Friend."

10. Ibid.

11. Ibid.

12. Ibid.

13. Ibid.

14. Ibid.

15. Ibid.

16. Ibid.

17. Stephen Miller, "Captain Haggerty, 74, Dog Trainer, Dog Author, Dog Cineaste." 18. John Rendel, "Student of Dog Psychology," *New York Times*, 3 February 1965.

19. Steve Dale, "A Salute to Captain Arthur Haggerty."

20. Ibid.

21. Margalit Fox, "Arthur Haggerty, 74, Master Dog Trainer, Dies," *New York Times* via News Bank, 18 July 2006.

22. Ibid.

23. Steve Dale, "A Salute to Captain Arthur Haggerty."

24. Ibid.

25. Ibid.

26. Ibid.

27. Ibid.

28. Steve Diller, "Dogs Lost a Champion But I Lost a Friend."

29. Sid Kane, "What's New in the Animal Business," *New York Times* via News Bank, 15 March 1987.

30. Steve Diller, "Dogs Lost a Champion But I Lost a Friend."

31. Ibid.

32. Steve Dale, "A Salute to Captain Arthur Haggerty."

33. Stephen Miller, "Captain Haggerty, 74, Dog Trainer, Dog Author, Dog Cineaste."

34. Steve Diller, "Dogs Lost a Champion But I Lost a Friend."

35. Steve Dale, "A Salute to Captain Arthur Haggerty."

36. Steve Diller, "Dogs Lost a Champion But I Lost a Friend."

37. Stephen Miller, "Captain Haggerty, 74, Dog Trainer, Dog Author, Dog Cineaste."

38. Steve Diller, "Dogs Lost a Champion But I Lost a Friend."

39. Ibid.

40. Mary Ellen Tarman, "Old *Dog Worlds*: A Bountiful Yield for the Canine Collector," *Canine Collectibles Quarterly*, Winter 1993.

41. Captain Arthur Haggerty, "National Dog Week," defunct website.

42. Ibid.

43. Ibid.

44. Ibid.

45. Ibid.

46. Ibid.

47. Ibid.

48. Ibid.

49. Ibid.

50. Ibid.

51. Ibid.

Bibliography

Books

Judy, Will. *Don't Call a Man a Dog.* Chicago: Judy Publishing Co., 1949.

_____. *Handy Dog Booklets: Anatomy of the Dog.* Chicago: Judy Publishing Co., 1948.

_____. *Handy Dog Booklets: The Dog in the Show Ring.* Chicago: Judy Publishing Co., 1950.

_____. *Handy Dog Booklets: Dog Shows and Rules.* Chicago: Judy Publishing Co., 1951.

_____. *Handy Dog Booklets: Feeding the Dog.* Chicago: Judy Publishing Co., 1950.

_____. *Handy Dog Booklets: Handling the Mating of Dogs.* Chicago: Judy Publishing Co., 1950.

_____. *Handy Dog Booklets: Housebreaking the Dog.* Chicago: Judy Publishing Co., 1948.

_____. *Handy Dog Booklets: How to Sell Dogs.* Chicago: Judy Publishing Co., 1951.

_____. *Handy Dog Booklets: How to Ship Dogs.* Chicago: Judy Publishing Co., 1951.

_____. *Handy Dog Booklets: Laws on Dogs.* Chicago: Judy Publishing Co., 1949.

_____. *Handy Dog Booklets: Puppies and Their Care.* Chicago: Judy Publishing Co., 1951.

_____. *Handy Dog Booklets: The Stud Dog's Care and Management.* Chicago: Judy Publishing Co., 1951.

_____. *Men and Things: Fifty Essays About Human Nature, the Ways of Men, and Their Private and Public Conduct.* Chicago: Judy Publishing Co., 1927.

_____. *Sayings of Rammikar: Being an Attempt in Publishing a Collection of the Words of Wisdom of the Mayan Filosofer Rammikar as Deciphered, Interpreted, and Modernized in Phrasing by Translator Wymar Port.* Chicago: Judy Publishing Co., 1927.

_____. *A Soldier's Diary: A Day to Day Record in the World War.* Chicago: Judy Publishing Co., 1930.

_____. *Training the Dog: Complete Instruction Suitable for All Breeds and All Purposes, Including Field and Outdoor Work.* Chicago: Judy Publishing Co., 1932.

_____. *Training the Dog: A Presentation of the Mentality of the Dog, with Instructions Suitable for Training All Breeds for All Purposes, Including Also Field and Outdoor Work.* 6th ed. Chicago: Judy Publishing Co., 1941.

_____. *Training the Dog.* Chicago: Judy Publishing Co., 1953.

Port, Weimar. *Chicago the Pagan.* Chicago: Judy Publishing Co., 1953.

Internet Sources

American Anti-Vivisection Society. "The Foremother to American Animal Advocacy: Caroline Earle White." Accessed December 2013. http://www.

203

aavs.org/site/c.bkLTKfOSLhK6E/b. 6452381/k.1E3C/The_Foremother_to_ American_Animal_Advocacy.htm.

American Humane Association. "How American Humane Association Began." Accessed December 2013. http://www. americanhumane.org/about-us/who- we-are/history.

American Society for the Provention of Cruelty to Animals. "Regarding Henry: A 'Bergh's-Eye' View of 148 Years at the ASPCA." Accessed December 2013. http://www.aspca.org/about-us/about- the-aspca/history-aspca.

Beautiful Joe Heritage Society. http:// beautifuljoe.org

Brethren Rivival Fellowship. "Basic Be- liefs Within the Church of the Breth- ren." 18 November 2009. http://www. brfwitness.org/?p=88.

Burch, Mary R. "The Evolution of Modern-Day Dog Training." National Animal Interest Alliance, 8 January 2012. Accessed January 2014. http:// www.naiaonline.org/naia-library/ articles/the-evolution-of-modern-day- dog-training.

"Campaign Dinner Address of Franklin Delano Roosevelt." Delivered 23 Sep- tember 1944. Accessed January 2014. http://www.wyzant.com/resources/ lessons/history/hpol/fdr/fala.

Chaffee, Dugald. "Edmund B. Chaffee and the Labor Temple." *The Courier: Syracuse University Library Associates* Vol. XI, no. 1. Accessed January 2014. http://surface.syr.edu/libassoc/31.

Derr, Mark. "Fala, the Presidential Dog: How a Special Little Dog Made Amer- ica's House His Home." *The Bark*. Ac- cessed January 2014. http://thebark. com/content/fala-presidential-dog.

"English-Word Information." Accessed December 2013, http://wordinfo.info/ unit/3465/page:2.

The Humane Society of the United States. "Pets by the Numbers." 27 Sep- tember 2013. Accessed December 2013. http://www.humanesociety.org/ issues/pet_overpopulation/facts/pet_ ownership_statistics.html.

Jalowitz, Alan. "Judy, William Lewis." 5 November 2009. http://pabook.libra ries.psu.edu/palitmap/bios/Judy_Will. html.

Juniata College. "Will Judy Lectureship Fund (1958)." http://www.juniata.edu/ services/activities/speakers/sponsors/ will_judy.html.

"Magazine Covers Archive—September 1928." Accessed November 2011. http:// www.whosdatedwho.com/sections/ magazines/archive/1928/September.

Oregon Poetic Voices. "Ben Hur Lamp- man." Accessed January 2014. http:// oregonpoeticvoices.org/poet/2.

Orphans of the Storm. "Our History." http://www.orphansofthestorm.org/ About/OurHistory.html.

Pearl, Nancy. "These Books Have Gone to the Dogs." National Public Radio audio. 6 November 2006. Accessed January 2014. http://www.npr.org/tem plates/story/story.php?storyId=6431059

Pietrusza, David. "Coolidge Pets." Ac- cessed December 2011. http://david pietrusza.com/coolidge-pets.html.

Presidential Pet Museum. "White House Pets." Accessed January 2014. http:// presidentialpetmuseum.com/white housepets-2.

Presidential Pet Museum. "White House Pets: Fala Biography." 29 December 2009. http://www.presidentialpetmuse um.com/Pets/fala.htm.

Santi, Pat. "The Maxwell Medallion." Dog Writers Association of America. Accessed January 2014. http://www. dwaa.org/dogwriters-maxwell_med allion.php.

"Who Won the 1928 Westminster Dog Show." Accessed 30 November 2011. http://whowonthe.com/westminster- dog-show/1928/winner.

Wikipedia. "Garrett, Pennsylvania." Ac- cessed December 2013. http://wikipe dia.org/wiki/Garrett,_Pennsylvania.

Wikipedia. "Lassie Come Home." Ac- cessed January 2014. http://en.wikiped ia.org/wiki/Lassie_Come_Home.

Wikipedia. "Vernon and Irene Castle." Accessed December 2013. http://en.

wikipedia.org/wiki/Vernon_and_Irene_Castle.

Periodicals

Boxer Review. "The Story Behind Dog World Magazine." October 1956.
Canine Collectibles Quarterly, Winter 1993 II (2).
Dog World. "*Dog World* Rate Card." February 1925.
Dog World, August 1947.
Dog World, August 1953.
Dog World, September 1958.
Dog World, December 1965.
Dog World, January 1991.
Dog World, October 2003.
Time, "Animals: Modern Doggery." 29 September 1930.
Time. "Animals: Poisoner Caught." 9 February 1931.

Newspapers

Becker, Bob. "Mostly About Dogs: National Dog Week Has Seven Aims." *Chicago Tribune*, 7 August 1938.
_____. "Chicago Joins U.S. in Paying Tribute to Dog." *Chicago Daily Tribune*, 19 September 1938.
Berkley Daily Gazette. September 1941.
Chicago Daily Tribune. "Dog Is Man's Friend, Give Him a Pound." 21 March 1928.
Dale, Steve. "A Salute to Captain Arthur Haggerty." *Hartford Courant* via Tribune Media Services, 5 July 2006.
Deseret News. September 1952.
Diller, Steve. "Dogs Lost a Champion But I Lost a Friend." Babette Haggerty's School for Dogs. Accessed January 2014. http://www.haggertydog.com/bio.html.
Eugene Register Guard. "This Is National Dog Week, a Fine Time to Teach Your Pet the Five Basic Commands." September 1961.
Fletcher, Walter R. "An Astute Dog Judge." *New York Times*, 20 July 1961.
Fox, Margalit. "Arthur Haggerty, 74, Master Dog Trainer, Dies." *New York Times* via News Bank, 18 July 2006.

Free Lance-Star (Virginia). "National Dog Week Almost Got by Unnoticed." 9 September 1934.
Kane, Sid. "What's New in the Animal Business." *New York Times* via News Bank, 15 March 1987.
Lakeland Leger. 18 September 1972.
Lodi News Sentinel. 15 September 1973.
Los Angeles Times. "Actress and Dog Friends: Alice Brady Will Direct National Dog Week Here." 14 September 1936.
Miller, Stephen. "Captain Haggerty, 74, Dog Trainer, Dog Author, Dog Cineaste." *New York Sun*, 17 July 2006. http://www.nysun.com/obituaries/captain-haggerty-74-dog-trainer-dog-author-dog/36127.
Milwaukee Journal. "Defense Will Be Stressed During Nation's Dog Week." 22 September 1941.
Milwaukee Journal. "Dog to Have His Day Here Marks National Week." September 1945.
Milwaukee Sentinel. "Hounded Reporter Wants People Week." September 1961.
Milwaukee Sentinel. September 1945.
New York Times. "A Canine Cavalcade in Plaza of Rockefeller Center." 24 September 1948.
New York Times. "Champions Parade in Dog Exhibition; Obedience, Retrieving Also Figure in City's Tribute to Thoroughbreds." September 1940.
New York Times. "Depression Felt by Homeless Pets; Women's League for Animals Reports Big Gain in Work as Result of Hard Times." January 1932.
New York Times. "Full of Mischief, Dog Steals Show." 28 September 1951.
New York Times. "Girl's Essay on Dog Wins Silver Medal." 5 October 1938.
New York Times. "It's National Dog Week and Pound Mutts Seek Homes." 24 September 1940.
New York Times. "Mrs. Jiggs to Aid Dog Week." 23 September 1940.
New York Times. "Paddy Is Star Model at Dog Fashion Show." 22 September 1938.
New York Times. "60 Polite Pets Star in Dog Week Show; Thousands See Var-

ious Breeds in Obedience Demonstration at Rockefeller Center." 26 September 1952.

New York Times. "21st Observance of Dog Week Set." 29 August 1948.

Ocala Star-Banner. "Whatever Happened to National Dog Week? We're in It— But It's Called Pet Responsibility Week," 18 September 1977.

Ottawa Citizen. "Every Dog in England Had His Day This Week in National Campaign." September 1928.

Palm Beach Post. "Canine Week Exhausts Master." September 1961.

Palm Beach Post. September 1948.

Peterson, Arthur. "Our Town." *Toledo Blade*, 20 September 1948.

Pittsburgh Post-Gazette. "National Dog Week Brings New Jewelry for Pet Protection Medallion." September 1944.

Pittsburgh Post-Gazette. "Small Dogs Sought for War Services." September 1943.

Pittsburgh Post-Gazette. "Stands by Helpless as 90 Dogs Burn." 2 February 1930.

Reading Eagle. "5 Dogs Accepted for Armed Forces: Kennel Club Officials Resume Tests Here." 13 September 1945.

Rendel, John. "Student of Dog Psychology." *New York Times*, 3 February 1965.

Somerset Daily American. "Native Son to Talk." 24 May 1938.

Spokane Daily Chronicle. "War Dogs Are Treated Kindly." 10 February 1944.

Spokesman-Review. "Champion of All Dogs." 31 July 1936.

Other

Judy, Will. "The Female." 3rd edition. Chicago: Judy, 1963.

Juniata College. Promotional material (possibly from a book cover), hand-dated 1945.

Juniata College Alumni File. *The Big 6.* Promotional material.

Juniata College Alumni File. "Capt. Judy Retires from Dog World After 36 Years." Promotional material, for release as desired, 1958.

Pollard Press Syndicate. "'Mr. Dogdom' of America." Undated press release.

Wall, John. Dir. Media Relations, Juniata College. E-mail message to author regarding the Will Judy Lectureship Fund (1958), 19 November 2009.

Index

www.ingramcontent.com/pod-product-compliance
Lightning Source LLC
Chambersburg PA
CBHW021141090426
42740CB00008B/883